Castaways of the
Kriegsmarine

First published 2017 by Derek Nudd.
Reprinted with minor correction 2021.

Copyright © 2017, 2021 Derek Nudd.

The right of Derek Nudd to be identified as the Author of this work has been asserted by him in accordance with the Copyrights, Designs and Patents Act 1988.

All rights reserved. No part of this publication may be reproduced, stored in a retrieval system, or transmitted in any form or by any means without the prior written permission of the author, nor be otherwise circulated in any form of binding or cover other than that in which it is published and without a similar condition being imposed on the subsequent purchaser.

A catalogue record for this book is available from the British Library.

ISBN 978-1548371012

Cover design by Art of Communication.

Although every precaution has been taken in the preparation of this book, the publisher and author assume no responsibility for errors or omissions. Neither is any liability assumed for damages resulting from the use of the information contained herein.

Dedication

I hope my mother, who sadly died while I was researching this book, would have thought it an adequate tribute to her father's panning the gold dust of intelligence from the river of bedraggled humanity flowing past him.

Most of all, as I type I approach thirty-five years of marriage to the woman whose love, heroic support and forbearance have made this, as so much else, possible.

A merciless editor is a treasure beyond price.

U-Bootsfahrer Lied

I. Ob Sturm uns bedroht hoch vom Norden,
Ob Heimweh im Herzen auch glüht;
Wir sind Kameraden geworden,
Und wenn es zur Hölle auch geht.
Matrosen die wissen zu sterben,
Wie immer das Schicksal auch spielt,
Und geht uns're Trommel in Scherben,
Dann singt uns der Nordwind ein Lied:
Refrain

   Auf einem Seemannsgrab,
   Da blühen keine Rosen,
   Auf einem Seemannsgrab,
   Da blüht kein Blümelein,
   |: Der einz'ge Gruß, das sind die weißen Möwen
   Und eine Träne die ein kleines Mädel weint :|

II. So manchen von uns sah'n wir sterben,
Doch keiner von uns hat geweint,
Scharfe Klippen – sie brachten Verderben,
Der Kahn ging zum Teufel derweil.
Es schlugen die eiskalten Wogen
Nach dem, den wir all' so geliebt;
Und als ihn der Tod von uns trennte,
Da sangen wir leis' dieses Lied:
Refrain

The U-boat Sailor's Song

I. Whether high storms threaten us from the North,
Whether homesickness glows in the heart;
We have become comrades
and when it also comes to hell
Sailors know how to die
As always fate also plays
And goes our drum in pieces
Then the north wind sings us a song:
Refrain
> On a seaman's grave
> No roses bloom
> On a seaman's grave
> No flowers bloom
> |: The single greeting is the white seagulls
> And a tear which a small maiden cries :|

II. So many of us saw death
But none of us cried
Sharp cliffs they brought us destruction
Meanwhile the boat went to the devil
The ice cold waves struck
All those that we so loved
And as death separated us
Then quietly we sang this song.
Refrain

Some of the *Scharnhorst* survivors claimed to have sung this cheerful ditty, adapted from a traditional German sea shanty, as they awaited rescue or death in the freezing waters of the Barents Sea.

Contents

Preface and Acknowledgements ix
Glossary and Abbreviations xv
U-Boats in the Mediterranean 1
Blockade Breakers in Biscay 9
Battleships in the Barents Sea 17
CSDIC – The System 25
The People 59
At CSDIC UK 95
"That Which Changes Us" 127
International Relations 163
Prelude to *Götterdämmerung* 183
Conclusion 193
Appendix A – Eavesdropping Timeline 197
Appendix B – *Scharnhorst* Survivors' Interrogation aboard *Duke of York* 199
Appendix C – Contents of NID U-boat Compendium, June 1944 203
Appendix D – Stool pigeons 217
Bibliography 223
Index 233

List of Illustrations

Figure 1: A relaxed moment for the naval staff at Latimer House. x
Figure 2: Sketches of T-25 & T-26 being shelled, and of MV Kerlogue rescuing survivors. 14
Figure 3: DMI Prisoner-of-War Organisation. 26
Figure 4: Latimer House today. 27
Figure 5: CSDIC UK Workload during the six years of war.. 28
Figure 6: Number of SR (eavesdropping) reports by year. 33
Figure 7: 1940/41 caricature of (then) Lt Burton Cope 61
Figure 8: The NID Team at Latimer House, 1943. 62
Figure 9: Merchant shipping vs U-boat losses in 1943. 72
Figure 10: Prisoner Morale January 1943 - March 1944. 74
Figure 11: Prisoners' Attitudes to Hitler from February 1943 to January 1944. 76
Figure 12: 'Fighting Spirit' of Prisoners from April 1943 to January 1944. 78
Figure 13: It could have been anywhere. 97
Figure 14: Eavesdropping and Reporting Timeline. 198

List of Tables

Table 1: GSR Fit 142

Preface and Acknowledgements

On 17th January 1944 Commodore Rushbrooke, Director of Naval Intelligence (DNI), wrote to his team leader at the Combined Services Detailed Interrogation Centre (CSDIC) Latimer House:

'Dear Cope
The heavy simultaneous influx of nearly 250 prisoners from SCHARNHORST, T.25, ALSTERUFER, U.593 and U.73 threw a greater strain than ever before during the war on your section.
2.   The results have nevertheless maintained the high standard to which I have become accustomed, and the speed with which they have been produced has been very creditable.
3.   You and all those concerned are to be congratulated on this very good effort. Please convey my thanks to those officers who were responsible for these satisfactory results.'[1]

CSDIC's work to recover intelligence from prisoners-of-war is covered elsewhere;[2] the fate of *Scharnhorst* is well known, that of the other vessels less so. This story draws together the threads of five desperate engagements in the closing days of 1943, from the balmy Mediterranean to an Arctic storm, the bedraggled survivors' journey to a Buckinghamshire country house, the intelligence gleaned and how it was used.

It looks at the men and women waiting to receive them: the disparate personalities thrown together and the techniques they used in what was by then a highly tuned intelligence production-line.

These five crews were not the only naval castaways enjoying CSDIC's hospitality at the time. Their stay overlapped at least in part with those of U-536 (sunk 20th November 1943), U-172 (13th December), U-848 (4th January 1944), U-231 (13th January), *Charlotte Schliemann* (12th February), U-406 (18th February), U-264 and U-386 (19th February), and U-257 (24th February) not counting the continued attrition from March onwards. The simultaneous surge was unprecedented and a considerable strain on the naval staff at CSDIC but was good practice for the flood that followed the Normandy landings just a few months later.

Figure 1: A relaxed moment for the naval staff at Latimer House.

The turn of 1943/44 was a moment when, with hindsight, the chance cards of war were falling consistently in the Allies favour. We shall see that this was not obvious to the people concerned. Germans' horror of defeat strengthened their denial of its possibility. Even a year later, when the Battle of the Bulge hit the news, many prisoners in Britain expected to be freed at any moment by an invading army. For their part, the interrogators were only too aware of their opponents' desperate advances in submarine technology and the garbled reports of immensely destructive secret weapons nearing completion.

Preface and Acknowledgements

This was also the period when the CSDIC model as it had evolved since 1939 was at its zenith. After D-Day the sheer volume of prisoners forced a shallower and more selective approach, while the capture of intact equipment and documents reduced the need for painstaking extraction of technical detail. At the same time the available staff shrank as officers were reassigned to forward intelligence duties, and the naval emphasis shifted from the Atlantic to coastal waters. Increasingly desperate German innovation threw half-developed equipment with half-trained crews into what were only theoretically *not* suicide missions. They still had to be understood and countered.

We leave the movers and shakers, the German generals and senior staff, having their egos massaged at Trent Park. Instead, we focus on the constant procession of ordinary matelots and seagoing officers who passed through Latimer House and Wilton Park, were drained of useful information, and dumped to regular prisoner-of-war camps.

The army ran the interrogation centres, but in the first half of the war the German navy and air force provided most of their raw material and their opposite numbers thus had the most experienced teams.

Naval Intelligence Division, apart from being arguably the most effective of the British service intelligence branches, was intimately involved in the only campaign that lasted from the first day of the war to the last, and the only one which could alone have handed the Nazis victory: the U-boat struggle. In the cramped, airless Operational Intelligence Centre and the adjoining Submarine Tracking Room under the Admiralty exhausted men and women synthesised all the information available to them – including from prisoners-of-war – in a desperate, multifaceted, intelligence-led chess game played on both strategic and tactical levels. A pawn taken from the board meant choking, burning, drowning death, somewhere in the merciless ocean.

All of which helps narrow the scope of what could otherwise be a thousand-page doorstop to something that I hope will be more manageable and less soporific. If that leaves you gasping for more, I can always keep going.

I am deeply indebted to Dr Helen Fry for exposing the seam which I mine here in her books *The Walls Have Ears* and *Spymaster: The Secret Life of Kendrick*, and for her support in my subsequent burrowing. I hope you will agree as we navigate the shafts and galleries together that there are useful and entertaining nuggets of insight to be teased out down here.

While writing this book I have been privileged to meet and correspond with some of the people who were there or their descendants. In particular I would like to mention Fritz Lustig, one of the last of the secret listeners, Franklyn E Dailey Jnr who served aboard USS *Edison* when she sank U-73, Tom Doležal son of Oldřich Doležal pilot of the aircraft that sank *Alsterufer*, and Lance Shippey whose father helped guard the *Scharnhorst* survivors aboard *Duke of York*, and who has researched their background and subsequent lives.

I was first drawn to this topic by curiosity about my grandfather, Burton Cope, who led the Naval Intelligence section at Latimer House. As is the way with these things the story quickly gained a momentum of its own.

More than one chance remark by a friend or relation has made me stop in my tracks, scrap or change cherished words, research and add a whole new section. Infuriating at the time but I am grateful. Yes, really!

I am further indebted to the reviewers who took the time and trouble, once I thought I had finished, to point out those areas where I really hadn't. I am deeply grateful for their generosity of time and professionalism. Any gaps remaining are

Preface and Acknowledgements

down to my stupidity or stubbornness, not their contribution. I would particularly like to mention here the author Michael Jago, and Dr Simon Trew at The Royal Military Academy, Sandhurst.

The National Archive at Kew is a priceless resource – efficient, accessible and free. It is the mark of a civilised and honest society to have its written memory open to researchers in this way. Long may it remain so.

When quoting German prisoners' conversations and statements I use the contemporary English translations. I leave the transcribers' practice of capitalising significant names unchanged, although it can be distracting to a modern reader. Speakers are identified in the transcripts by a CSDIC index number; up to then a simple sequence beginning 'A' for air force, 'M' for military or 'N' for navy. The suffix '(Am)' indicates a prisoner taken by US forces. A more complex system was adopted after D-Day.

If you need a trigger warning it might be best to stop reading now. I repeat here the unexpurgated, unguarded comments of people brought up in the service of a vicious regime. I name them, as well as their colleagues who turned their backs on the system. We can learn from history, but only by looking at it with a clear and steady gaze.

Any author knows you can stare at manuscripts and proofs until your eyes spin, but the moment the irretrievably printed book lands on your doorstep the howlers leap out at you. I take sole credit for all the mistakes and idiocies that follow and will try to post corrections and clarifications on my web site (www.dnudd.co.uk) as I find them. The site also features downloadable transcriptions of some of the sources I used.

---

[1] Original in the author's possession.
[2] Helen Fry; *The Walls Have Ears* (Yale, 2019).

Glossary and Abbreviations

All full stops are removed for consistency.

Term	Expansion
AB	Able Seaman
ACNS	Assistant Chief of Naval Staff
A/C	Aircraft
Active Sonar	Apparatus to find the range and bearing of a submarine by transmitting an acoustic pulse and listening for the reflected sound
A/S	Anti-Submarine
Aphrodite	German code name for radar decoy balloons (RDB).
Asdic	British active sonar
ASV	Anti-Submarine Visualiser (radar)
B-Dienst	*Beobachtungsdienst* (observation service): the German naval intelligence department responsible for interception, decryption and analysis of enemy radio transmissions.
BAOR	British Army of the Rhine
BDM	*Bund Deutscher Mädel* – League of German Girls, related to Hitler Youth
BdU	*Befehlshaber der U-Boote* (U-boat central command)
Blitzmädel	Uniformed female armed-forces helper, usually a Hitler-Youth graduate.
BOLD	See SBT
CB	Confidential Book
CO	Commanding Officer
CPO	Chief Petty Officer
CSA	Consular Shipping Adviser. See NCSO below.
CSDIC	Combined Services Detailed Interrogation Centre

Term	Expansion
DASW	Director of Anti-Submarine Warfare
DDMI	Deputy Director of Military Intelligence
D/F	Direction Finding
DNI	Director of Naval Intelligence
DTM	Director of Torpedoes and Mining
E-Boat	German fast torpedo boat (*Schnellboot* or *S-boot*), equivalent to a British Motor Torpedo Boat
ERA	Engine Room Artificer
FO(SM), FOSM	Flag Officer (Submarines)
GAF	German Air Force (*Luftwaffe*)
GHQ	General Headquarters
GSR	German Search Receiver (a radar countermeasure)
HTP	High Test Peroxide
IO	Intelligence (or Interrogating) Officer
JIC	Joint Intelligence Committee
KDB	*Kristalldrehbasisgerat*: a type of German passive sonar
KK	*Korvettenkapitän* (equivalent to Lieutenant-Commander)
Klt	*Kapitänleutnant* (equivalent to Lieutenant)
LTO	Leading Torpedo Operator
MG	Machine-Gun
MV	Motor Vessel
NCO	Non-Commissioned Officer
NCSO	Naval Control Service Officer: the network of naval liaison officers in friendly and neutral naval ports who, together with the Consular Shipping Advisers (CSAs) in civil ports formed a more-or-less overt worldwide British naval intelligence network.
NID	Naval Intelligence Division
OIC	Operational Intelligence Centre
ONI	(US) Office of Naval Intelligence

Glossary

Term	Expansion
PAC	Parachute and Cable
Passive sonar	Underwater detection of a target by listening for the noises it makes.
Pfadfinder	German youth organisation, later absorbed into the *Hitler Jugend* (Hitler Youth).
PO	Petty Officer, Pilot Officer
PO Tel	Petty Officer Telegraphist
P/W, PW, PoW	Prisoner of War
PWE	Political Warfare Executive, a secret Foreign Office department briefed to undermine enemy morale and resistance by propaganda.
PWIB	Prisoner of War Information Bureau
PWIS	Prisoner of War Interrogation Section
RDB	Radar Decoy Balloons, also known as '*Aphrodite*'
RDS	Radar Decoy Spar-Buoy, also known as '*Thetis*'
RMLI	Royal Marines Light Infantry
RPS	Royal Patriotic Schools (also known as Royal Victoria Patriotic School), Wandsworth, used from January 1941 to June 1945 as an interrogation centre for refugees, escapees and defectors from occupied Europe.
SBT	Submarine Bubble Target (aka BOLD): a metal canister filled with calcium hydride which gave off large quantities of gas when mixed with sea water. The resulting bubble cloud looked very like a U-boat to Allied sonar.
SOI, SO(I)	Staff Officer (Intelligence)
SOE	Special Operations Executive: the reconnaissance and sabotage organisation created by Churchill to "Set Europe ablaze."
SP	Stool Pigeon
S/R	Send / Receive

Term	Expansion
SR	Special Report: transcript of a 'bugged' conversation
SS	Steam Ship
Starshell	Ordnance deploying a flare and parachute to illuminate a battle area.
Tel	Telegraphist
Thetis	See RDS
TNA	The National Archives (Kew, London)
U-Boat	*Unterseeboot*; German submarine
UC	Possibly 'Urgent Communication;' Naval Intelligence one and two-page reports flagging up the latest information on a single topic
UJ boat	German anti-submarine vessel; typically a converted trawler
W/T	Wireless Telegraphy
WEC	War Establishments Committee

German Naval Ranks and British Equivalents

Rank	Equivalent
Bootsmannsmaat	Leading Seaman.
Fähnrich zur See	Junior Midshipman.
Feldwebel	PO (Mechanical)
Fregattenkapitän	Commander.
Funkegefreiter	Telegraphist.
Funkmaat	Leading Telegraphist.
Funkobergefreiter	Telegraphist.
Kapitän zur See	Captain.
Kapitänleutnant	Lieutenant.
Korvettenkapitän	Lieutenant-Commander.
Leutnant zur See	Junior Sub-Lieutenant.
Marinestabarzt	Surgeon Lieutenant.
Maschinengefreiter	Stoker, 1st Class.
Maschinenmaat	Leading Stoker and ERA, 5th

Glossary

Rank	Equivalent
	Class.
Maschinenobergefreiter	Stoker, 1st Class.
Matrose	Ordinary Seaman.
Matrosengefreiter	Able Seaman.
Matrosenobergefreiter	Able Seaman.
Mechanikersmaat	Leading Seaman (S.T.)
Oberassistenzart	Surgeon Lieutenant.
Oberbootsmannsmaat	PO (Seaman's Branch).
Oberfähnrich zur See	Senior Midshipman.
Oberfunkmeister	CPO Telegraphist
Obergefreiter	Able Seaman
Oberleutnant zur See	Sub-Lieutenant.
Obermaschinenmaat	Acting Stoker PO and ERA, 4th Class
Obermaschinist	Chief Stoker and Chief ERA, 1st or 2nd Class.
Obermechanikersmaat	Acting Petty Officer
Obersteuermann	CPO (Navigation)
Steuermann	Helmsman
Steursmannsgefreiter	Able Seaman (Navigator's Yeoman)
Zimmermannobergefreiter	Shipwright AB Rating

(*ing*) denotes engineering branch.

U-BOATS IN THE MEDITERRANEAN

U-593

U-boat successes were unevenly distributed: the top fifty 'ace' commanders out of 1,400 who put to sea accounted for about 6.2 million of the 14.1 million tons of Allied merchant shipping sunk by German submarines.[1] All ran the same risks. Estimates vary but between seventy and eighty percent of the men who went to sea in U-boats died in them, the highest attrition rate for any branch of any armed force in that brutal conflict. Between forty and fifty percent of the survivors were taken prisoner.

As *Kapitänleutnant* (Lieutenant) Gerd Kelbling took U-593 out of Toulon on 3rd December 1943 he had reason to be confident. A professional naval officer since 1934 he had transferred to the submarine arm on the outbreak of war and commanded U-593, a Type VIIC U-boat, since her commissioning in 1941. He and the boat had already sunk 50,000 tons of shipping. He was not a big star like Otto Kretshmer (by then captive), the late Joachim Schepke or the late Günther Prien; but earned his keep well enough for an Iron Cross 1st Class and Knight's Cross. More importantly from his crew's perspective he was *not* going to be easy depth-charge fodder. But, thanks to a U-135 survivor captured the previous September, the Royal Navy knew he was there.[2]

On this, his fifteenth operational trip with the boat, Kelbling reached his patrol area south of Majorca and attacked a merchant ship without success. His luck changed early in the morning of 12th when he sighted convoy KMS-34 outbound from Liverpool to various Mediterranean ports. He fired a T5 'Gnat' homing torpedo at the Hunt class destroyer HMS *Tynedale*, sinking her with the loss of 73 out of her 155 crew. Dodging counterattacks he stayed with the convoy for five and a half hours until a new opportunity presented. HMS *Holcombe*, another Hunt class, was busy chasing a sonar contact when Kelbling put another T5 into her stern. She sank quickly; just 80 of the 164 men aboard survived.

U-593 spent the rest of the day evading the convoy's four surviving escorts. That evening the boat surfaced to charge her batteries and was immediately surprised by a searchlight-equipped Wellington bomber. Kelbling's crew beat off the attack; the aircraft was forced to retire with severe damage and its searchlight out of action. The rattled U-boat stayed under water most of the night, her batteries perilously low.

At 11:00 next morning a sonar operator heard propeller noises: the convoy escorts were back and in a vengeful mood. Three and a half tense hours later a depth-charge pattern exploded very close, followed by another before the crew could react. The boat shipped water fast as they worked frantically to save her. In a near-fatal misunderstanding the engineer officer reported that they were shipping 400 (*vier hundert*) litres of water per minute; the captain misheard that as a quarter litre (*ein viertel*). With the stern now dropping and the main motors in danger Kelbling blew ballast tanks and ordered all spare hands to the fore ends. It wasn't enough, and the boat continued sinking until the engineer managed to get the motors working and drove her to the surface as yet another depth-charge pattern exploded around her.

Her nemesis, the destroyers HMS *Calpe* and USS *Wainwright*, were waiting and opened fire: *'The next few minutes were rather hectic and there was a distinct danger of "Wainright" and*

"*Calpe*" hitting each other in their exhuberance [sic].'[3] It was soon clear that the U-boat's crew were abandoning ship and the destroyers ceased fire. As they did so Kelbling and *Obermechanikersmaat* (Acting Petty Officer) Günther Hünert calmly set scuttling charges and wedged the aft torpedo hatch open to ensure the boat would go down quickly. They picked up submachine guns and warned the approaching pinnace crew that the boat was about to blow. No boarding party was going to grab her Enigma machine or code books.

All 51 officers and men aboard survived and landed at Algiers in the small hours of 14th December. Kelbling and three others were flown to the UK for urgent interrogation while the rest of the crew waited for surface transport. During his brief stay in Algiers Kelbling was overheard bemoaning the fact that he had never yet managed to spend Christmas with his wife, and then:

'N 43/1578: *I don't really care whether they send me to ENGLAND or not; the only thing is, it won't be exactly a picnic there when we start our reprisals.*'[4]

Intensive bombing of Peenemünde and the planned launch sites had already delayed the V-weapon programme, and when it arrived it would be on nothing like the scale envisaged. But the clock was still ticking.

Despite – or perhaps because of – a harsh regime at the Algiers camp the prisoners kept their high morale. They left warnings about a suspected stool pigeon (informer) in their midst and a later guest found 'Kelbling's Crew' written on the wall.[5]

There was a short delay due to inter-Allied bickering about whether the survivors should be sent to Britain or the US. This allowed the second watchkeeping officer and his opposite number from U-73 to escape two days before the rest embarked for the UK. It was depressingly easy – they hid in a latrine during roll call while two petty officers answered their names and then resumed their place in the 'other ranks' line. They eventually made their way back to Germany via Spain.

Experienced petty officers had ample time to drill the others on the long haul to Britain, so they arrived in good spirits and very security conscious.

U-73

U-73, a Type VIIB U-boat, left Toulon for a patrol area off Oran and Algiers on the same day as U-593. *Oberleutnant zur See* (Sub-Lieutenant) Horst Deckert had served with the boat since her commissioning in 1940 and succeeded her first commanding officer, Helmut Rosenbaum, whose impressive record he was desperate to match. Under Rosenbaum U-73 had sunk nearly 58,000 tons of shipping including the aircraft carrier HMS *Eagle*, which had earned him the Knight's Cross. Deckert's actual tally to date was some 25,000 tons plus, according to his crew, some spurious claims. Nonetheless he was an efficient commander.

The boat herself was getting old by then: her design had been overtaken by later marks and according to one prisoner she was due to be broken up after her last patrol.[6]

In a frustrating fortnight U-73's crew fruitlessly attacked two corvettes which didn't even seem to notice, had to extract a flooded torpedo from a tube, was inconclusively depth-charged by a destroyer and collided at periscope depth with an unknown vessel. On the morning of 16th December, they sighted an Italian cruiser leaving Algiers but were too far away for any hope of an attack.

That afternoon their luck seemed to improve. At about 3:30 PM they sighted GUS 24, a slow westbound convoy picking up ships on its way from Port Said to Hampton Roads, Virginia, *via* Gibraltar. Better yet, the convoy had stopped zig-zagging while ships joining from Oran formed up.[7] U-73 closed to attack and torpedoed the 7,200-ton Liberty ship SS *John S Copley*. The crew mistakenly believed they had also hit two escorts, while a fourth torpedo went astray and circled unnervingly above the submarine.

John S Copley was badly holed. Non-essential crew took to the boats and were picked up by convoy escorts as three destroyers (USS *Woolsey*, USS *Trippe* and USS *Edison*) scrambled from Mers El Kébir to look for her attacker.

U-73 was still at the scene when the destroyers arrived at about 5:15 PM. Deckert, perhaps hoping for another crack at the crippled merchantman, was held down by two escorts detached from another convoy. When the reinforcements arrived he made a run for it with the unfortunate effect that his sonar operator couldn't hear the destroyers' approach. An hour later after one inconclusive contact, USS *Woolsey* got a good Asdic (active sonar) bearing and dropped a depth-charge pattern which exploded below U-73's keel.[8] The boat started shipping water both in the motor room and the forward torpedo room, lost trim and sank to a depth between 160 and 230 metres.

As the boat's crew struggled to save her *Woolsey* couldn't get a clear enough ping for a second attack. Deckert blew all ballast tanks and forced the submarine to the surface at 7:00 PM with her one remaining motor. Firing up his diesels he tried to escape at full speed in the night. Darkness was no shelter from the destroyers' radar; *Woolsey* found her straight away. A searchlight stabbed the gloom and as U-73 tried to shoot it out the destroyers opened fire with everything that would bear. The doomed submarine sank in less than five minutes with the loss of sixteen crew members, one of whom was picked up but could not be revived. *Woolsey*, with the other two destroyers screening her in the calm sea, found the officers and about two-thirds of the enlisted men. *Edison* then spent another two hours scouring the area in the dark for the remaining survivors, who claimed the officers had taken the only dinghy and left the other ranks to find their own way out and swim for it. They were cheerful enough to be safe and dry, and much more interested in their 'survivor kits' than in their comrades' fate.

Thirty-four survivors were put ashore at Mers El Kébir at midnight on 16th/17th. Usefully, and strictly against orders, some had drawings and notes of the boat and its new homing torpedoes from on-board training sessions in their pockets.

Both boats had lasted longer than they had any right to expect in the increasingly lethal Mediterranean killing ground. By the end of 1943 52 U-boats had successfully run the gauntlet of the Straits of Gibraltar but 39 had been lost, leaving just thirteen of them operational. Another thirteen tried in 1944 with three sunk at Gibraltar. By the end of September the last of them had gone. They fought hard and as their numbers dwindled the *Luftwaffe* redoubled its efforts, attacking shipping with dumb and smart bombs, torpedoes and mines. By the end of the year it was over: shortly after the fall of Toulon and Marseilles convoys entering the Mediterranean were allowed to disperse and proceed independently.

---

[1] Web site uboat.net. *Greatest U-boat Commanders*. Consulted 12th May 2017.

[2] TNA ADM 223/142; *Summary of statements by German prisoners of war 1943 July-Sept*. Report for week ending 19th September 1943.

[3] U-boat Archive: *Narrative of A/S Attack of H.M.S. "Calpe" in company with U.S.S. "Wainwright" and Sinking of U. 593*, July 2014.

[4] TNA WO 208/5508; *Interrogation reports on German and Italian prisoners of war: AFHQ 1-107 1943 May 30 - 1944 Mar 27*.

5 TNA WO 208/4200; *Special extracts from interrogation reports on German and Italian prisoners of war 1942 Dec – 1945 Mar*. Extracts from SR Draft Nos 837, 951A, 1454, 1487, 1509, 2580, 3346, 4695/9, 9289.
6 TNA ADM 223/144; *Summary of statements by German prisoners of war (January-March 1944)*, summary for week ending 8th January 1944.
7 TNA ADM 199/1032; *Various convoys: reports*: GUS 24
8 U-boat Archive; *Woolsey Action Report*, July 2014.

BLOCKADE BREAKERS IN BISCAY

Alsterufer

MV Alsterufer was a 2,729-ton blockade runner, originally designed as a fast fruit ship and converted in 1941 to a naval supply ship. In the process she lost some of her hold space to accommodate prisoners-of-war, extra crew, and a magazine for her heavy defensive armament of one 75 mm, two 37mm, four 20mm and four machine guns. She also carried four launchers for anti-aircraft rockets which dangled a long wire from a parachute in the attacking aircraft's path.

She had left Bordeaux in March 1943 with supplies for a U-boat base at Penang (Malaya) and cargo for Japan, along with two passengers: a priest whose religiosity and prudishness made him thoroughly unpopular, and a mysterious aircraft engineer from Heinkel. The return journey was laden with a precious cargo of rubber, tungsten concentrates and tin ingots.

She left Batavia (Djakarta) for home on 10th November, a few days behind the larger SS *Osorno* making the same perilous run. Both sought the cover of the long winter nights to mask their final approach.

Captain Paulus Piatek was an experienced merchant seaman under no illusions about his chance of completing the trip, especially since the British had been granted the use of an air base in the Azores the previous August. Morale was further depressed by heaving-to for ten days to avoid two Allied convoys crossing ahead of the ship.

Burning fuel recklessly at her maximum speed of fifteen knots, *Alsterufer* was only a day behind schedule entering Biscay. A day too late.

Evidence had been mounting from intercepts and reconnaissance. U-boats were ordered not to attack single merchant ships from 1st December in the swathe of ocean through which *Osorno* and *Alsterufer* were due to pass.[1] A vessel spotted in mid-Atlantic by an air patrol on 8th December identified herself as a British ship known to be in Bombay (Mumbai) at the time. NID concluded this was probably *Osorno* leading a string of attempted breaks. On 9th December a U-boat reported sighting a steamship of 'Antilla' type (presumably *Alsterufer*).[2] U-boats in the Biscay area were given more information about *Osorno* on 22nd, warned to expect friendly warships escorting her, and ordered to report any sighting of the blockade-runner or Allied forces.

An Admiralty signal of 19th December reinforced the importance of keeping Germany starved of war material, instructing that *'Search for blockade runners is to have priority over all other air operations.'*[3] The First Sea Lord (Admiral Andrew Cunningham) followed that with a personal message to the Commander-in-Chief, US Navy (Admiral Ernest King, a vitriolic Anglophobe) on 22nd asking if he could spare one or more escort carriers to help look for them. His reply is not recorded, but on 23rd aircraft from the American carrier USS *Card* spotted *Osorno* and the hunt was on.

As Allied ships formed a cordon across her path and aircraft tried to regain contact a flotilla of twelve German destroyers and torpedo-boats set out from Bordeaux to bring her in. They met *Osorno* and, with strong air support, escorted her into the Gironde estuary where she hit a wreck and had to be beached to save her cargo.

As this was happening *Alsterufer* entered the Biscay hornets' nest stirred up by *Osorno*. U-305 sent in a sighting report at noon on Christmas Day. It was promptly decrypted by Bletchley Park. On 27th December a tired German force, reduced to eleven ships, sailed again to look for her. *Luftwaffe* reconnaissance aircraft patrolled Biscay with orders to contact the blockade-runner directly on a special frequency, which didn't work.[4] In the meantime the ship had been spotted by a RAF Sunderland which was soon joined by others. From 11:45 AM to 1:45 PM *Alsterufer* beat off repeated attacks while the promised *Luftwaffe* support failed to materialise: in a classic failure of inter-service co-operation the ship and aircrew had been given different contact frequencies. Better yet, she was told she could not expect a destroyer escort until next morning. At 4:07 PM her luck ran out: a Czech-crewed Liberator, aircraft H of 311 Squadron (Pilot Officer Doležal) found her with radar. In a blistering half-minute the aircraft attacked with bombs, rockets and guns through vicious defensive fire and fatally damaged the vessel, which began to settle by the stern.

'N 2146 [2nd Officer Johannes Nissen, *Alsterufer*]: *They (the bombs) went through hatch 4, where all the naval crew had their quarters. We had a Merchant ship's crew and a Flak crew, but they were all at the guns already, which was a blessing. Everyone who was on deck, all the seamen and everyone, stood by the guns and helped. No one was wounded. Two men in the magazine probably never got out. I was standing aft at the 10.5 cm. gun – we had a 10.5 cm. gun as well – and shouted to them to come up; that was before the attack, but they didn't come up. One fellow, SCHERESTOCK(?), came flying out through hatch 4, but he'd been hit in the small of the back and killed immediately. The other fellow on the gun was wounded in the knee, his knee-cap was smashed, pushed out of place. His leg will probably remain stiff. The carpenter had his arm broken in two places, but that was whilst lowering a boat, not by the aircraft. Three of our men were killed; all the rest were saved.*'[5]

The crew abandoned ship after setting fire to the radio office and mistakenly throwing the captain's emergency grab-bag onto the pyre. She sank in four hours with the help of two more Liberators. When picked up the crew unanimously praised the fair and courageous conduct of the attack, Captain Piatek describing PO Doležal as a 'cunning old fox.'[6]

In desperation U-415 (*Kapitänleutnant* Kurt Neide) and U-309 (*Oberleutnant zur See* Hans-Gert Mahrholz) were ordered that night to try and draw off the attackers with dummy sighting reports,[7] but *Alsterufer* was already beyond help.

After two days in their rafts the 74 survivors were found at 5:00 PM on 29th December by Canadian Escort Group 6, shepherding combined convoy SL 143 / MKS 34.[8] All but three of the crew survived. On Admiralty orders a Special Interrogation Officer (Sub Lieutenant Williamson) transferred to the ship carrying *Alsterufer*'s commander to try and glean information about the other ships following her.

Three more homeward-bound blockade runners (*Weserland*, *Rio Grande* and *Burgenland*) were sunk in the first week of January 1944. From then on only U-boats, with their much smaller cargo capacity, attempted the hazardous run.

T-25

The futile sortie to bring in *Alsterufer* comprised five 'Narvik' class destroyers of the Eighth Destroyer Flotilla from Bordeaux and six 'Elbing' class ships of the Fourth Torpedo-Boat Flotilla out of Brest. The terms are deceptive: T-Boats were 1,200-ton ships armed with four 105 mm guns, a variety of smaller calibres and two sets of triple torpedo tubes – destroyers in Royal Navy parlance. Similarly the 'Narviks' gun armament was roughly equal to a British light cruiser.

At about 1:00 PM on 28th December, nearly a day after *Alsterufer* was abandoned, orders came for the flotilla to turn back. Almost immediately two British cruisers and 17 destroyers (the latter in fact imaginary) were reported in the area. The phantom warships undoubtedly influenced German behaviour; gunnery officer Günther Schramm later observed ruefully,

> *'I should just like to know where the report originated that there were seventeen English destroyers there. The captain told me that at the end, just before we abandoned ship.'*[9]

The cruisers HMS *Glasgow* and *Enterprise* were sighted at 1:30 and opened fire at extreme range. A short, bloody running fight developed in which the nominally stronger German force was hampered by the heavy seas while the cruisers simultaneously fought off an attempted *Luftwaffe* attack with glider bombs.

T-25 was the tail-end 'guard' ship of the torpedo-boat flotilla. Hits from *Glasgow's* third salvo destroyed one set of her torpedo tubes and put both engines out of action. With the rest of the force disappearing over the horizon T-25 was in deep trouble but kept firing and, having restarted one engine, attempted a torpedo attack. It was all to no avail and she sank under *Glasgow's* battering, perhaps helped by scuttling charges, at about 4:00 PM. The crew were not the pick of the *Kriegsmarine*: admittedly exhausted after nearly five days at action stations the two aft 105mm gun crews abandoned their weapons early in the action and, while most on deck remained calm, there were several reports of men shooting themselves. The emergency gear was missing, broken or damaged in the fight and a number of rafts were lost by being thrown out before the ship had stopped.

Sixty-two survivors packed into a pinnace designed for 24 and drifted for two and a half days until rescued by the minesweeper HMS *Seaham* on 31st. They were delivered to Falmouth the next day.[10]

Figure 2: Sketches of T-25 & T-26 being shelled, and of MV Kerlogue rescuing survivors.
Drawn by Hans Helmut Karsch while interned in the Curragh. Reproduced by kind permission of the National Maritime Museum of Ireland.

The German force split defensively into four to make its escape. As the battle faded east two more ships (T-26 and Z-27) were sunk and four damaged before the battered remnants of the flotilla made it back to France. Six survivors from T-25 and 159 from the other casualties were picked up by the tiny Irish freighter MV *Kerlogue* (142-foot, crew of ten), landed at Cobh on 1st January and interned for the rest of the war.* Fifty-five survivors were rescued by U-505 and U-618.

---

[1] TNA HW 18/250; *Teleprinted translations of decrypted Second World War German U-boat (or U-boat command) radio messages*.

[2] TNA ADM 199/549; *German - Japanese blockade running: reports*. Message 131557A dated 13/12/43. National Archives record ADM 223/8; Special intelligence summaries. OIC/SI 796 (13th December 1943).

[3] ibid. Message 190852A dated 19/12/43.

---

* The story of the *Kerlogue* is remarkable in its own right. The National Maritime Museum of Ireland's web site (http://www.mariner.ie/kerlogue/) is a good starting point.

4. TNA WO 208/4132; *Interrogation reports on German prisoners of war (CSDIC)*, SRA 4832.
5. TNA WO 208/4148; *Interrogation Reports on German Prisoners of War 2451-2699.* SRN 2668 dated 9th January 1944.
6. TNA ADM 186/809; *Interrogation of German naval survivors.* Personal correspondence with Tom Doležal, son of PO Oldřich Doležal.
7. TNA HW18/250; *Teleprinted translations of decrypted Second World War German U-boat (or U-boat command) radio messages.* Subject: Orbona & Alsterufer (1943 Nov 26 - 1944 Feb 3) – message dated 28/12/43; 02:37. One of the transmissions appears to have been picked up by the escort carrier HMS *Striker*, which flew off a patrol at daylight the next morning to investigate (TNA ADM 199/978; *K.M.S., M.K.S., W.S., O.S. and S.L. convoys: reports.*)
8. TNA ADM 199/966; *SL, KMS and MKS convoys: reports MKS 1 - 32 MKS 34, SL135, SL 136, SL 137, SL 138, SL 139, SL 140, SL 141, SL 142, SL 143, SL 144.* MKS 34 was one of the two possible convoys bringing home the survivors from U-73 and U-593.
9. TNA WO 208/4163; *Interrogation Reports on German Prisoners of War 1738-1949.* SRX 1919 dated 1st February 1944.
10. BBC WW2 People's War: *The Wartime Experiences of an RNR Officer*.

BATTLESHIPS IN THE BARENTS SEA

Scharnhorst was arguably the *Kriegsmarine's* most active and successful capital ship. Commissioned early in 1939 she and her sister ship *Gneisenau* started their war spectacularly by sinking the armed merchantman HMS *Rawalpindi* in November. During the Norwegian campaign of spring 1940 the two ships had an inconclusive run-in with the battle-cruiser HMS *Renown*, then sank a British corvette, the aircraft carrier HMS *Glorious* and her two escorting destroyers. *Scharnhorst* and *Gneisenau* sank nineteen merchantmen and captured three in a 1941 Atlantic sortie; it might have been more but for orders to avoid tangling with Allied capital ships. They then retired to Brest for repairs.

Early in 1942 German high command decided to move the ships north, where they could threaten the Russian convoys and use the better ship repair facilities at home. Accordingly in February *Scharnhorst*, *Gneisenau* and the heavy cruiser *Prinz Eugen* made their famous dash up the Channel, one of the Royal Navy's greatest humiliations of the war.

In September 1943 *Scharnhorst* and *Tirpitz* led a raid on Spitsbergen which, while calling to mind the words 'sledgehammer' and 'nut,' successfully destroyed military and port facilities including the important weather station there. Still the disparity of forces left an unpleasant taste behind for *Maschinenobergefreiter* (Stoker First Class) Paul Schaffrath.

'N 2175: *After the SPITZSBERGEN operation, they cursed like anything on board the SCHARNHORST. No-one was in favour of firing at those cardboard houses. The ratings cursed.*

> *Everyone cursed. They were really defenceless. If there had been anything there! We thought there were at least land torpedo tubes and torpedo batteries and that sort of thing, but there was nothing. Just a few old '8.8's and '10.5's and one 15 cm gun, but that was all. We went in with nine 28 cm guns.*
> N 2110: *Was the TIRPITZ there, too?*
> N 2175: *Yes. She remained outside. They sent us in. The swine were too cowardly to go in with the TIRPITZ.*[1]

Although thought to be a lucky ship the luck didn't always run *Scharnhorst's* way. She took heavy damage from a torpedo hit by one of *Glorious'* escorts, and again from an air raid at La Pallice (La Rochelle) in 1941. Two mine strikes during the Channel dash put her out of commission for six months. She then collided with a U-boat when working-up, forcing another spell in dry dock. An unexplained explosion in March 1943 killed 34 men and meant more repairs. Despite – or perhaps because of – her heavy armour protection *Scharnhorst* was vulnerable to weather damage. Her initial trials revealed a tendency to ship water in heavy seas, which delayed her commissioning while a raised bow was fitted. This mitigated the problem but didn't cure it: the ship sustained flood damage after the *Rawalpindi* action, escaping from *Renown* in 1940 and again during the passage to Norway in 1943.[2]

Christmas Day 1943 was rudely interrupted at 13:00 when *Scharnhorst's* loudspeakers blared out the order to prepare for sea at three hours' notice. Russia-bound convoy JW 55B had been spotted three days earlier and was approaching the area of maximum danger, north of Norway. Rear-Admiral Bey came aboard with his staff and at 19:00 the ship, her crew still frantically clearing away stores, put to sea with five escorting destroyers. Her departure was reported by Norwegian resistance and confirmed by Bletchley Park's code breakers.

JW 55B comprised nineteen merchant ships escorted by seventeen destroyers, four of them detached from westbound convoy RA 55A which hadn't been noticed. In addition, Force 1 (cruisers HMS *Belfast*, HMS *Norfolk* and HMS *Sheffield*) and Force 2 (battleship HMS *Duke of York*, cruiser HMS *Jamaica* and four destroyers under Admiral Bruce Fraser) were converging on the area. The convoy was the terrifyingly vulnerable bait in a deliberate trap.

As he approached the convoy's path Admiral Bey sent his destroyers ahead to find and shadow it. In the increasingly vile weather Force 1 found him first, opening fire at about 9:00 on 26th December; a lucky – and crucial – early hit by HMS *Norfolk* disabled *Scharnhorst's* forward radar.

It is worth taking a moment to contemplate the storm conditions, which had a profound effect on the battle. Few people got any rest aboard *Duke of York* during her dash to the east and many of *Scharnhorst's* crew were working through the miseries of seasickness. U-boat and *Luftwaffe* operations were severely constrained, and life aboard the smaller ships must have been deeply unpleasant.

Encouraged by signals from Admiral Dönitz, Bey turned south in an attempt to loop around the obstacle and find the convoy. In the heavy seas now running his ship was much faster than the cruisers, who fell back to protect the merchantmen. Another sharp engagement followed when *Scharnhorst* ran into the screen again and turned away after damaging *Norfolk*. Without radar Bey had no idea that he was running onto *Duke of York's* fourteen-inch guns until starshell flamed overhead and the battleship's salvoes started to fall around him, quickly disabling his forward gun turret. In a fatal mistake, anti-aircraft gun crews were ordered to take cover while the first and second gunnery officers quarrelled about using the secondary armament as combat batteries or to illuminate the scene with starshell.

Scharnhorst turned east and used her speed to open the range from *Duke of York*, which ceased fire at 18:24 when some twelve miles distant. One of her last salvoes destroyed a boiler room, reducing Scharnhorst's speed to ten knots. Minutes later *Scharnhorst's* crew saw 'shadows' in the night which turned out to be *Duke of York's* escorting destroyers closing each side for a torpedo attack, helped by the silence of her secondary armament.

'N 2131 [*Mechanikergefreiter* Johann Wiest]: ...... *transmitted: "Enemy shadows on starboard side." The Gunnery officer sent through: "We can't fire at shadows, we must have targets."*
N 2132 [*Mechanikergefreiter* Horst Zaubitzer]:*(ironically) The shadows fired torpedoes.*
N 2131: *The shadows sank us, beautifully!*'[3]

At least three torpedoes hits brought *Scharnhorst's* speed, which had started to recover, back down. The doomed ship was caught between *Duke of York* and *Jamaica* to the south and *Belfast* and *Norfolk* to the north, with destroyers all around. Racked by shellfire and torn by torpedoes she capsized and sank at about 19:45, her surviving guns firing to the last.

Duke of York's fourteen-inch heavy guns fired 77 salvoes during the battle; her secondary armament and the cruisers' six and eight-inch guns shot at an even higher rate; the British cruisers and destroyers fired 55 torpedoes between them, of which eleven to thirteen hit *Scharnhorst*. Despite this savage battering the survivors were unanimous in their belief that the ship could not have been sunk by gunfire alone. They claimed that no shells had penetrated the central citadel, and the ship's armour and multiple damage control compartments would have allowed her to survive a gun battle almost indefinitely. Nonetheless the critical disabling of her radar, destruction of two-thirds of her main armament and the speed reduction which allowed the destroyers to close were all achieved by gunfire. One survivor who witnessed the engagement from the crow's nest described the accuracy of *Duke of York*'s fire, and its ability to track *Scharnhorst*'s every move, as uncanny.

Prisoners shipped to the UK aboard *Duke of York* were dismissive of her overly large compartments but amazed at how little damage she had suffered, almost all of which was due to the shock and blast of her own guns.

Scharnhorst's life-rafts were poorly maintained, many were destroyed in the unimaginable carnage of the battle, her abandon-ship drills were skimpy to non-existent, and a floating man had short life expectancy in the freezing sea.

'N2127 [*Matrosenobergefreiter* Günter Bohle]: *No-one knew on which raft he should go or whether to put on a lifejacket.*
N2128 [*Matrosenobergefreiter* Helmut Backhaus]: *I didn't know how to put on my lifejacket; I had never put on my lifejacket since I joined the SCHARNHORST.*
N2127:   *And we had no instruction in lifesaving drill.*'[4]

★ ★ ★

'N2145 [*Matrosenobergefreiter* Nicolaus Wiebusch]:   *No preparations had been made in the SCHARNHORST in the event of the ship's sinking. The cases with provisions and signal pistols ought to have been on the rafts.*'[5]

The destroyers *Scorpion* and *Matchless* recovered just 36 survivors, all enlisted, from *Scharnhorst's* crew of 1,968. After about fifty minutes Admiral Fraser took the brutal and still controversial decision to leave the scene. The battered fleet found its way to the Kola inlet where *Scharnhorst's* survivors transferred to *Duke of York* on 27th December.

The circumstances of Fraser's choice bear examination. His first concern was to confirm that his quarry had in fact sunk, which *Scorpion* was able to do from survivors' testimony.

He then had to balance the dwindling chance of rescuing more at night in an Arctic storm against the growing possibility of a U-boat or *Scharnhorst's* escorts finding him. After an extended high-speed action in appalling weather he must also have been concerned about his destroyers' fuel state.

His staff would certainly have known – not least from earlier prisoner-of-war interrogations – that U-boats had been receiving steadily improved radar-warning receivers with rudimentary direction-finding ability since summer 1942. His battleship, four cruisers and nine destroyers stopped or milling around slowly in the open and broadcasting radar emissions were vulnerable targets whereas a surfaced U-boat would be near-invisible to radar in 'sea clutter' from the 6-8 metre waves.

U-boats had already used their radar detectors to shadow convoy escorts in the Atlantic. For example, Purkhold's U-260 tracked ONS 154 through the foggy night of 27/28 December 1942 while a wolf pack assembled. The convoy lost fourteen ships for the destruction of one submarine. I have found no evidence that Naval Intelligence knew this but the Admiral's staff, knowing the performance of their own radar detectors, could reasonably have inferred it.

The situation had the potential to turn from triumph to disaster in seconds. Fraser was not to know that the nearest U-boats were seventy nautical miles away, *Scharnhorst's* destroyers ninety.

We should also remember how finely balanced an operation it was. Fraser had to time his departure from Iceland with care: too early and his destroyers could run out of fuel or his force be detected; too late and *Scharnhorst* might find the convoy first. As it was, he had to order the convoy to double back on itself and then skirt the ice pack – luckily, for the cruiser squadron first detected *Scharnhorst between* themselves and the convoy. If the weather had been less bad; if Bey's staff had been quicker aboard, allowing an earlier departure; if *Norfolk's* lucky hit hadn't blinded *Scharnhorst* or that from *Duke of York* slowed her at the critical moment the cards might have landed horribly differently.

It must have been a particularly poignant moment for Admiral Fraser, who had been the penultimate commander of HMS *Glorious*. He praised the handling of the German ship to his officers later that night saying:

> *'Gentlemen, the battle against Scharnhorst has ended in victory for us. I hope that if any of you are ever called upon to lead a ship into action against an opponent many times superior, you will command your ship as gallantly as Scharnhorst was commanded today'*

The interrogating officer later repeated Fraser's comments to the survivors.

In Germany Admiral Dönitz lashed out at the *Luftwaffe* for misleading reconnaissance. As a later captive reported,

> *'They should have ascertained, with the aid of their apparatus, what sort of enemy forces were present. They reported nothing. Whereupon they* [the Kriegsmarine] *at once withdrew the destroyers, otherwise they would have been lost too.'*[6]

In atrocious weather with unreliable equipment it is difficult to see what more the German Air Force could have done and the excuse for *Scharnhorst's* escort being so far out of place is clearly specious.

---

[1] TNA WO 208/4149; *Interrogation Reports on German Prisoners of War 2700-3050.* SRN 2821 dated 20th January 1944.

[2] Wikipedia; *German battleship Scharnhorst*, 13th April 2017. Consulted 12th May 2017.

[3] TNA WO 208/4148; *Interrogation Reports on German Prisoners of War 2451-2699.* SRN 2641 dated 5th January 1944.

[4] ibid. SRN 2575 dated 4th January 1944.

[5] TNA WO 208/4149; *Interrogation Reports on German Prisoners of War 2700-3050.* SRN 2807 dated 19th January 1944.

[6] TNA WO 208/4150; *Interrogation Reports on German Prisoners of War 3051-3359*. SRN 3075 dated 14th March 1944.

CSDIC – The System

How it Worked

The Combined Services Detailed Interrogation Centre was a remarkable intelligence resource. Teams from all three services were integrated under army management, at first as MI9 responsible both for enemy prisoners in British hands and British and Commonwealth prisoners held by the Axis. In December 1941 the two were separated with interrogation of enemy prisoners becoming the responsibility of a separate section, MI19. The following month the naval CSDIC team was reorganised with its German and Italian speakers assigned to the relevant geographical sections.

Their focus was very different from that of interrogation centres run by MI5 at Camp 020 (Latchmere House near Richmond) for suspected spies and by Military Intelligence at the Royal Patriotic Schools in Wandsworth for refugees and defectors. These two were interested in the individuals passing through their hands, to assess their sincerity and determine their fate. Those found to be agents faced a stark choice: work for the British as part of the celebrated 'Double-Cross' system or submit to a court's pick between prison and the hangman.

CSDIC on the other hand developed a highly tuned intelligence production line, taking in captives thought to have useful information as raw material, separating and processing it, then 'dumping' the subjects back to conventional prisoner-of-war camps. The guests passing though were uniformed servicemen who came with a package of Geneva Convention rights that could be stretched a little but never ignored.

Director of Military Intelligence (DMI)

Deputy Director of Military Intelligence/Prisoners of War (DDMI/PW)

MI9 (Brigadier Crockatt)
Intelligence policy regarding British P/W
Collection & distribution of information from P/W camps and escapers
Facilitating escape & evasion
Ancillary tasks and support

MI19 (Lieutenant-Colonel Rawlinson)
Intelligence aspects regarding enemy P/W and alien refugees, excluding security
Policy of Inter-Allied and Inter-Service P/W interrogation organisations
Policy of CSDIC (UK) and PWIS (Home) in respect of detailed and long-term interrogation of enemy P/W
Policy and organisation in respect of interrogation of alien refugees and infiltrators in UK
Dissemination of the resulting Army P/W and alien intelligence

Outside Organisations
Intelligence School No 9
RAF Intelligence Course "B"

Outside Organisations
CSDIC (UK) (Colonel Kendrick)
(Long-term, technical examination of specially selected P/W of all Services)
PWIS (Major Scotland)
(Prisoner of War Interrogation Section: Interrogation of Army P/W in UK and selection of P/W for CSDIC)
MI19 (RPS) (Major Acton Burnell)
(Interrogation of Alien refugees and escapers)

Figure 3: DMI Prisoner-of-War Organisation.

At times they sorely tried their hosts' patience. A low-level fighter-bomber attack on 20th January 1943 caught London unprepared and hit Sandhurst Road School in Catford. An interrogator threw the toll in a *Luftwaffe* NCO's face.

'A 1158:   *He (I.O.) told me that during the daylight raid with the Jabos* [fighter-bombers] *one bomb landed on a girls' school and killed 150 of them.*'
'A 1170   *That's good, that will make them sick of the whole business.*'[1]

The service was originally based at the Tower of London but quickly outgrew its facilities and took over country houses at Trent Park near Cockfosters (December 1939), then Latimer House (July 1942) and Wilton Park (December 1942) in Buckinghamshire. By spring 1944 the latter two, known as No's 1 and 2 Distribution Centres to disguise their purpose, were running at full capacity.

CSDIC – The System

Figure 4: Latimer House today.
The Library was then the Officers' Mess.

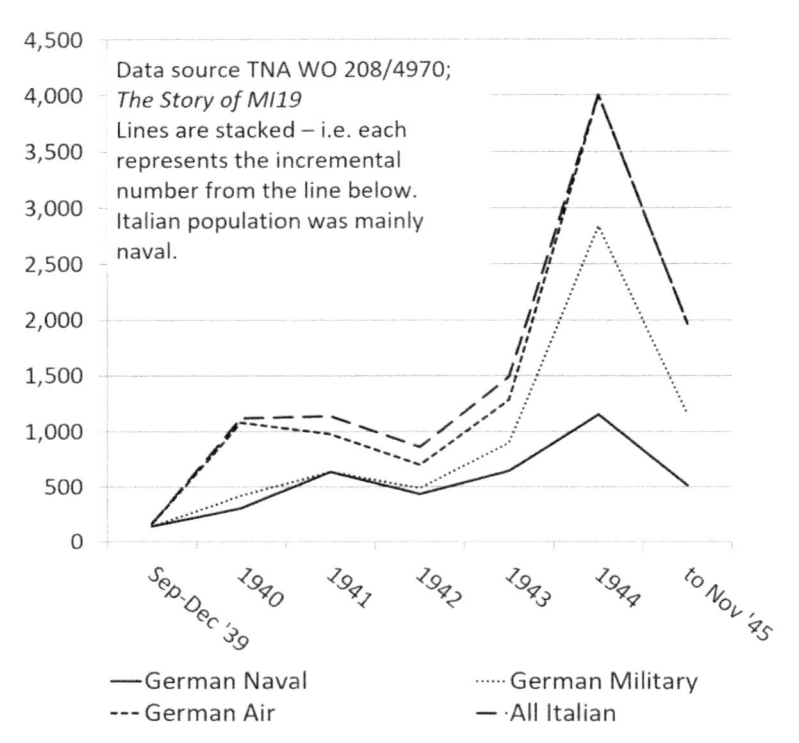

Figure 5: CSDIC UK Workload during the six years of war.
Note the paucity of army clients until 1943.

After this Trent Park was kept for the most senior prisoners who knew most and took up long-term residence there as a kind of operatic chorus, to give a running commentary on the war from the enemy's point of view. They were encouraged to live in a fantasy world of their own significance – *Alles in Wonderland*.

Red Cross inspectors were kept well away from all of them in a juggling act which required ever more ingenuity as time passed. By early 1943 it is easy to discern the Prisoner of War Information Bureau's frustration at being cold-shouldered by MI19 while fending off the Protecting Power (Switzerland). PWIB made its point in a terse memo:

> '1. It is considered that the Bureau should know the physical location as distinct from the notional location of every prisoner of war in the U.K. because that is their function and it is information essential to be known.
>
> They are fully aware that prisoners of war in the Distribution Centres [CSDICs] are not to be notified save as at a permanent camp. It is erroneous to presume that all information given to them is notified to the Protecting Power.
>
> After all, Distribution Centres differ from ordinary cages in this important particular that prisoners of war are held there for a longer period than can be permitted to elapse without notifying the prisoners of war [sic] capture.
>
> This requires the collusion of the Bureau.
>
> 2. The name Distribution Centres seems adequately to convey their transitory nature.
>
> Their safety from inspection by the Protecting Power depends not on any denial of entry on the grounds of their being a cage, but on their official non-existence.'[2]

The eventual ruse was that Trent Park was owned up to but prisoners at the other centres were assigned to a 'notional' overt internment camp.

Equally strenuous efforts were made to keep all mention of the process out of the press. There were limits to the scope of a formal stop because international law permitted the searching and interrogation of prisoners. Censors were briefed to look for anything that gave away the place, methods or results of searching or interrogation, or allowed individual identification. Editors were informally contacted to ensure there was no published suggestion of prisoners being asked for more than their name, rank and number.[3]

Early in the war MI9 evaluated refugee Polish intelligence officers as potential interrogators on the assumption that their language and culture would give them a head start in dealing with German captives. This proved unwarranted and it was felt that their burden of incandescent anger created too high a risk of trampling Geneva Convention rules to allow their use except in the case of 'Action Stations' (invasion) when all normal constraints would vanish. The offer was revived in 1943 when there happened to be a Polish intelligence officer in Algiers as Poles in German service were captured in Tunisia.[4]

In the mature system prisoners could be brought directly to CSDIC or first taken to one of nine reception cages run by the Army's Prisoner of War Interrogation Service (PWIS). The cages needed a lot of space. Some were at Kempton Park, Catterick, Lingfield, Newmarket and Doncaster racecourses, or Preston North End football ground. Other sites were at Loughborough and Edinburgh. They skimmed off those deserving CSDIC's attention and sorted the rest for dispersal to the hundreds of accommodation camps in Britain and abroad, trying to segregate people who were likely to kill each other (for example separating virulent Nazis from regime opponents and pressed foreigners). This involved preliminary interview, sometimes by CSDIC staff on detachment, and was supposed to complete within 48 hours.

The notorious London District Cage (LDC) in Kensington Palace Gardens seems at times to have taken things much further. *Funkgefreiter* (Telegraphist) Alfred Wernard of U-187, captured in February 1943, described an interview with an army captain who kept a revolver on the desk. Every time Wernard stonewalled a question he rotated the gun a fraction, eventually informing him 'When this points at you I will pull the trigger.' It didn't happen but the threat was plausible enough. Prisoners were also shown what they were told was an open grave in the grounds, and frequently woken for interrogation in the small hours of the morning.'[5]

As the number of captives ballooned after D-Day Kempton Park, Lingfield and LDC (plus Devizes for US prisoners) were used for preliminary interrogation and selection of candidates for CSDIC.

Interrogators had to be good linguists, not necessarily bilingual but able to follow a technical, colloquial conversation. They needed to be familiar with the interviewees' world and able to adapt their approach to the personality they were dealing with. They also had two secret assets to help them.

German servicemen had been warned to expect multiple interrogations. *Funkobergefreiter* (Telegraphist) Hans Ewald of U-264 told a stool pigeon,

'N 2245: *In GERMANY we were told that you go through several interrogation camps before reaching your permanent camp.'*[6]

They had also been told their conversations were likely to be bugged.

'N 2332: *A Kapitän zur See MEISSNER, holder of the Oak Leaves, who was exchanged, reported that they used microphones to a very great extent.'*[7]

In March 1944 Rudolf Spitz, a stool pigeon formerly of U-444, was naturally curious about the current state of their briefings.

'N 1552: *What do they say in the security lectures?*

N 2243: *So far it has been correct: "You will come to a camp where you will be interrogated from all quarters, by English and American officers and when you are in your rooms you mustn't speak about your U-boat or about any service matters. There is apparatus installed through which they hear everything, even the slightest sounds."*[8]

---

*   Helen Fry's book *The London Cage: The Secret History of Britain's WWII Interrogation Centre* (Yale University Press, 2017) explores this topic in detail.

Despite all advance preparation the microphones, which were hidden in the light fittings, were often suspected but never found. At least, not at CSDIC UK. The cages were a different matter. Alfred Wernard found microphones at LDC and *Matrosenobergefreiter* (Able Seaman) Theodor Lange of U-264 spotted them in the racecourse cage he passed through.

> 'N 2247: *In the cell, at the racing stables where I was first of all, microphones were concealed in the pillars. They have them in the first place you go to. They don't have them here.'*[9]

Bugs were also spotted in the Middle East centres. This from *Leutnant zur See* (Junior Sub-Lieutenant) Fitz of U-223:

> 'N 2401: *In the interrogation camp at ALGIERS there were microphones. There were two German officers who were probably stool pigeons; we had to go on daily walks with them.'*[10]

Prisoners were kept two to a cell, preferably men from different services or branches to encourage full explanation of a topic. Selected newspapers were available to provoke discussion, as were writing materials with which they surprisingly often drew explanatory sketches.

Their conversations were systematically recorded and transcribed by listeners, typically German-Jewish refugees, hidden in a separate 'M' (for microphone) room.[11] Each listener monitored two cells, keeping an ear open for topics of interest. When something came up he set a disc recorder going as long as necessary, then handed over to a colleague while he transcribed the material.

Gossip about people and places was as welcome as material of obvious military interest such as equipment, tactics and plans. It all helped add to the interrogators' air of omniscience. As time progressed it became clear how widely known the regime's atrocities were, and how many were complicit.

Some prisoners, either through conscience or convenience, agreed to become stool pigeons: to lead their colleagues' conversation in interesting directions and report back. They didn't know about the microphones but could compensate for the eavesdroppers' key limitation. Sharing the background and expertise of their subjects they could follow a highly technical discussion about, say, gunnery, torpedoes or radar in a way that the 'M' Room listeners could not. For instance the report of a long talk about the new T5 torpedo with a leading seaman from U-73 begins with the candid admission that *'The German text of this report is very obscure, but an attempt has been made to translate it.'*[12] Luckily his cellmate was a stool pigeon and radio specialist, who could presumably fill in the missing or corrupt detail.

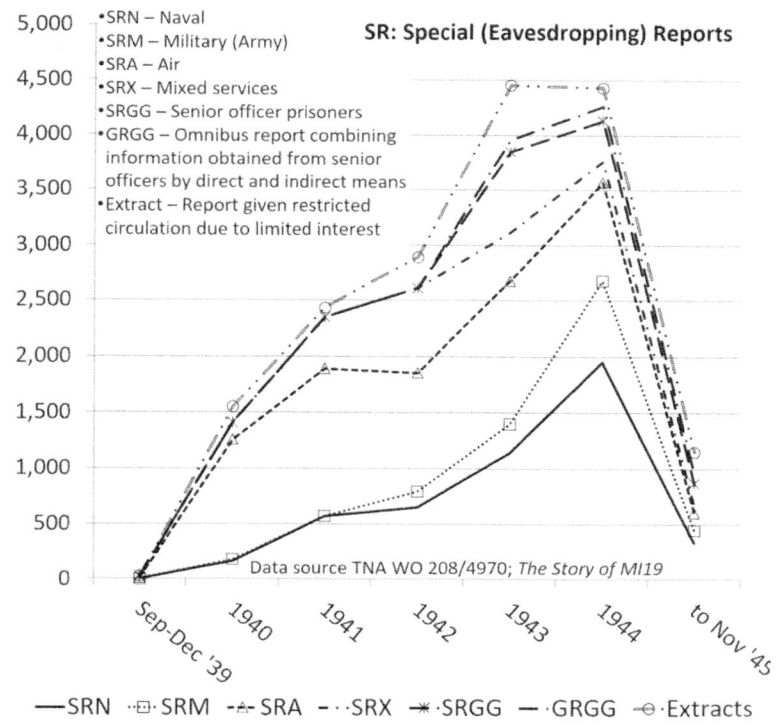

- SRN – Naval
- SRM – Military (Army)
- SRA – Air
- SRX – Mixed services
- SRGG – Senior officer prisoners
- GRGG – Omnibus report combining information obtained from senior officers by direct and indirect means
- Extract – Report given restricted circulation due to limited interest

Data source TNA WO 208/4970; *The Story of MI19*

Figure 6: Number of SR (eavesdropping) reports by year.

Each service team helped the others as needed but had its own culture and methods. RAF interrogators used microphones largely to confirm what they had already discovered whereas the smaller naval team used the interview to pump-prime for later eavesdropping or stool pigeon conversations:

'N 2125:   (Re loading of shells). I told him (IO) that I load twelve of them (a minute), whereas I load twenty-one.'[13]

In Admiralty a central department (NID 1/PW for Germany and NID 3/PW for Italy) filtered the information required from and the context provided to the CSDIC crew to preserve security and segregation of different intelligence sources, whereas the Air Force team were given wider access.

They all found the task became easier as they went along. The interviews were not always recorded but notes were taken. The interrogator skilfully used his knowledge to hide the gaps he was interested in. A prisoner facing an interviewer who already seemed to know everything about his tactics, equipment, home port and favourite bars was tempted to relax and enjoy the drink, smoke and gossip offered. After all, what point was there in holding back? In this conversation between Kurt Böhme and Heinz Hungershausen, captains of U-450 and U-91 respectively, both officers are clearly aware of the trick but unable to resist being drawn into it.

'N 2364 [Hungershausen]:   *They keep on talking about 'Walter' boats here. As far as I know, they have withdrawn them again already, whether to allow for more thorough development or to allow of quicker building of another type, I don't know.*

N 2344 [Böhme]:   *I should be very surprised if the people here didn't know all the details about them.*

N 2364:   *Perhaps there is a traitor on the staff somewhere, after all.*

N 2344:   *I think that is the most important thing that must be passed on to GERMANY.*

N 2364:   *It's well known. That is what is mentioned in all the pamphlets we get. If we are taken prisoner: "The enemy have very accurate information; don't be deceived by that into thinking that, when they are carrying on a friendly conversation with you, they only want confirmation of facts they already know, and don't let yourself be surprised into speaking about things which they may not know about at first(?)". Our people over there know that they know such a lot here. The joke is that we are told much too little about everything that is going on.*

N 2344:   It is all secret, but only to U-boat captains.'[14]

This also illustrates another technique, which was planting seeds to germinate in later cellmate conversations: 'Oh they know all about X but they haven't a clue about Y.'

The interrogators scrupulously avoided physical mistreatment, not through ethical qualms but because it was ineffective and might affect the fate of British prisoners in Germany. There were however psychological levers available for the recalcitrant prisoner. A spell in solitary confinement, the suggestion that the Russians were interested in him or he would be sent to Canada through the (supposedly) lethal U-boat infestation of the Atlantic could work wonders. A frequently successful tactic was requiring him to show enough knowledge to prove he was who he said he was and not a spy or saboteur – liable to trial and execution.

A serviceman's natural respect for rank could also be exploited. A *korvettenkapitän* (lieutenant-commander) U-boat skipper would be interviewed by a commander or captain – or at least by someone who appeared to be. Interrogators kept a selection of jackets with appropriate rank insignia for different occasions.

Early in the war NID experimented with a combination of drugs (Evipan or hexobarbital, a barbiturate derivative) and hypnosis using volunteers as guinea-pigs. The approach was abandoned for a number of reasons, again to do with effectiveness. It was essential that the subjects should never realise, then or later, what had been done to avoid word getting out; a doctor whose ethics were flexible enough to administer the treatment might not be reliably discreet; and – critically – it didn't work. Or at least not well enough.[15]

There was always the risk of giving away more than you learnt. Prisoners' letters were censored and NID knew the code they had been given to feed back information, but were not so naive as to believe they were catching everything. More than once a German officer with valuable tactical information was accidentally included in a prisoner swap. And Franz von Werra – 'The One That Got Away' – a *Luftwaffe* officer shot down in September 1940 eventually made it back to Germany in April 1941 having been fruitlessly exposed to every technique in the toolbox at the time. It did no good. For most, time and familiarity wore down the warnings they had been given, especially when the more colourful predictions of torture proved false.

Von Werra's escape led to the immediate classification of prisoners as 'X' or 'Y' according to whether they were captured before or after his return. Experience showed this to be an unnecessary precaution but the distinction was kept to allow segregation of captives who had and had not undergone the full CSDIC experience.

The toolbox contained carrot as well as stick. Although it was fatal to relax the discipline which Germans expected, their civility would be reciprocated and bring small kindnesses – a seat, a cigarette – in return. Alcohol could be used to reward a prisoner or put him off his guard. Once the team had his measure he might be taken to a pub (perhaps with a Wren officer along) or for a slap-up dinner in London as a special treat, and to give the lie to German propaganda of smoking rubble and a starving population. A tour of the city, carefully routed to avoid the worst damaged areas, was sometimes enough on its own to bring home the brutal reality of Germany's situation, as in this conversation between N2189 *Matrosengefreiter* (Able Seaman) Wolfgang Blumenberg and N2191 *Funkhauptgefreiter* (Telegraphist) Hans Dabelstein of U-386.

> 'N 2191: (*Having returned from a visit to LONDON*): *It is really sickening the way they lie in the German broadcasts. One should speak directly to GERMANY on the wireless -*
> N 2189: *Yes.*
> N 2191: *I should like to tell them, I should like to rub it in, honestly I would.*
> N 2189: *It is scandalous.*
> N 2191: *The Germans call these attacks large-scale ones. Compare the attacks the German population has to put up with, and these so-called 'large-scale attacks' are a mere bagatelle. They hit three or four houses and a small fire is the result, that is their 'large-scale attack'. Later on, when I go home, I shall tell them what I saw here with my own eyes.*
> N 2189: *It has made a tremendous impression on me.*
> N 2191: *Yes, on me too.*
> N 2189: *You can depend on it, I shall tell them in GERMANY exactly what it was like. I won't have the slightest hesitation.*
> N 2191: *I never thought they would let us walk about so freely.*
> N 2189: *That shows that they trust us.*'[16]

Both later agreed to work as stool pigeons.

Many who had spent their professional lives trying to strangle Britain's supply lifeline in the 'tonnage war' found it dispiriting to discover how little they had succeeded. Standard rations at camp were beyond the experience of most while a meal out, off ration, left Kurt Böhme (commander of U-450) stunned.

(After an outing):

'*N 2344: They simply don't know what war is! You should just see the cake which was put before us. There hasn't been anything like that in GERMANY for a long time.*'[17]

An occasional trick was for the host to match the guest glass for glass. They would then be joined by another interrogator who had been 'delayed' and was stone-cold sober.

These trips had their own perils. Colonel Kendrick, in overall charge at Latimer, was entertaining at Simpsons in the Strand one day when Winston Churchill walked in. Churchill was incandescent at this 'pampering' of Germans, which he instantly forbade. MI19 duly moved their operations to the Ritz.[18]

As far as the naval team was concerned the cost of the expeditions, as well as of lubricating interrogations and a few small comforts for the stool pigeons, was borne by DNI's secret fund. Toward the end of the war it averaged £15 per month (about £615 at 2016 prices) but swelled to double that at the end of 1944, which brought a pained rebuke from Captain Clanchy, one of the Director's deputies to Lt Cdr Cope, at Latimer:

'There are several items which are objectionable, viz: entertaining at the Ritz and purchase of considerable quantities of gin. If these facts became generally known, there might be good cause for scandal. Furthermore, I and many others are quite unable to enjoy these luxuries and it is out of all proportion that our enemies should.
An occasional outlay of this kind is a different matter but the objection is the continuity of this treatment.'

Cope, no doubt knowing that he was soon to move on, made a suitably anodyne reply.[19]

From the start NID used a standard classification for intelligence reliability comprising a two-character code: A to E for the reliability of the source and 1 to 5 for the probability of the news (0 where it could not be assessed). Thus, a radio technician talking willingly about his own subject might be rated A, but only C when he discussed torpedoes. His views on equipment he had handled would be rated 1 but that would drop to 3 or 4 for dockside gossip. This and clear separation of different sources of intelligence – wireless intercepts, captured documents, reconnaissance, friendly and enemy spies – allowed intelligence consumers such as the Operational Intelligence Centre (OIC) to make rational judgements on how to build them into an overall picture. This sophisticated evaluation system helped guard against DNI (1939-42) Admiral Godfrey's *bête noire* – 'wishfulness' – and was probably ahead of its time.

The 'point' officers were supported by a photographic section who took prisoner 'mug shots,' copied maps and documents and processed any undeveloped film captives had on them. Commissioned Wren (Women's Royal Naval Service) specialists wrote the final reports, assisted by non-commissioned clerical staff. The interrogator dictated a rough report as soon as possible after an interview; one copy of this went to the Admiralty along with the current batch of 'M' Room transcripts by a frequent despatch-rider service. Other copies were filed in the CSDIC master file, subject files and kept handy to aid report preparation. Any particularly urgent news was phoned through.

The Wren officers combined the interrogation reports, stool pigeon feedback and 'M' Room transcripts into preliminary reports (designed to flag the intelligence likely to be produced and provoke questions from consumers) and a Weekly Summary of Prisoners' Statements, with each nugget of intelligence tagged by source and estimated reliability.

Once the information reached 1/PW and 3/PW at Admiralty it was used to produce a series of Confidential Books in the CB 04051 series, generally one for each vessel whose survivors passed through the system. The books took several months to produce however and, despite their wide distribution (over 500 copies), seldom reached the destroyer, frigate and corvette officers who had most urgent need of the information. They were later replaced by simply-produced, subject-specific technical reports with wider distribution.

Where a result was likely to affect operations NID issued 'UC' (possibly 'Urgent Communication') reports. These were one or two-page documents on a single topic, quickly multigraphed and widely issued. They were based on one or several sources which were often but not always disguised.

When Pilot Officer Doležal and his crew sealed *Alsterufer's* fate they were too busy to pay much attention to the storm of anti-aircraft fire they were flying through. It was only when their photographs of the engagement were developed that they realised they had ignored about twenty 'PAC' rocket-deployed parachutes, each dangling about 300 feet of wire. A Naval Intelligence UC report had warned of this possibility the previous August and survivors in due course provided more technical detail, leading to an updated warning in February 1944.[20] Luckily many of the cartridges were affected by damp and proved useless when needed.

The CSDIC interrogators travelled a long and tortuous road to gain credibility with their Admiralty customers. Flag Officer (Submarines) and the naval constructors, for example, did not believe their reports that U-boats could dive beneath the maximum setting of British depth charges until the capture in August 1941 of U-570 (later HMS *Graph*) and her subsequent evaluation. Equally the constructors long denied that a ship as small as the Narvik class destroyer could carry gun armament matching a British light cruiser. Many refused to believe this, even after an Admiralty warning, before the Biscay battle with HMS *Enterprise* and *Glasgow*, and the final doubters were not satisfied until one fell into our hands after D-Day.

The key lay in reducing the mass of material coming out of the centres to a series of relevant, reliable and digestible alerts tailored to the information consumers' needs. One such, the Operational Intelligence Centre (OIC), was a small group of men and women working day and night to maintain the best available picture of the Atlantic battle. This 'working fiction,' produced through a fog of exhaustion and integrating all available sources of intelligence, was used to re-route convoys, reinforce escorts, and set traps for U-boats. One OIC writer put the problem succinctly:

> *'Unfortunately P.O.W. dockets tended to be very verbose and as the questioning process covered pretty well every aspect of the prisoner's life, private and otherwise, it sometimes took a long time to find the precise information one was looking for. Another factor limiting the amount of research which could be expended on these P.O.W. dockets was the necessity to check up on the statements made therein. An interrogation might have an A grading judged by purely external standards but when guaged [sic] by the touch stone of intercepted W/T might prove to be valueless. On the other hand one completely erroneous statement of fact need not prejudice the whole and as a result the task of extracting value from these interrogations was extremely laborious. It is true to say that P.O.W. reports never received the attention they merited for the simple reason already so frequently stressed, namely lack of time.'*[21]

Some CSDIC staff were more conscious than others of the need to sell their product, and ruffled official feathers by skipping the official chain of command. As time progressed the team's presentation was refined both by Wren writers at the CSDIC sites and by the co-ordinating Admiralty section, NID 1/PW, which also integrated intelligence from captured documents. Godfrey's successor as DNI, by then Rear Admiral Rushbrooke, observed:

'There are always people who regard Intelligence as a Cinderella. They will be converted only when they have found in practice that she makes a good partner at the ball.'[22]

CSDIC's growing track record of accuracy and reliability did produce some glass slippers. In 1942 the organisation alerted the Admiralty to the Submarine Bubble Target (SBT, an acoustic sonar decoy) and the German Search Receiver (GSR) designed to warn the submarine when it was illuminated by radar. Both gave time to think about tactical countermeasures and, in the case of GSR, to argue the case for the new centimetre-band radar. Steadily accumulating evidence since 1942 about German development of acoustic homing torpedoes was used to develop countermeasures but not widely promulgated until the September 1943 attack on convoy ON 202 confirmed they were being used offensively. The Admiralty promptly issued messages describing the torpedo, its capabilities and limitations, and put the countermeasures into effect (see *Torpedoes, and how to dodge them*, P.136 below).[23] Foreknowledge was not however a certain shield: on her last patrol U-593 sank HMS *Tynedale* and HMS *Holcombe* with heavy loss of life to both.

The CSDIC system was not error-proof. Premature release of information about German midget submarine development led to a rash of panicky 'sightings' in the Channel long before they were operational. Even more disruptively, an able seaman captive in the US gave a convincingly detailed but entirely imaginary description of anti-escort mines which could be discharged by a U-boat under attack to float in the path of the following destroyer. This migrated from a US Spot Item to the NID weekly report, was promulgated by C-in-C Western Approaches and caused alarm and despondency among the ships under his command. In the meantime CSDIC interrogators and stool pigeons tried fruitlessly to confirm their existence:

> '*N 2203:   There is now also an apparatus of which he (IO) said, that it looks like a periscope on top, and a mine is attached to it underneath.*
>
> *N 2385:   I haven't seen that yet.*'[24]

As well as receiving the output from CSDIC, NID1/PW and 3/PW acted as a conduit for information fed to them – either questions from the information clients or intelligence fed to the interrogators from other sources (suitably disguised) to strengthen their hand. They were *not* for instance in on the secret of Special Intelligence (the Bletchley decrypts), so anything from that source had to be delayed and presented as though it had come from an agent.

This chain of communication was shortened on occasion, mainly to allow direct discussion of engineering and technical topics with the relevant Admiralty and Air Ministry specialists – provided the latter understood the limitations of prisoner-of-war intelligence. For example, a consolidated report on German Naval Gunnery was produced jointly by CSDIC and Naval Ordnance specialists at the end of January 1944. It comprised 'M' Room transcripts from T-25 and *Scharnhorst* crewmen, a coastal artillery gunner and (acting as a naive chorus) a bomber pilot and U-boat radioman, pasted together under a number of subject headings, with occasional commentary where helpful.

Other Places, Other Ways

Middle East

The success of the UK CSDIC model led to the establishment of similar interrogation centres at Al Maadi (Cairo) in 1940 and at Birkhadem, a village south-west of Algiers in 1943.[†] Their focus was different: keen to extract immediate operational value from a transient population they simply did not have time for the painstaking, methodical tactics of the home units.

Reporting was intermittent and slapdash with none of the careful integration and analysis that characterised the treatment of intelligence in Britain. SR (eavesdropping) transcripts, for example, were tagged only with the date they were typed up, which could be several weeks after the conversation. They relied heavily on the listener's notes; recordings were taken only where the subject's speech was indistinct or seemed particularly important. Reports were also heavily edited, almost down to 'sound bites' reflecting what the transcribers thought significant, rather than placing the talk in context.

In another break from British practice 'M' Room operators posing as reception or welfare NCOs were allowed to meet their subjects, the better to recognise their voices. As in the UK the supply of bilingual officers quickly proved inadequate, so operators were recruited from Jewish refugees living in Palestine.

The static camps were supplemented by mobile units to keep pace with a fluid campaign. They used 'M' lorries, and hid microphones in the tent pole or 'Turk's Head' inner sheet support. They were very successful and pioneered the use of 'binaural' (stereo) microphones, which made the listener's job easier and allowed him to pick out a single conversation from several going on. The use of tents had the twin benefits of avoiding the reverberation issues inevitable in a permanent building and setting the subjects' minds at rest.

[†] There were smaller and/or temporary camps at Alexandria, Malta, Baghdad, Bethlehem, and Khartoum, later near Naples and Rome.

CSDIC Middle East also had to cope with the sometimes-fractious relationships between the multinational forces of the North African campaign. In particular, French demands for access were stalled and referred to the Joint Intelligence Committee (JIC) for political direction, on fears both of lax security and of prisoners' mistreatment. Since Germany recognised only the Vichy government Free French officers were in an ambivalent position *vis-à-vis* the Geneva Convention; the concern was that any suggestion of improper action by French interrogators would lead to instant reprisals against British prisoners.

The French set up an entirely separate system in response, with inevitable prejudice to goodwill and intelligence sharing. In an eventual compromise three French officers were attached to CSDIC Algiers to work under the direct supervision of the commanding officer. CSDIC UK remained strictly off-limits.[25]

The hasty, unsubtle approach of Middle Eastern static camps raised prisoners' suspicions that cannot have made later interrogators' task any easier. An engineering officer from U-450 (captured 10th March 1944) related:

'This is probably a special camp, such as I have already experienced in ALGIERS. The things that went on down there! A paratroop Leutnant had to dig his own grave; he got to a depth of 60 cm. During that time they took him away three times for interrogation. He would not give away his unit. He was interrogated for fourteen hours at a stretch in a dark room, and there were three different lots of interrogating officers. Each one who asked him a question shone a searchlight lamp on to his face, then turned it off again, and that went on for fourteen hours! The fellow didn't give way an inch. Then they let him go. He was given back his pay-book, which had his unit clearly written in it. Someone else had given it away. There was a Russian major as interrogating officer. The soldiers who came here told me that. I believe they also interrogated them for two nights long,

also shining their lamps into their faces. He said that on a table there was a long list which was headed, heavily underlined in red: "Transport to SIBERIA." The transport never really went to SIBERIA.'[26]

Several conversations revealed that guests in transit had found the microphones at Algiers and seen through the clumsy use of stool pigeons. The inmates had to go for walks with a 'German' officer who was suspiciously inquisitive and well-stocked with cigarettes, chewing-gum and newspapers – and had an English handkerchief in his pocket.

A1474   Before I left ALGIERS I wrote on a piece of paper: "Beware of Hauptmann So-und-So!" I put that under the W.C.'
A1459   I was in a room in which was written in large letters beneath the ceiling: "Beware! The enemy is listening!"'[27]

The results were unsatisfactory from the Admiralty's point of view because interrogators could not cross-check their results against a history of interviews and other sources of information. Haste begat waste. There was also more evidence of service parochialism, with the navy struggling to obtain the priority it felt its candidates deserved. Indeed CSDIC had fought off an attempted 'land grab' earlier in 1943 when an army paper suggested a multi-layered interrogation structure with little regard for other services' needs. A reviewer observed:

'I have only one comment to make and that is that, in view of the extreme shortage of manpower and transport, it will very substantially facilitate obtaining W.E.C. approval of your proposed P.W.I.S. establishments, for a G.H.Q. as well as for an Army working independently, if something approximating to a corresponding reduction in C.S.D.I.C. U.K. could be shown.
It seems to me that it is reasonable to anticipate that the war is about to enter a phase when short-term tactical interrogation of P.Ws. will assume increasing importance and at the same time the long-term work carried out by C.S.D.I.C. may well tend to lose some of its

present importance. I do not know what D.D.M.I. (P/W)'s view may be on this point, but it seems to me that it is one which merits consideration, and one which the War Establishments Committee are likely to raise, particularly in view of the substantial increase in your establishments which have recently been approved.'[28]‡

This was over two years before the end of the war.

In contrast, a small team of experienced naval interrogators – without the technological toys – was attached to 30 Assault Unit (brainchild of Ian Fleming, assistant to the DNI and future James Bond novelist) after the Normandy landings and achieved superb results. This carefully-selected and well-briefed Forward Interrogation Unit and their muscular friends went with (sometimes ahead of) the assault troops to grab anything and anyone of naval intelligence value. Even then, prisoners were sent back very quickly to CSDIC for detailed interrogation.[29]

USA and Canada

A US Office of Naval Intelligence (ONI) representative was attached to CSDIC even before Pearl Harbour and returned enthused by what he had seen, and in particular by the advantages the Royal Navy derived from prisoner interrogation. The ONI applied pressure for an equivalent facility in the USA which led to the opening of interrogation centres at Fort Hunt near Washington in August 1942, and Byron Hot Springs ('Camp Tracy') in California in March 1943, intended mainly for German and Japanese prisoners respectively. Few Japanese surrendered until late in the war however, so Camp Tracy took a substantial number of German guests.

---

‡ WEC – War Establishments Committee; PWIS – Prisoners of War Interrogation Section; GHQ – General Headquarters; DDMI – Deputy Director of Military Intelligence.

The Royal Canadian Navy's experienced team in Ottawa handled censorship of mail addressed to German prisoners in the US. A six-monthly interrogator exchange programme was maintained with the UK until D-Day, after which the number of Americans in Europe swelled enormously.

As in the UK, candidates for in-depth interrogation who seemed to have technical or strategic information were selected at reception and screening camps as soon as possible after capture. Temporary camps in North Africa, Italy and France were built with segregated compounds for CSDIC use to prevent contamination of newly arrived prisoners by the 'old-timers.' Survivors landed in Canada were sent to the US for interrogation so as to avoid wasteful duplication of effort.

Unfortunately, inter-service rivalry rigidly segregated Army and Navy operations and reporting (there was no independent US Air Force until after the war), partly undermining the benefits of co-location. This was however less damaging than it might have been because the US Navy jealously kept the Army away from maritime operations. Looking back at the Admiralty's constant struggle with the RAF for resources and priority to Coastal Command their attitude is perhaps understandable.[30]

The Americans frequently eavesdropped on the interrogations as well as the prisoners in their cells. Before bringing someone in for formal interview they checked that there was no interesting conversation going on in the cell and, if necessary, delayed the session until it had finished. Cells were routinely monitored for an hour after the interview.

It seems to have been more difficult to prevent extraneous noise such as passing aircraft making life difficult for the listeners. MI19 in the UK managed to block construction of one airfield and have another downgraded from operational to training use to preserve their peace. However, instead of a single microphone in the light fitting the Americans used a stereo pair above the ceiling to aid intelligibility.

A post-war review by Colin McFadyean, head of NID1/PW, was caustic about the US effort:

Despite the well-known American capacity for concentration, organisation and hard work, for some reason the American interrogation section was to a certain extent lacking in all these three qualities. It had far more officers than we did and probably more than it needed; those who were not first class were retained in the section, whereas we never kept or accepted officers who were not 100% useful. Although particuar [sic] interrogators made themselves interested in various technical subjects, no fully qualified technical officer was ever appointed to the section. The American methods were slow in comparison with ours. Their hours of work were circumscribed whereas our interrogators often worked through the night, and their methods were not sufficiently intensive. They generally employed two officers to do an interrogation where we only used one.

This comparative failure of the United States interrogation section was probably largely the result of the different status which it held in the Navy Department in Washington in comparison with ours in the Admiralty. It was kept rigidly separate, its officers were never properly encouraged to consult and visit the users of p/w Intelligence who themselves often did not appreciate the value of the Intelligence available and certainly never pressed for minute-to-minute and immediate results such as the Admiralty always expected of us. The United States naval interrogators therefore lacked the incentive which Admiralty give to C.S.D.I.C., and consequently took less interest in their work than did the British interrogators. This reflection is not made in a spirit of idle criticism but rather to reinforce the lesson which we learned that naval interrogation can never be successful unless it is closely correlated not only with all other sources of intelligence but also with the day to day work of those responsible for formulating technical and tactical strategy.

A margin note, apparently by Winston Churchill, vehemently disagreed. For their part, the Americans thought it essential to have the time and resources to try a number of different approaches to a recalcitrant prisoner rather than feeling pressured to move on to the next candidate or the next batch of arrivals.[31]

CSDIC (UK)'s insistence on priority access to the more interesting prisoners also created resentment. For example U-593 was a shared RN/USN 'kill' while U-73 was despatched entirely by the US Navy but both crews were shipped to the UK, a decision that provoked some bickering at the time.

In September 1944 the Director of Naval Intelligence (Canada) approached his UK opposite number about the feasibility of setting up a twenty-cell 'M' Room installation at one of his own camps. The reply was an estimate of £950 (about £39,000 at 2016 prices) for hardware, forty staff to operate and four to maintain a twenty-room installation. Assuming the right people could be found it would take ten weeks to train them. At this late stage of the war, it seems the subject was let drop.[32]

Germany

The nearest the Germans had to CSDIC was the *Durchgangslager der Luftwaffe* or air force transit camp, shortened to *Dulag Luft* at Oberursel near Frankfurt-am-Main. The camp contained 200 soundproofed cells for captured airmen. On arrival, from days to weeks after being shot down, they were issued ill-fitting clothing to replace their uniforms, tweaking their natural anxiety and disorientation. They were given a 'Red Cross' form to fill in and told that everyone did so, making it easier for their families to know of their fate and for Red Cross parcels to find them. This was of course a trick, which fooled many.

The forms were matched with any documents found on the prisoner, his crewmates or in his crashed aircraft; any information on file about his squadron, home town; aircraft type and tactics; the operations on the day he was shot down; and not least the daily list of questions arriving on the centre's teleprinter. The prisoner was then assigned to one of up to 65 interrogators at the unit's peak who, just like his British counterpart, would do his best to build partial information into an impression of omniscience. As well as the *Luftwaffe* personnel there was a small Gestapo contingent who undertook political interrogations, though their main task seemed to be watching the military staff.

Longer-term residents were kept two to a cell. Stool pigeons were used, and one of the barrack blocks was quickly discovered to be wired for sound.[33]

Psychological tricks were widely used but physical violence was rare. However, while co-operative subjects were offered cigarettes those suspected of holding out might suffer loss of privileges, extended solitary confinement or 'baking' in overheated and vermin-ridden cells. There were reports of prisoners being denied medical treatment or interrogated in hospital. The evidence was strong enough to lead to a post-war investigation by LDC and war-crimes charges against five former staff. The commandant (*Oberstleutnant* Erich Killinger) was convicted along with two others, and later committed suicide.[34]

Depending on their perceived intelligence value prisoners were kept there between five and thirty days before transfer to a permanent *Stalag Luft* prison camp.

The *Kriegsmarine* operated a similar but less sophisticated facility, *Dulag Nord*, at Wilhelmshaven until February 1942 when it was moved to Westertimke to escape Allied bombing. It fed permanent naval prison camps, *Marlag und Milag Nord* (for naval and merchant seamen respectively) near Bremen.

Lieutenant K G Patterson RANVR, captured after a beach reconnaissance at Anzio, spent a total of three months at *Dulag Nord*. The whole time was in solitary confinement which suggests that stool pigeons and microphones were not used. The conditions he experienced were harsh, not brutal, but the entire population was moved out when a Red Cross inspection was in the offing. He recalled that direct interrogations were infrequent and apparently amateurish. He also spent four weeks in hospital where it is possible that friendly nurses were playing 'nice cop.' When he was finally discharged from the *Dulag* to the regular prison camp at *Marlag Nord* he found the population very much on their guard for stool pigeons.[35]

The combination of solitary confinement and persistent questioning was typical of the *Dulag Nord* approach. Leonard Hall, a RAF officer detained there for several weeks in early 1943 had the same experience. He eventually simulated capitulation and gave detailed answers to the questions asked. His information was accurate, but eighteen months out of date.[36]

They may have been the lucky ones. *Matrosenobergefreiter* Hermann Schütz of *Scharnhorst* recalled seeing prisoners manacled at Wilhelmshaven.[37] A U-593 survivor had heard from a member of Dönitz' staff that prisoners suspected of espionage were given thirst-inducing food but nothing to drink, then interviewed by an officer who kept helping himself from a pitcher of water on his desk. If they were thought to be lying they were severely beaten, sent to hospital to recover, then the process was repeated.[38]

Captives and deserters in the hands of the German Army could look forward to several interrogations working back from the front. The local command post would be interested in matters of immediate tactical relevance – paths through a minefield, location of observation posts, how much barbed wire in front, how many tanks and guns behind. Fear and disorientation were the key: the unfortunate would be only too aware that he was at the mercy of people who, perhaps minutes before, had been trying to kill him and might not have entirely abandoned the idea.

Passed back to divisional level he would meet a professional intelligence officer for the first time, working to a standard questionnaire and trying to find out more about order of battle, new weapons and their performance, and tactical developments. For most it was a cursory experience. This conversation between a Luftwaffe flights registration corporal and supply sergeant was recorded at Algiers on 27th December 1943:

A 43/1643: Does the German Army interrogate prisoners as they do here?'

A 43/1642: Not in the same way. What we do is to pick out certain men, who are then sent to HQ. There they are interrogated by someone from the Intelligence Service and then allowed to go again. But we don't do it as it's done here; this is an absolute form of arrest.'[39]

Senior prisoners might then be interviewed in depth at corps or army level, or those with specialist knowledge by one or other of the Party's or State's Byzantine intelligence organisations.

There is a key distinction between prisoners taken on the western and the eastern fronts. The former could rely to some extent on the protection of the Geneva Convention, which Russia never signed. The absence of legal constraints combined with a baked-in view of the enemy as *untermensch* led to a level of sustained brutality matched only in the Pacific. The fear of the newly captured Russian soldier was wholly rational.

Equally, prisoners who fell into the hands of the parallel intelligence organisations operated by the SS might expect a rougher time. This conversation between a *Luftwaffe* wireless operator and bomber mechanic was recorded by CSDIC Middle East:

'A 44/1743   *If our prisoners won't talk, do we treat them badly?'*
'A 44/1751:   *They're beaten and kicked, and they get nothing to eat for days on end, until they fall ill. An SS man once told me that when we were drinking. Sometimes they let them go, but an air crew who have been shot down, like ourselves, would never get through without talking.'*[40]

On an even more sinister note SS *Sturmbannführer* Zorn, captured in November 1944, was overheard saying:

'If one uses measures against a PW, which are contrary to international law for instance, if one puts him to work at the sandheap and then lets him off again, then in the end one must do away with him. As the bearer of a secret, a man like that must be rendered harmless.'[41]

The Germans knew or at least suspected the use of microphones by the British and warned their servicemen about them. They used the technique themselves in prisoner-of-war camps and at least at *Dulag Luft*.

<u>Re: Microphones in German PW Camps.</u>
N 2196 [Dr Greven, a GSR specialist captured from U-406] states that:-
One is fitted into the electric light rose on the ceiling and a further six are grouped in the ceiling round this. A further four microphones are fitted, one in each corner of the ceiling of the cell.[42]

At its best their handling of prisoner intelligence was very good but it never approached the honed slickness of CSDIC. There seems to have been little sense of urgency about selecting candidates for extended, strategic examination and, despite occasional warm words, the interrogators were constantly up against the military hierarchy's ingrained disdain for intelligence. Above all the fractured, suspicious, competitive nature of the Nazi state made any idea of a joint service approach a non-starter.

Japan

The Far East theatre deserves a book or several of its own and I do not attempt to tackle it here. There is however a document in the UK National Archives, translated from Japanese, giving instructions for the interrogation and handling of prisoners of war. It contains the following interesting snippets:

'It is important to vary strictness in response to the nature and character of the man being questioned. The application of torture which would menace the maintenance of military discipline will be avoided from the very beginning.'

'There will be no senseless countermeasures against P'sW, such as useless murder caused merely by anger toward the enemy, or cruelty caused by a man seized by emotion. This procedure will be observed particularly in the case of high-ranking officers.'

'Items interrogated will be clearly written down. It is advantageous to use leading interrogation. Form questions depending on the condition of the person to be interrogated and obtain written answers or sketches. Interrogation will be conducted in response to the man's mentality, nature, and character, and from the very beginning there will be no threats of application of the "third degree".'[43]

From all accounts these worthy sentiments were honoured more in the breach than in the observance.

---

[1] TNA WO 208/4129; *Interrogation Reports on German Prisoners of War 3500-3900*. SRA 3559 dated 23rd January 1943. The reported casualties were somewhat exaggerated but still unpleasant.

[2] TNA WO 208/3524; *Inter Service Detailed Interrogation Centres described as transit*.

3   TNA WO 208/3525; *Publication in the press of information regarding the interrogation of POWs.*
4   TNA WO 208/3515; *Use of Polish officers for interrogation, 1940 Dec-1941 July.* WO 208/3461; *CSDIC's: inclusion of Allied personnel.*
5   IWM Audio Record Cat No 18573; *Wernard, Alfred Conrad (Oral history).* Reel 5.
6   TNA WO 208/4149; *Interrogation Reports on German Prisoners of War 2700-3050.* SRN 2990 dated 4th March 1944.
7   TNA WO 208//4200; *Special extracts from interrogation reports on German and Italian prisoners of war 1942 Dec – 1945 Mar.* Extract from SR Draft No 855 dated 26th March 1944.
8   ibid. Special Extract from SR Draft No 2065 dated 2nd March 1944.
9   ibid. Extract from SR Draft No 2062 dated 2nd March 1944.
10 ibid. Extract from SR Draft No 951A dated 10th April 1944.
11 Helen Fry; *op cit.* There were also a few mobile M-units built into converted buses, partly for field operations and partly as a backup in case the CSDIC centres were bombed.
12 TNA WO 208/4148; *Interrogation Reports on German Prisoners of War 2451-2699.* SRN 2569 dated 31st December 1943.
13 TNA WO 208/4149; *Interrogation Reports on German Prisoners of War 2700-3050.* SRN 2762 dated 17th January 1944. The speaker was Hermann Schütz who worked in one of the starboard 105mm. anti-aircraft gun turrets.
14 TNA WO 208/4150; *Interrogation Reports on German Prisoners of War 3051-3359.* SRN 3220 dated 21st March 1944.
15 TNA ADM 223/475; *Intelligence collection methods.*
16 TNA WO 208/4149; *Interrogation Reports on German Prisoners of War 2700-3050.* SRN 2978 dated 2nd March 1944.
17 TNA WO 208/4200; *Special extracts from interrogation reports on German and Italian prisoners of war 1942 Dec – 1945 Mar.* Extract from SR Draft No 3197 dated 3rd April 1944.
18 Helen Fry; *Spymaster: The Secret Life of Kendrick* (Marranos Press, 2014). P.386.
19 Exchange of letters dated 28th – 30th October 1944, in TNA ADM 223/475; *Intelligence collection methods.*
20 TNA ADM 223/877; *NID UC Reports: Nos 315-500 (incomplete) 1943 Apr 01 - 1944 Jun 28.* NID UC Report No 357 dated 5th

August 1943. TNA ADM 223/120; *Naval Intelligence Division Reports UC 251-500 1942 Sept – 1944 June*. Report No 425 dated 5th February 1944.

[21] TNA ADM 223/209; *Photocopies of Papers Cited in History of Intelligence 1939-1945 Vol 3 Pt 1* P.43.

[22] TNA ADM 223/286; *Operational Intelligence Centres: formation and history* P.iv.

[23] These examples are from paper *P/W Interrogation 1939-45*, by Colin McFadyean, included in TNA records ADM 223/84; *Photocopies of Papers Cited in History of Intelligence 1939-1945 Vol I* and ADM 223/475; *Intelligence collection methods*.

[24] TNA ADM 223/144; *Summary of statements by German prisoners of war (January-March 1944)*, Summary No 66, for week ending 11th March 1944. ADM 223/475; *Intelligence collection methods*. Paper *PW Interrogation 1939-45*, section D(c); *No Interrogation in Ships effecting Capture*. WO 208/4150; *Interrogation Reports on German Prisoners of War 3051-3359*. SRN 3178 dated 24th March 1944.

[25] TNA WO 208/3461; *CSDIC's: inclusion of Allied personnel*.

[26] TNA WO 208/4200; *Special extracts from interrogation reports on German and Italian prisoners of war 1942 Dec-1945 Mar*. Extract from SR Draft No WG 837 dated 26th March 1944.

[27] ibid. Extract from SR Draft No 1487 dated 17th February 1944. See also SR Extracts 951A, 1454, 1509, 3346, 4699/4695 4932, and 9289, in the same record.

[28] TNA WO 208/3458; *CSDIC's and PWIS's: general policy, 1943*. Letter from Lt Col J C S Barrow to Lt Col A R Rawlinson MBE dated 29th March 1943.

[29] TNA ADM 223/475; *Intelligence collection methods*. Paper: 'The German Prisoners of War Interrogation Section in N.I.D. During the 1939-45 War' by C Mitchell, May 1947.

[30] Major Steven M. Kleinman USAFR; *The History Of MIS-Y: U.S. Strategic Interrogation During World War II*. Unclassified MSc thesis submitted to the Faculty of the Joint Military Intelligence College, 2002.

[31] TNA ADM 223/475; *Intelligence collection methods*. Contrast a memorandum from Lt Cdr Ralph G. Albrecht, USNR to Lt. Cdr. J.L. Riheldaffer, U.S.N., (RET) dated 22nd April 1942 (http://www.uboatarchive.net/POW/POWInterrogationAlbrechtVisit.htm).

[32] TNA WO 208/3468; *CSDIC (Canada): fitting POW's with microphones*.

[33] TNA WO 208/3269; *Dulag Luft (Oberusel): RAF personnel*.

[34] TNA WO 208/4642; *Dulag Luft, Oberursel, Germany: ill-treatment of allied airmen*.

[35] IWM Documents.7766. *Private Papers of Lieutenant K G Patterson RANVR*. PP. 366-368.

[36] IWM recording Catalogue No. 27271; *Hall, Leonard (Oral history)*.

[37] TNA WO 208/4149; *Interrogation Reports on German Prisoners of War 2700-3050*. SRN 2703 dated 9th January 1944.

[38] TNA ADM 186/809; *Interrogation of German naval survivors*. BR 1907(94) P.9.

[39] TNA WO 208/5508; *Interrogation reports on German and Italian prisoners of war: AFHQ 1-107 1943 May 30 - 1944 Mar 27*. Special Report CSDIC AFHQ No 92(G) dated 27 Dec 43.

[40] ibid: *AFHQ 1-107 1943 May 30 - 1944 Mar 27*.

[41] TNA WO 208/4140; *Interrogation Reports on German Prisoners of War 1111-1264 (December 1944-July 1945)*. SRM 1124 dated 15th December 1944.

[42] TNA WO 208/4200; *Special extracts from interrogation reports on German and Italian prisoners of war*. Extracts from SR Draft No 83 dated 13th March 1944.

[43] TNA WO 208/2525; *Procedure in interrogating and handling prisoners of war*.

THE PEOPLE

The Naval Intelligence Team

Apart from two Marines the NID group were naval volunteer reservists, many of them 'Special Service'. In terms of the regulars' sniffy crack the Royal Navy Reserve were sailors pretending to be gentlemen and the Volunteer Reserve were gentlemen pretending to be sailors. Special Service didn't have to be either, they just needed skills useful in wartime. Even the most landlubberly of them was however expected to acquire some sea time or at least visit HMS *Graph* (formerly U-570) and learn something of their interviewees' lives.

They were an eclectic and irreverent mix, using cover names and often adopting a rank of convenience. Operational experience was valuable because it allowed the interrogator to empathise with his victim. So, in a technological war, was familiarity with engineering terms and principles. The Admiralty also liked a background in journalism giving them the versatility to draw out people of differing personalities and classes. Donald Welbourn recalled that when he arrived in March 1943 his colleagues included an artist, a Canadian diplomat and an openly gay officer.[1] They were predominantly young men in their twenties and thirties.

In a relatively recent development there were Women's Royal Naval Service (Wren) officers, also fluent German speakers, whose role was to integrate the intelligence from interrogations, stool pigeons and secret listeners; and to write intelligence reports for the group's customers. By the end of 1944 they were supported by a clerical staff of six Wren POs.

The team leader, Lieutenant-Commander **Burton Cope** was by far its oldest member. He was born to a British family in Munich, where his father worked as a stained-glass painter, in 1885. On the outbreak of the First World War he returned to Britain with his parents and German wife. He joined the RNVR in 1916 and, as a native German speaker, was rapidly recruited by Naval Intelligence, gaining his first experience of prisoner interrogation under (then) Major R M Trench RMLI. Between the wars he worked for Cunard-White Star Line in Paris where he probably had a covert role as well. After his first wife's death he married and seemed well settled, but the family had to leave France hastily in early 1940. Back in Britain he resumed his NID career and commissioned the Latimer team when the centre opened in July 1942. His colleagues did not think him the brightest star in the firmament but he could turn on an impressively intimidating manner when needed.

Late in 1944 he left to form Naval Party 1735, briefed to take over the port of Wilhelmshaven when liberated. He entered the town with the reconnaissance party in two jeeps on 5th May 1945 and moved on to the secure communications complex at Sengwarden. The party then clarified the status of the occupants by marching in and ordering lunch. This apparently convinced the staff that they must have surrendered, and shortly afterwards a parachute regiment turned up to remove all doubt.[2]

He served there until released from the Navy in 1946. After demobilisation he made several trips to Germany for the Control Commission, including a stint at BAOR Hohne-Bergen (formerly Bergen-Belsen concentration camp). Somehow he came to know John Bingham, on whom John Le Carré's George Smiley was partly modelled, and who was working in Hannover on secondment from MI5 at the time.

The People

He died in 1952 but one of his sisters, who married a German in August 1914, lived in Munich until her death in 1986.

Figure 7: 1940/41 caricature of (then) Lt Burton Cope

The two other veterans of the team were **Wilfred Samuel** and Dick Weatherby. Samuel, based in Ottawa, was responsible for liaison with Canadian CSDIC and censorship of prisoners' mail from the USA and Canada.

In a curious example of the compressed hierarchy at Latimer he, Ralph Izzard and Charles Everett had all achieved the same rank (Acting Temporary Lieutenant-Commander) as their boss by the time of this study. The navy was very firm in its view that promotion came with seagoing-equivalent responsibility, and if a lieutenant was fit to command a submarine or sloop, he should have the character and intellect to hold his own with any rank in the other services.[3]

Figure 8: The NID Team at Latimer House, 1943.
Burton Cope is centre, standing. Richard Weatherby is third from camera-right with Donald Welbourn next to him. Ralph Izzard is the tall officer at rear left. The Wrens in the front row are (from the left) Jean Flower, Evelyn Barron, Esmé Mackenzie, and Gwendoline Neel-Wall. Helen Fry has identified the seated officer at centre as George Blake, who was later a notorious spy.

Dick Weatherby had previously served in destroyers. He was, after Cope, the most experienced member of the NID CSDIC team and took over its command at the end of 1944. As CSDIC

The People

(UK) wound down in 1945 he transferred to the naval staff in Berlin. He and his elder brother John were members of a large family of Wykehamists (graduates of Winchester College) who joined the services on the outbreak of war and distinguished themselves. He was born in 1917, married twice (in 1942 and 1952) and died young in 1959, at which time he was a 'Member of H.M. Foreign Service.'[4]

In the first half of 1944 he followed several of his colleagues in a secondment to the US station (HMS *Saker*) and so may have been absent for the events of this book.

John Weatherby, an artist and graduate of Magdalen College Oxford, joined the Royal Marines in November 1942 and NID in early 1943. In 1967 Weatherby was awarded a MA in History by Makarere University College, Uganda.[5] He died in 2003.

After graduating from Queens' College Cambridge in 1931 **Ralph Izzard** joined the *Daily Mail* as Berlin correspondent. He had a narrow escape on 11th November 1939 when, following up reports of German soldiers kidnapping British intelligence agents at Venlo in the Netherlands, he himself was almost trapped.[6] Hiding in the toilet of the Café Backhaus and preparing to destroy his passport he was saved by a quick-thinking landlady who assured the searching troops there was no-one there but Dutch and Americans.

He returned to Britain and joined the RNVR as an Ordinary Seaman gunner. Despite a German-born wife he was swiftly commissioned and recruited – supposedly by Ian Fleming – to NID. While working at CSDIC he travelled to America between March and July 1942 to help the US Navy set up an equivalent organisation (Op-16-Z). Initially frustrated by lack of staff, premises and real prisoners to practise on he established close co-operation with Canadian NID, helped select Fort Hunt and was finally saved from an endless round of lectures and role-play exercises by the arrival of captives from U-85 in April and U-352 in May.[7]

Back with CSDIC UK his background in journalism fitted him well to be the unit's link with NID 17Z: the psychological warfare branch led by Donald McLachlan.

Shortly after D-Day he crossed the Channel with Ian Fleming's 30 Assault Unit (30AU), briefed to grab anything and anyone with naval intelligence value. His role was formalised as leader of a specialist group integrated with but separate from 30AU: the Forward Interrogation Unit (FIU). As the interrogator attached to 30AU Team Six he entered Wilhelmshaven on 6th May 1945 to find Cope, his old boss, just setting up as Staff Officer (Intelligence) there. The meeting must have been interesting.

At the end of the war FIU shared the mammoth, essential but pedestrian task of de-nazification which was probably less to Izzard's taste. By February 1946 he had resumed his career in journalism with, it is widely speculated, a sideline in espionage. He died in 1992.

Colin McFadyean came to NID with extensive operational experience under his belt. Joining the RNVR in 1939 he had first served in the armed merchantman HMS *Dunottar Castle* then the Royal Naval Air Service station at Dartmouth Nova Scotia. Late in 1940 he was posted to HMS *Cameron* (formerly USS *Welles*) a 'destroyers-for-bases' ship which was so severely damaged in an air raid while refitting in Portsmouth that she never saw active service. This was followed by convoy duty in two more old US ships: HMS *Lancaster* in the Atlantic and HMS *Leeds* on the east coast – the latter so abysmally capricious that the transfer to NID in March 1942 must have come as a relief. That posting took him to the US before he found his niche at CSDIC and rapid promotion to acting lieutenant-commander. By the end of 1943 he had returned to NID headquarters in charge of the prisoners-of-war section where he remained into the post-war years, though returning to sea from time to time to keep his hand in.

Australian-born **John Marriner**, another journalist, seems to have gained much of his experience snooping informally in small craft. He was probably in the US at the time of our focus.

Donald Welbourn graduated from Emmanuel College, Cambridge in 1937 and joined the English Electric Co. Ltd. in Stafford, where he became Assistant to the Works Superintendent. He had travelled in Germany and Austria before the war, observing the rise of Nazism at first hand and learning some German in the process. He joined the Royal Navy as an electrical branch officer in 1942 and found himself working on magnetic mine sweeps. With boundless self-confidence boosted by a matching intellect and the spur of knowing there was no room for mistake, he fleshed out his sketchy knowledge of electromagnetism by self-study while waiting for trains between east-coast bases.[8]

Early in 1943 he was unceremoniously pulled from his perilous experimental minesweeping duties and told to report to London. In an increasingly technological war CSDIC needed a German-speaking engineer.

At first his role was confined to advising interrogators and helping them frame their questions, but as he gained familiarity with the work he took on interrogation duties himself.

After the war he was sent to Germany to assist with the intelligence take there and was able to reacquaint himself with some of his pre-war friends. They commented on his vastly improved command of the language, his new Hamburg accent and much fruitier vocabulary![9]

The team's engineering expertise was further strengthened by the recruitment of **Leslie Atkinson** in 1943 and **Harry Scholar**, a Czech, in 1944. Atkinson may not have been suited to the work, moving on after about a year. Sadly, Scholar received a spinal injury in a car accident on New Year's Eve 1944.

Charles Everett was born in Britain in 1908 to an American father and Polish mother. He was educated and spent most of his youth in Germany. He worked as a teacher at Catholic college in Manchester until 1937, then for a student travel company in Lucerne, Nice, Innsbruck and other places. The war brought a radical change: he left England for Bucharest in December 1939 and worked for SOE in Romania and Yugoslavia from January 1940 to April 1941. In June 1941 he resurfaced in Portugal, as Naval Control Service Officer for Oporto, which covered his SOE activities scouting beaches for landing, evacuation and sabotage. His past caught up with him however, and in October 1942 he was asked to leave in a case escalated to Dr Salazar, the dictator, himself.

In a place where almost everyone seemed to be a spy of one persuasion or another, this seeming clumsiness might not have been accidental. German military intelligence was clear that the Allies were building up to an offensive landing somewhere, but where? Almost anywhere from the Finnmark to Dakar via the Balkans was possible but Portugal was one of the favoured guesses. It may be that Everett had something to do with that. In the event, the Axis powers were taken completely by surprise when Operation TORCH troops waded ashore – in Algeria and Morocco.

Despite allegations of pro-German leanings he formally joined the Navy in July 1941 and Naval Intelligence in December 1942.[10] Not, by all accounts, the easiest person to get along with he found himself later in 1944 at the Kempton Park cage sorting out prisoners worth CSDIC's attention from the post D-Day tsunami.[11] After the German surrender he was Staff Officer (Security) at Emden.

The People

A 1941 NID paper observed, *As the German antipathy towards Jews has been fostered by propaganda to such an extent that the sight of a Jew has an adverse effect on the mental attitude towards prisoners' captors and hardens the prisoners' resistance, it is considered a mistake to employ interrogators of Jewish appearance. The Germans seem to have developed a special instinct, which enables them to recognise the slightest Jewish strain; it has also been found that this fact has the effect on Jewish interrogators, possibly subconsciously, of making them feel somewhat inferior. It is thought unwise to allow prisoners to come into contact with Jews before interrogation.'*[12]

This policy had clearly eased by the time **Julius Lunzer** joined the team in September 1944. He was a Canadian citizen of Dutch-Jewish extraction and had joined the Royal Canadian Navy Volunteer Reserve in 1940. He had barely got his feet under the table at CSDIC before joining Ralph Izzard in the Forward Interrogation Unit. While there he managed to trace some of his relatives, who had survived Belsen, a few months after their liberation.[13] He emigrated to the US in 1951, giving Chorleywood (a couple of miles from Latimer) as his place of birth, and died in New York in 2006.

Claudia Furneaux typifies the Wren analysts who vastly improved the quality and focus of the unit's reports from about 1943 onward. They synthesised the different sources of data available to CSDIC: the reports that came with the captives, their effects, their interrogations and the 'M' Room transcripts to produce a single view of the intelligence product and, importantly, of its reliability. The finest intelligence is useless unless it is believed and acted on and, comparing later with earlier reports, it is difficult to avoid the conclusion that the Wrens were largely responsible for closing CSDIC's initial credibility gap.

She interrupted a modern languages degree at Somerville College Oxford to join the Navy on hearing of the fall of

France in 1940. After a period listening to German radio transmissions from various stations on the South Coast she was commissioned and posted to Latimer. One of her more bizarre duties was to help escort two U-boat officers on a pub-crawl to London – to reward them for good behaviour and no doubt to relax their tongues.

At CSDIC she met and married Harry Lennon, one of the American interrogators rotating through the site. After the war she returned with him to New York where she taught French in a Catholic girls' school and significantly broadened the reading list.

On the death of her parents, being already widowed, she returned to run the family farm in Essex until her own death in 2011. She never did complete her degree.

The other Wren officers in the team at the time were Evelyn Barron and Jean Flower, later joined by Celia Thomas and Betty Colls. Relationships within the service were not uncommon. Jean Flower married NID officer Charles Mitchell. Esme McKenzie, an earlier Wren resident described as 'vivacious and exceptionally bright,' married Brian Connell who was a member of Forward Interrogation Unit and went on to become a successful television journalist.

The Pollsters

A staff psychologist (Lt Col Henry Dicks, RAMC) conducted regular, overt opinion surveys among the prisoners to track German morale statistically, as far as possible, and inform the Allies' psychological warfare efforts (see Figures 10-12). The quarterly snapshots measured prisoners' views on the likely outcome of the war, service conditions, the home front, the effect of bombing, their attitude to Hitler and the regime (not always the same), the Allies and the effect of propaganda – both Allied and German. For consistency only air force and navy prisoners (for much of the earlier war the only ones available) were included, with army views added separately for illustration where helpful. In the quarter from November 1943 to January 1944 survivors of the five vessels we are considering made up six of the ten officers, and 41 of the 62 other ranks interviewed. Thirty-five out of fifty-four naval interviewees, an unusually high proportion, were from surface ships. To complicate the analysts' task further the fourteen *Scharnhorst* survivors' buoyant morale made them, *en bloc*, a statistical outlier which had to be allowed for.

One key indicator was the popularity of listening to the BBC. This could be personally very comforting, as the service broadcast prisoners' names after a delay to ensure the information had lost its tactical value. Domestically, however, it was dangerous. The – accurate – perception was that breaking the law against listening to foreign stations could bring the Gestapo down on your head with horrific results. For many the need to know overcame caution. *Funkhauptgefreiter* (Telegraphist) Hans Dabelstein of U-386 confessed,

'N 2191: *My mother said that she would listen in to all the British broadcasts if ever my U-boat should be overdue. She told me that in that case she wouldn't care any more about regulations.*'[14]

In the services, however, it was a different matter. While some U-boat skippers rigidly enforced the ban others turned a deaf ear or even broadcast the service over the boat's public address system. Radiomen like *Funkegefreiter* Theodor Essman of U-73 (N2155) were in a privileged position, as he explained to a stool pigeon:

'N 1552: *Have you ever listened to the English news?*
N 2155: *Yes, I heard it fairly often in the MEDITERRANEAN.*

> N 1552: *The English are allowed to listen to German broadcasts.*
> N 2155: *Yes, but an Englishman is quite different from a German, he doesn't let himself be influenced.*
> N 1552: *Yes, that's just it.*[15]

Generally over half of U-boat and *Scharnhorst* survivors were familiar with the broadcasts while the only conspicuous exceptions were the T-25 crew, who were felt to be more war-weary and of lower intellectual standard than the others. On the other hand Paulus Piatek, *Alsterufer's* skipper, had listened extensively to Allied propaganda on the long haul back from Japan (including ten interminable days hove-to while two convoys crossed ahead of him). It didn't affect his determination or professionalism for the last, lethal dash across Biscay but can't have improved the mood of resigned fatalism with which he set out.

Overall, the BBC had lost 'market share' over the previous year from 88% who had heard it and 30% regular listeners in the second quarter of 1943 to 57% and 21% respectively in the five months to February 1944. One clear warning was that exaggerated claims of Allied success undermined the station's credibility quicker than anything else.

Such BBC 'white' propaganda which didn't pretend to be anything else was sponsored by the Political Warfare Executive (PWE), reporting to the Foreign Office. The PWE had several other tricks up its sleeve. Since May 1941 German listeners had been able to pick up 'GS1,' apparently clandestine transmissions from a disaffected senior army officer. They continued until November 1944 when they were rudely interrupted by shouting and the sound of machine-gun fire as the 'sedition' was wound up. In the meantime 1943 brought *Deutsche Kurzwellensender Atlantik* (*Atlantiksender*), a short-wave forces' station aimed squarely at U-boat crews which mixed the best of popular music with news items, gossip and tips. This was quickly joined by *Soldatensender Calais* (later *Soldatensender West*), aimed at the army. All were broadcast from Britain in an operation masterminded by a German-born journalist, Sefton Delmer, and greatly helped by apparently trivial scraps of information from prisoners-of-war.

The fake services were originally short-wave only but from late 1943 had been allowed to use the enormously powerful 'Aspidistra' 600 kW medium-wave transmitter (named after Gracie Fields' song *The Biggest Aspidistra in the World*) near Crowborough in Sussex. This allowed them to beam their message into Germany itself on a frequency close to the official German medium-wave channel.[16]

Even when the pretence wore thin it kept its excuse value for *Maschinenobergefreiter* Breuker of U-406.

'N 2200: *(re British broadcasts in German): We often listened to them. We didn't know whether it was being sent from GERMANY or to GERMANY. That is what we used to tell the officers and they couldn't say anything.*'[17]

In the previous year the *Wehrmacht* had suffered the hammer-blows of Stalingrad, Tunis, Kursk, and the surrender of Italy. Between the dismal (for the Allies) month of March and the Germans' 'Black May' 1943 U-boat losses soared and results faded (see Figure 9). In June the *Kriegsmarine's B-Dienst* decoding service lost the ability to break the British convoy code. From then on U-boats were groping half-blindly for their targets.

Little wonder that from February to October 1943 the proportion of prisoners claiming to believe in ultimate victory had shrunk from 27% to just 5%. Yet, almost unbelievably, in the quarter from November 1943 to January 1944, this very satisfactory trend reversed – fully 21% claiming to believe in

Germany's eventual triumph. Or, perhaps more accurately, refusing to contemplate defeat.

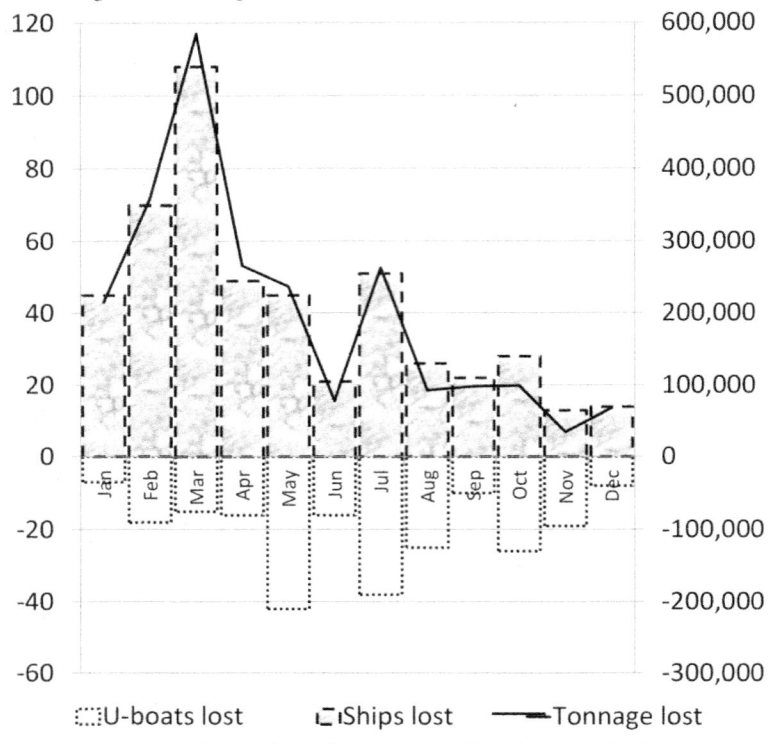

Figure 9: Merchant shipping vs U-boat losses in 1943.

The analysts, scratching their heads, first tried removing the *Scharnhorst* survivors from the results. Isolated, with little direct experience of the blockade and air raids pummelling Germany, well-led, well-fed and confident they were the elite of the navy, thus unrepresentative of the centre's normal customers so it was a fair move. That helped, bringing the quarter's result down to 16%, but not enough to mask the worrying trend reversal. The next trick was to try looking at the question from another angle: were the respondents railing against the possibility of utter defeat rather than believing in triumph? As the report put it:

> *'Refusing to admit, even to themselves, that defeat is certain, although possessing no positive faith in victory, many Germans fight on with considerable determination in the vague hope that time, if unlikely to be wholly on the German side, may impose a tolerable compromise on the belligerents.'*

Unfortunately:

> *'But if we take the ability to recognise coming defeat rather than belief in victory as our yardstick for measuring the German will to resistance, we still find a significant stiffening of that will in recent months. Defeatism increased suddenly at the time of the Tunis surrender and MUSSOLINI's fall, afterwards steadied-out, and in recent months has fallen to a level only slightly above that prevailing before those events. This remains true – although the trend is a little less striking – if we omit the Scharnhorst Ps/W from the most recent sample.'[18]*

On deeper probing the prisoners struggled to give reasons for their confidence. There was some desperate expectation of secret miracle weapons to be produced with a flourish from Hitler's hat – but recognition that he was cutting it a bit fine. U-boat crews hoped that new torpedoes, better electronics, improved stealthing and Dönitz' wild exhortations might tip the balance back in their favour. *Kapitänleutnant* Hans Harold Speidel of U-643, caught in October 1943, certainly bought the brochure.

> *'To-day we are technically so far advanced in our weapons that we can sink any destroyer. We are no longer afraid of them. … you'll see that U-boat warfare is coming back again. DOENITZ said: "Well, gentlemen, what can you expect? We realised clearly that the enemy, whose life is hangs on a thread, would make every effort to achieve something. But what they have done in three and a half years, we shall put right in six or nine months…" That's what we call the 'black U-boat' … It is invisible; that is to say it can't be D/F'd.'[19]*

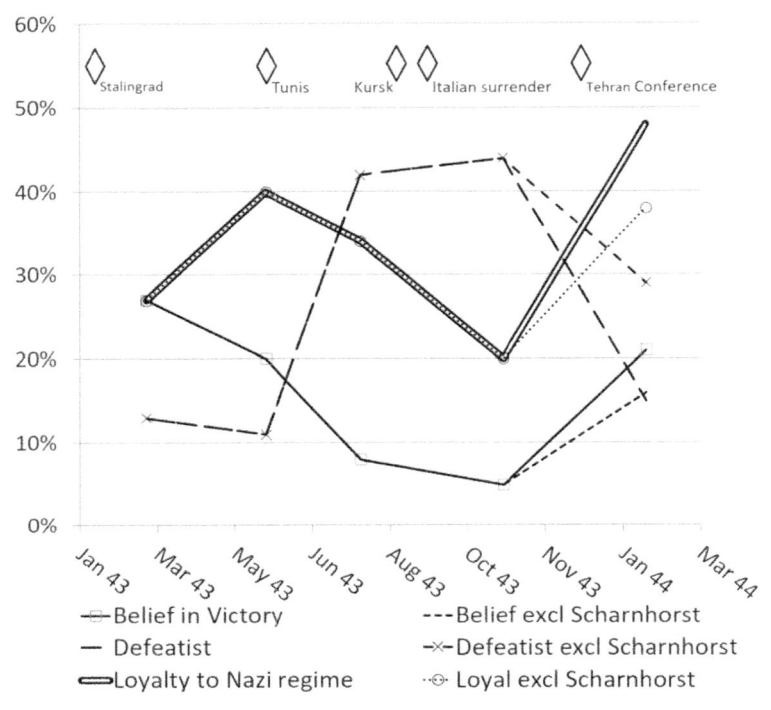

Figure 10: Prisoner Morale January 1943 - March 1944.

Above all there was a gathering fear of the consequences of defeat leading to the stubborn feeling that 'We must win and therefore we shall.'

The united front and the demand for 'unconditional surrender' presented at the Casablanca and Tehran Conferences in January and November 1943 were above all to reassure the eastern and western Alliance partners – but especially Stalin's paranoia – that neither would cut a deal without the other.

They were also a gift for Nazi propaganda, allowing the party machine to present the conflict as a fight to the death in which there would be no victors and defeated, only survivors or annihilated. They took away the hope of an Alliance split and the expectation that the US and Britain would not allow Russia to enter Germany.

The People

The older ones perhaps remembered the collapse of the state after the Versailles treaty, many feared the possibility of forced labour in Russia, and all had a dawning consciousness of the untrammelled vengeance that might be stored up for German atrocities, about which servicemen were often well-informed. Not all this fear was irrational: there was a substantial body of opinion in Britain and America that twice was enough; Germany should be thrown back centuries to a purely agrarian economy.

The analysts concluded that:

'It would seem that at this stage Allied propaganda would most effectively disintegrate the German will to resist by affording to the German "little man" some faint ray of hope making the prospect of defeat appear, if not exactly welcome, at least not wholly unendurable. And the chief concern of the German "little man", of the type frequently found among Ps/W, is undoubtedly his personal economic security; not necessarily fixed at a very high standard of living, but at least guarding him from the terrors of unemployment, inflation, and utter impoverishment through the physical destruction of his property in air-raids. Less universal, but occupying an important place in the minds of many, particularly of the older generation, is the yearning for a society governed by law and order – a "Rechtsstaat" – in which the guilty will be punished but the ordinary law-abiding citizen allowed to live his private life in peace.'

A similar pattern emerged in the prisoners' attitude to the National Socialist regime. The interviewers felt that the solid core of true believers remained fairly constant as did the much smaller population of convinced anti-Nazis. A significant number of 'floating voters' drifted between belief and an apolitical stance according to where they saw their interests lay and were easily influenced by propaganda.

A more interesting group was described as 'belief with reservations.' It comprised the substantial proportion of captives who were fundamentally loyal but had reservations about one or more aspects of National Socialist policy. It covered a range of views, from lapsed Catholics rediscovering their consciences to a U-boat petty officer who thought it was counter-productive to expel Jewish doctors and scientists but described the massacre of 75,000 Jews in Vilna (Vilnius) without turning a hair. Such chinks at least opened up the possibility of bringing about a change of heart through argument.

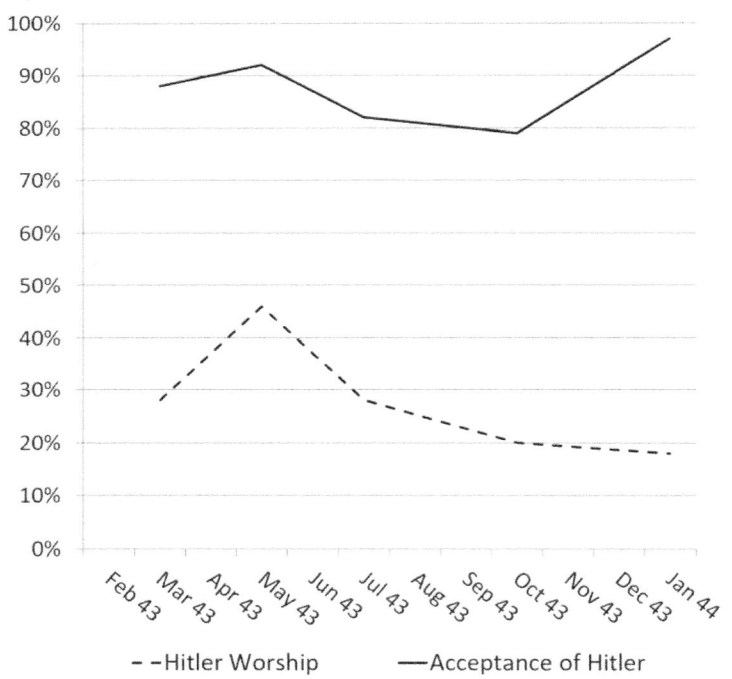

Figure 11: Prisoners' Attitudes to Hitler from February 1943 to January 1944.

The analysts were at pains to point out that their sample was not representative of the German population. The armed forces were male, young, and getting younger as combat casualties thinned out experienced men (the average age of this sample was 22.6 years) and so had little memory of life before Hitler.

The People

They lived in a close-knit community with clear standards of behaviour and sense of purpose, and were sheltered from the worst effects of the blockade on Germany.

From our perspective it seems extraordinary that, even with varying views of National Socialism, there was almost no criticism of Hitler from the respondents.

As recently as October, *Oberleutnant zur See* Georg of E-boat S-96 had grimly opined,

'I'm not expecting victory, but the shattering of all our dreams. It is a good thing that we have got time now to collect our thoughts a bit. I hope that DOENITZ will set up a military dictatorship, so that there won't be a fight between the Reichswehr and the SS – that's what I fear most. The FÜHRER is a dreamer, who is driving the German people to destruction. That talk about a secret weapon is bluff. They must say that, because they are afraid.'[20]

Now none expressed hostility to him and only 8% (6 out of 72) admitted to doubts, in contrast to 21% and 12% from the two previous cohorts.

There was however an encouragingly consistent decline in the number displaying a quasi-religious dedication in which all accusations against him were blankly denied, explained away, or blamed on his subordinates. Accepting that he was only human and capable of error opened another psychological chink. The report advised:

'The argument most likely to weaken the allegiance of those Germans who accept Hitler's authority but fall short of looking on him as a god, would emphasize Hitler's personal inability to retrieve Germany's fortunes. It would hint at rather than dwell on Hitler's responsibility in the past, but show that as a national leader – compared with Bismarck for example – he has lost control over the situation. Faith in the original good intentions of Hitler runs deep, even among convinced anti-Nazis, and it is generally an unrewarding task to try to displace it.'

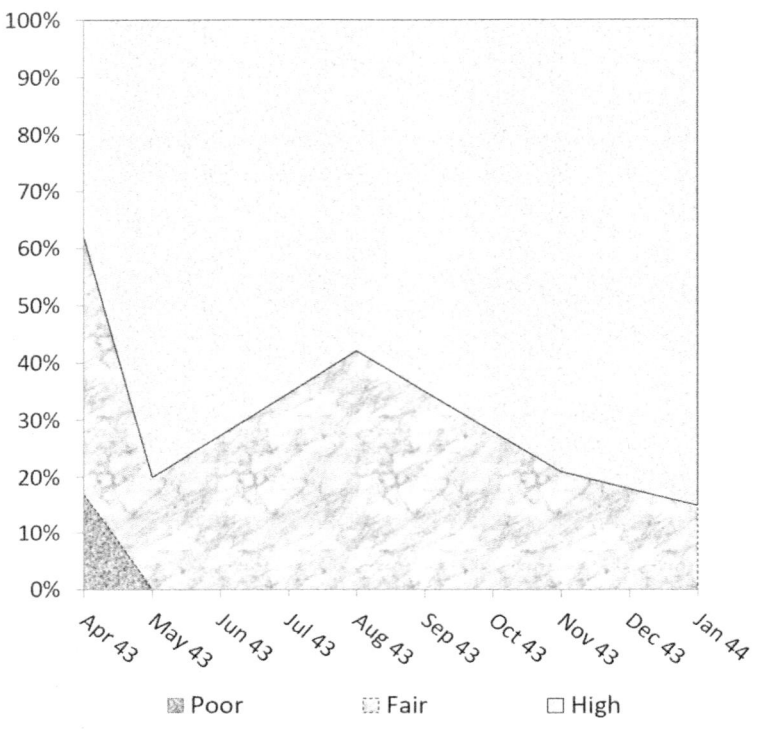

[Chart: Fighting Spirit percentages from Apr 43 to Jan 44, with categories Poor, Fair, High]

Figure 12: 'Fighting Spirit' of Prisoners from April 1943 to January 1944.

Less surprising in hindsight was their attitude to Allied air-raids: bitterness mixed with a determination to endure. It was predictably like the attitude of Londoners four years earlier and, like them, they were convinced that only the other side bombed civilians.

The pollsters' view of German fighting qualities must have been as unwelcome as unsurprising to their audience. They had previously found no indication of widespread failure and now observed:

'We suggested in GRS9 that to many Germans, military resistance seemed the only way of retaining respect in the eyes of the world and in their own eyes. This motive still operates, but it is now strongly reinforced by a lively and personal fear of the consequences of defeat.'

Too many had seen or heard of the 'consequences of defeat' as applied to the Nazis' victims and dreaded their stored thirst for vengeance; too many remembered Versailles or believed Goebbels' take on 'unconditional surrender.' For them the stark choice of victory or death must have seemed all too real.

Stool pigeon: Traitor or Patriot? Conscience or Collaboration?

The soldier who changes sides has few friends. His new companions never quite trust him, his former mates despise him. Yet what do we make of one who turns his back on a system that has become a byword for evil? About fifty captives passing through CSDIC chose to throw in their lot with their hosts.

An 'M' Room listener recorded *Maschinenmaat* (Leading Stoker) Wilhelm Görs, one of four survivors (all ratings) from U-444, telling this rather laboured joke shortly after arrival.

'N 1553:   *Who is the biggest farmer in Germany?*'
'N 1558 [*Obermaschinenmaat* Philipps, U-432]: *I don't know.*'
'N 1553:   *Adolf; and do you know why? He's got a herd of eighty-five million cattle, a great fat pig, and a dog.*'

The crack would have been distinctly unwise before his capture a few days earlier.

His crewmate *Maschinengefreiter* Gerhard Wengefeld mentioned a casualty from the boat whose two brothers had already died, one at Stalingrad and the other in a dive bomber. *Funkgefreiter* Rudolf Spitz observed that if all the English were as humane as the interrogating officer it was all the same to him whether Germany won or lost the war.[21] All three denied any close connection with the Nazi Party and two were easily persuaded to work as stool pigeons.* Spitz kept going in that role, using several identities, for nearly a year.

Some of the intelligence consumers at Admiralty were uneasy with the ethics of using information obtained by 'traitors' and suspicious of its reliability. The latter concern was easy to allay: 'M' Room listeners validated the reports of 'stoolies,' who were sublimely ignorant of the microphones.

CSDIC UK, unlike the US equivalent, gave its stool pigeons no special status while they worked (apart from separate accommodation for obvious reasons) and no promise of preferential treatment after the war. Their motivation had to come from something other than self-interest.

The earliest recruits were refugees, followed by communists who had been drafted to the U-boat service from concentration camps because of their technical skills and needed little encouragement to switch sides. Others, separated from their crewmates, felt their military duty was done and pondered the tension between their duty to Germany and their forced oath of fealty to Hitler. In all, four refugees and 49 prisoners took up the role during the course of the war. The refugees, unlike the prisoners, were paid. Between them all they 'serviced' 1,506 prisoners.

Sönke Neitzel and Harald Welzer in their book *Soldaten – On Fighting, Killing and Dying* (translated by Jefferson Chase) explore the way in which the Nazis incrementally shifted Germany's frame of reference as a whole and that of her armed forces in particular to normalise horror. Some prisoners, particularly those old enough not to have been indoctrinated from their youth, allowed their earlier values to bubble to the surface on release from the mental stockade. We earlier met

---

* The term 'stool pigeon' to describe an informer originated in the USA in the mid 19th century. It probably recalls earlier usage for decoy birds in hunting.

The People

Blumenberg and Dabelstein of U-386, who were recorded the day before their London treat:

> '*N 2191: I should never have made a good National Socialist, because I still remember what it was like previously. I soon found out that they consider us to be fools, they forbid us to read the books we want to read. I am capable of forming my own judgment and won't be put into blinkers. If we lose the war I shan't bother about anything any longer. I shall grow my cabbages and that's all.*
>
> *N 2189: If we lose the war I shan't bother about politics any longer either. In the Hitler Youth Movement I was an idealist and was enthusiastic. But through my father's profession* [diplomat] *and his free thinking I have acquired a broader outlook. I want to see foreign countries and form my own opinion of them. I won't have any views dictated to me. A man like GOEBBELS lays down to a sixty-year-old professor which books he may read. That's a scandal!*'[22]

In short, despite the unimaginable pain CSDIC's guests had caused in service of one of the most vicious regimes the world has seen, they were not two-dimensional caricature villains but human beings, with the complex and often contradictory bundle of motives that go with that condition. Some bought the whole, sick story; many rejected the excesses of the Nazi Party while clinging to some or all National Socialist ideals; some were profoundly anti-Nazi while retaining an almost religious belief in Hitler. As *Maschinenmaat* Theodor Averkamp of U-91 put it,

> '*N 2390: I'm no Nazi either, but what ADOLF has done: "Not for myself but for the people," and if anyone talks against him, he should be shot!*'

Inevitably, as the dream of National Socialism segued into nightmare, some felt Germany's best chance lay in hastening her defeat as quickly and cleanly as possible. Others were convinced their military duty was to escape or make life difficult for their captors. Yet others found the conflict irresolvable.

Nor did anti-Semitic views map conveniently onto this spectrum. Some anti-Nazis felt the racial laws were its only redeeming feature while a few devout National Socialists thought them at best stupid and counter-productive, at worst plain wrong.

While on active service the differences were masked by a combination of aligned factors: loyalty to Germany, Party conditioning and coercion, military training, their oath of fealty, and above all the mutual trust, dependence and loyalty of a crew. Taken out of that context the cracks began to show, more easily if they had come from an unhappy ship. Officers' behaviour could reinforce or quickly undermine team spirit. For example a leading seaman in U-135, a deeply discontented boat, described their selfishness while the survivors were at Freetown awaiting transport to Britain.

'N 1877:   *In our first P/W camp our own officers swindled us out of our cigarettes. They received everyone's ration and divided them into half, which meant that five officers kept exactly the same quantity as they gave to thirty-five men. Fine gentlemen those were!'*

Which ran true to form. The captain was first to abandon ship, then tried to steal someone else's lifejacket when his own didn't inflate. The first lieutenant could not make the simplest chart entry without help and the second lieutenant, though competent, was a virulent Nazi.

Their shipmate *Oberfunkmaat* Edmund Meyer happily shared his knowledge of German codes and 'stated his readiness to serve in a merchant ship in convoy, or even in one of our submarines, he would do anything *'except actually fire a gun against Germans!'*[23] In fact he became stool pigeon N1878 who had a long and successful career in the role.

The People

On the other hand *Scharnhorst* survivors came from a large and stable community. Many had been with the ship since her commissioning and had almost unlimited faith in her, and in each other. *Matrosengefreiter* Rudi Birke put it like this:

'You'll seldom find such peculiar people as there were on the SCHARNHORST. For an old SCHARNHORST hand who commissioned with the SCHARNHORST there was nothing but the SCHARNHORST. The GNEISENAU was nothing by comparison. You know, they swore by the SCHARNHORST, that's why no-one jumped overboard, they said: "The SCHARNHORST will never sink!"'[24]

Consequently, they presented a solid, coherent front to the interrogators. Almost. *Maschinenobergefreiter* (Stoker 1st Class) Paul Schaffrath (N2175) was a member of the repair party, and war-weary to start with.

'N 2175:   *...POLDI wanted to get his Knight's Cross. He went on clamouring until we went up to NORWAY. ... He always thought he had done us a favour by that; he always used to promise us that we should see action. We had no wish to do so!'*[25]

★ ★ ★

'N2175:   *I am absolutely fed up with the services, with all the Prussianism. Do you think I would escape from here if the opportunity ever occurred? No, never! If I did I would get eighteen days' leave, after which I would have to go to NORWAY, join the TIRPITZ and be sunk again. I want to be left in peace and not have to listen to perpetual orders.'*[26]

Officers' abuse of privilege in a supposedly meritocratic organisation, combined with their disdain of normal ethical standards, chipped further away at his resolve.

'N 2175:   *Do you know that very strong complaints were about officers in connection with that Joy ship. A case came before the courts – Leutnant HOFFSTÄDTER (?) was courtmartialled concerning*

a woman. The battery deck patrol caught him in the act with a woman in the bakery, he had her lying on the sacks of flour.
*N 2129 [*Zimmermannobergefreiter Martin Wallek*]: That isn't the place I'd choose to do it in.*
N 2175: The anti-splinter bulkhead was closed. And at three o'clock in the morning the 'Kommandant' was behind it with the woman; he had gone right through the compartments. We have a sentry there, but they had sent him away.
N 2129: They can't send you away if you're on sentry duty.
N 2175: Well that's what he did. And the First Signals Officer (?) saw it, and there was a row about it, and the sentry was sent back to his post. They danced with the women on the quarterdeck. The woman gave old BERGER (?) a sock on the jaw. "Give me another kiss, Miss." Plonk! He caught it! He was a Korvettenkapitän. And the sailors, the Flak watch at the after quadruple guns, saw that. What a to-do! That sort of thing makes me sick of the service. Plenty of women came up there all the time. The Joy ship was first of all to have been a floating brothel, but they turned that down. DERHOFEN (?) turned it down. So that the officers should have something, they built a 'Strength through Joy' ship. That's a nice name to give it. The ratings have to applaud. We got boys on board who had never been with a woman, seventeen-year-olds.'[27]

Two weeks after their arrival the hopelessness of Germany's military situation was beginning to sink in, and with it a willingness to question the judgement of those who had led her into such a catastrophic dead-end. Schaffrath, in conversation with Able Seamen Alsen and Wallek (N2129), clearly felt he was with a receptive audience for sentiments which would be treasonable at home.

'*N 2175: We missed an opportunity then in 1939 when AMERICA offered to mediate. We ought to have made full use of that.*

N 2129: Yes, HITLER is a bit of a megalomaniac. He wanted to do everything by himself without accepting any outside help.

N 2175: Yes, but there can never be a revolution in GERMANY, even if the allies smash up the whole of GERMANY. I have always had some sympathy for the English, but these terror raids are a foul business. After all the German people ought not to be made to pay for the fact that our leaders are incapable.

N 2129: Our leaders are too young and inexperienced. The chances of victory are 100 to 1 against us. We are fighting against the three mightiest peoples of the earth.

N 2175: It was madness to start the war, and I simply can't understand how they think they are going to win now; but we have a lot of people who can't think for themselves and can't see that. The invasion will certainly come this year and then they will march straight into GERMANY.'

Schaffrath's last illusions were left in the chill of the Barents Sea. Despite belonging to a tightly knit, elite community his loss of faith in the war, the military and his national leadership was complete enough for him to start working as a stool pigeon, one of the more surprising conversions. Another unusual feature is that we can date the switch precisely: his last recorded conversation with his crewmates and his first as stool pigeon were both on 25th February 1944 and he remained in harness until 16th May. Intriguingly, the first work name picked for him was Paulsen, who was Kelbling's training skipper when he converted from minesweepers to U-boats.

Willi Alsen on the other hand was unconvinced. He had remained silent during the above conversation but was overheard the next day saying,

'*N 2130: We ought to fire shells on LONDON for days on end and give then a real blood bath. I have no sympathy for those swine. When once the SS marches in here, they will clean things up. They'll get a hell of a shock.*'[28]

It is instructive to look at a failed recruitment. *Oberleutnant zur See* Kurt Böhme was a professional naval officer, commander of U-450 sunk in the Mediterranean in March 1944, and should have been a prime candidate. Eavesdropping revealed that he was a Protestant Anti-Nazi who had lost his house in an air raid and whose parents were close friends of the controversial Pastor Niemöller who, despite his strongly nationalistic views and previous record as a successful First World War U-boat captain, had renounced his initial support for the Nazi Party.

Böhme fumed at the inhumanity, abuses and corruption of the Nazi establishment. His mother was harassed and had windows broken in a dispute with an official; a neighbour was reported for saying 'Good morning' instead of '*Heil Hitler*;' a man was condemned to death for doubting the existence of reprisal weapons while others walked free on the strength of Party membership. Niemöller was released after his trial for 'Activities against the State' in 1938 but immediately re-arrested and packed off to a concentration camp, where he remained until the end of the war.

A conversation with a stool pigeon produced the following outrage:

'I know, for example, from my sister-in-law in the Labour Service, where they were asked "Who among you will present the FÜHRER with a child?" that twenty-two out of thirty-five volunteered, that things were arranged accordingly and that it was said: "Two women" (to one man). I've often heard it said "That can be justified from every point of view because we have lost so many men." Thank God I've not yet seen the effects of it. In accordance with that view the woman is no longer a being with whom you share your life, physically and spiritually, but just a piece of flesh.'[29]

This was no isolated perversion. Günter Schramm of T-25 described an acquaintance at Berchtesgaden where his mother had been evacuated after their home in Hamburg was destroyed.

'N 2074   *She was a BDM [Bund Deutscher Mädel] leader and told her girls that it is an honour now for every German girl to lose her virginity when she is fourteen or fifteen years old and to give birth to her first child at the age of sixteen, seventeen or eighteen; and that it is no longer of importance for a girl to wear pretty clothes and so on, that is all a secondary matter. The main thing is to keep their underclothing clean and tidy and, if possible, they must be made of silk, of course. These words haven't been exaggerated in the telling, they are the very words. The woman had a very close relationship with an SS-Führer and immediately became pregnant, whereupon this factory owner of course divorced her. It was very shattering because my mother, and particularly my friends, knew this lady – I got to know her too. It all came as such a surprise that we couldn't believe it. But those are actually the ideas the SS are spreading.'*[30]

Böhme was happy to defend the official line in public but privately recognised the moral equivalence between the RAF bombing raids on Germany and the *Luftwaffe*'s earlier blitz, and between the Royal Navy's blockade and the U-boat campaign.

N 2344 [Böhme]:   *I keep reminding the IO here of the bomb which the English first dropped on the heath in WESTERLAND, by which we try to prove that the English started indiscriminate bombing, but I haven't got a clear conscience about it.*

'N 2364 [Oberleutnant zur See Hungershausen, U-91]:
   But they tried to starve out our civilian population by the blockade.

N 2344:   *And what is the purpose of our U-boat warfare?*'[31]

He argued in political and military discussions that a quick Allied victory was the best hope to minimise Germany's inevitable torment:

   '... *what will 'beaten' mean for us? That the whole of GERMANY will be reduced to rubble and a further million will lose their lives.*'[32]

But his profound sense of duty left him unable to take the final step into helping it happen. Nonetheless he parted on friendly terms with Donald Welbourn, the interrogator who had failed to convince him over many long country walks. The pair kept up intermittent contact during Böhme's post-war business career in South Africa, during which he reversed his originally pro-apartheid views. He died in 1984.[33]

A Boatswain's Mate from U-506 in conversation a few months earlier was clear that his only reason for *not* giving information to the interrogating officer was to avoid endangering the lives of comrades still at sea.[34]

If the interrogators were unsure, they had the option of testing the water at a 'nursing home' set up for anti-Nazi prisoners at the beginning of 1942. It was a secure facility where prisoners potentially willing to work for the Allies could be cultivated and evaluated. If rejected, they were returned to camp 'cured' of their ailment with no-one the wiser. The home was at Broughton Rectory; it is unclear whether this was Broughton in Hampshire or Oxfordshire.[35]

Stool pigeons typically worked for a few months until their first-hand knowledge became dangerously outdated. They were given an idea of the information needed and placed with a prisoner of similar specialty but often from a different branch or service, to cover any naive questions the 'stoolie' might ask. They were usually given a cover story involving recent capture from a genuine casualty and always worked under a false name. Their CSDIC index number remained constant.

Apart from the working alias there were creative exceptions to all rules. Stool pigeons were known to risk posing as survivors of boats still in service (U-425 and U-178 for example), which might have been embarrassing if they had really been sunk at the time.

The People

Rudolf Spitz from U-444 stayed in harness for almost a year. Günter Grüter† was a telegraphist survivor from the tanker SS *Germania*, sunk in December 1942. He started working as a stool pigeon by February 1943, keeping to his original role until May that year, and continued right up to April 1945: a remarkable feat of endurance. A versatile *Luftwaffe* officer, index number A713, had been in harness at least since 1940 when most Germans would have expected to win the war quickly.‡ He must surely have earned an acting award as well as a prize for brass neck by stretching his repertoire to impersonate a U-boat commander, even when paired with genuine U-boat officers. These three plus a naval radioman (N1878, *Oberfunkmaat* Edmund Meyer of U-135 recruited in September 1943) were deeply involved with the castaways in our story, and were helped on occasion by at least three others.

A good first step was to talk about the prisoner's own survival and capture, which few would see any harm in recounting. An increasingly common trick as the pool of stool pigeons grew was to place them in pairs with a single target. A prisoner might be suspicious of one overly-curious cellmate but drop his guard in a three-way conversation, a relaxation that worked almost as well with one stool pigeon and two guests. Certain successful pairings were used repeatedly.

As with microphones, prisoners had been intensively briefed on stool pigeons and even seemed to have specific clues as to who was involved.

'*N(Am)52: Just before we put to sea we were told about the German officer who asks questions here.*
N 2409:   Yes, things like that have often come through. In the beginning GAF people were mentioned, first a GAF officer, then

---

† Not his real name. He could have been any one of three telegraphist survivors.
‡ He may have been one of the original refugee volunteers.

another, and quite recently a 'Maschinenmaat' and an 'Obergefreiter' were reported to be doing things like that. According to the things one hears here, I don't know – it strikes me as being rather peculiar, because it would really have to be here; afterwards at the base-camp –
N(Am)52: It would be no use.'[36]

And, as with microphones, no amount of advance warning seemed to help. Cover names and legends changed faster than they could be blown and the need to talk almost always won through in the end. It helped to take a lively interest in the specifics of local gossip; a stool pigeon could too easily be tripped up by reminiscing fondly about a bar that had been bombed before he was supposed to have left port. Every so often he might be forcibly reminded of the outcast status he had embraced.

N 2243 [Matrosenobergefreiter Georg Kugler, U-264]: At the base we were always hearing that such and such a person would be sentenced after the war for betraying their country and for disclosing military secrets. It happened a few times every month.

N 1552 ['Funkobergefreiter Schüpler, Scharnhorst']: Are they supposed to be PW?

N 2243: Hm. They're here now.

N 1552: Was there ever anyone among them whom anybody else knew?

N 2243: The Obersteuermann once knew an Obersteuermann. He was said to have been on a boat which was sunk, to have been taken prisoner and to have given away information.

N 1552: What was his name?

N 2243: SCHMIDT, I believe, or SCHMITZ. I'm not certain, but it was something like that.

N 1552: How do they find out when someone here talks?

N 2243: I don't know how they find out.[37]

This was too much like Spitz' real name for comfort.

The People

The question remained what to do with a stool pigeon once he had outlived his usefulness. He could hardly be dumped to a regular prisoner-of-war camp where he risked being unmasked with very unpleasant consequences. In July 1943 the original British camp, Grizedale Hall in Cumbria, was set aside to house such helpful prisoners. By 1944 it was becoming overcrowded and was evidently too remote from London so they were moved to a section of No 7 Camp at Ascot.[38] Some found continuing employment with Sefton Delmer's propaganda radio service.

The misfortune of U-444 and her companion U-432 (sunk immediately afterward) happened in March 1943 which was otherwise a catastrophic month for the Allies in the Battle of the Atlantic. By May the tables were turned by the availability in quantity of escorts, improved weapons and sensors, and – finally – long-range patrol aircraft and escort carriers. U-boat losses for the rest of the year were unsustainable, almost matching merchant sinkings in some months. Although the fighting spirit of crews at sea was unaffected this had an unavoidable effect on morale ashore and on the reactions of those captured. In the final months of the war the supply of stool pigeon volunteers exceeded the need.

See Appendix D – Stool pigeons for an account of the technique extracted from the MI19 history.

---

[1] Donald B Welbourn F R Eng; *An Engineer in Peace and War – A Technical and Social History, Volume I 1916-1952* (Lulu, 2008). P.183.

[2] *Building and Launching of* HMS *Royal Rupert* – The Royal Rupert Times, Souvenir Xmas Number 1947.

[3] TNA ADM 223/467; *NID monograph: NID (I) 1938-1943.* J H Godfrey memo NID 1755 dated 16/3/1942.

[4] *Findmypast;* The London Gazette, <u>Notices under the Trustee Act 1925</u>.

5. J.M. Weatherby, 1967. *Aspects of the Ethnography and Oral Tradition of the Sebei of Mount Elgon*. Unpublished MA Thesis, University of East Africa.
6. *Dutch Border Clash Blamed on Nazi Police* – The Pittsburgh Press, 12th November 1939
7. *Processing and initial interrogation of U-352 POWs at Charleston Navy Yard, South Carolina, May 10, 1942;* http://www.uboatarchive.net/POW/POWU-352Photos.htm. See also an exchange of memos between Izzard and Admiral Godfrey in TNA ADM 223/475; *Intelligence collection methods*.
8. D.B. Welbourn F.R.Eng.: *Op Cit.* P.174.
9. D.B. Welbourn: *Op. Cit.* P.182.
10. TNA HS9/491/1; *Charles William EVERETT - born [1908]*.
11. TNA ADM 199/2478; *Director of Naval Intelligence: movements of small craft and personnel to Mediterranean, questionnaires and Prisoners of War statements: includes CX material*.
12. Extract from *Notes on the Interrogation of Prisoners of War* in TNA ADM 223/475; *Intelligence collection methods*.
13. United States Holocaust Memorial Museum Photograph no 79272; *The Joshua family stands outside the Jordanbad sanitorium near Biberach a few months after their liberation*.
14. TNA WO 208/4149; *Interrogation Reports on German Prisoners of War 2700-3050*. SRN 2947 dated 1st March 1944.
15. ibid. SRN 2476 dated 13th January 1944.
16. TNA FO 898/45 transcribed by Sefton Delmer Archive at https://www.psywar.org/delmer/8420/1001 (accessed 28/5/2017).
17. TNA WO 208/4149; *Interrogation Reports on German Prisoners of War 2700-3050*. SRN 2933 dated 26th February 1944.
18. TNA WO 208/5522; *Interrogation reports on German prisoners of war: GRS 1-11 1942 Jun 21 – 1944 May 27*. The comments here specifically relate to GR10 dated 24th February 1944.
19. TNA WO 208/4147; *Interrogation Reports on German Prisoners of War 2200-2450*. SRN 2388 dated 29th October 1943.
20. ibid. SRN 2333 dated 17th October 1943.
21. TNA WO 208/4145; *Interrogation Reports on German Prisoners of War No's 1489-1900*. SRN 1546 dated 20th March 1943, 1513 and 1512 dated 15th March.

The People

[22] TNA WO 208/4149; *Interrogation Reports on German Prisoners of War 2700-3050*. SRN 2947 dated 1st March 1944.

[23] TNA WO 208/4146; *Interrogation Reports on German Prisoners of War No's 1901-2199*. SRN 2179 dated 13th September 1943. TNA WO 208/5158; *Enemy PoW interrogation reports: wireless and signals intelligence 1939 Oct-1946 Mar*. Everett note dated 18th September 1943.

[24] TNA WO 208/4148; *Interrogation Reports on German Prisoners of War, SRN 2451-2699 (November 1943-January 1944)*. SRN 2663 dated 6th January 1944.

[25] TNA WO 208/4149; *Interrogation Reports on German Prisoners of War 2700-3050*. SRN 2829 dated 20th January 1944.

[26] ibid. SRN 2808 dated 19th January 1944.

[27] ibid. SRN 2810 dated 19th January 1944.

[28] ibid. SRN 2768 dated 17th January 1944, 2767 dated 18th January 1944.

[29] TNA WO 208/4151; *Interrogation Reports on German Prisoners of War No's 3360-3650*. SRN 3382 dated 18th April 1944.

[30] TNA WO 208/4163; *Interrogation Reports on German Prisoners of War 1731-1949*. SRN 1929 dated 1st February 1944.

[31] TNA WO 208/4150; *Interrogation Reports on German Prisoners of War 3051-3359*. SRN 3228 dated 23rd March 1944.

[32] ibid. SRN 3229 dated 24th March 1944.

[33] D B Welbourn; *Op. Cit.* and IWM Collection Cat No 18777: *Oral History Interview with Donald Burkewood Welbourn* (Reel 2). TNA WO 208/4200; *Special extracts from interrogation reports on German and Italian prisoners of war 1942 Dec-1945 Mar*. SRN 3309 dated 1st April 1944.

[34] TNA WO 208/4196; *Interrogation Reports on German and Italian Prisoners of War SP/F 1-142 May 1941-August 1944*. SP/F 121 dated 22nd July 1943. TNA WO 208/4150; *Interrogation Reports on German Prisoners of War SRN 3051-3359 (March-April 1944)*. SRN 3186, 3191, 3226-3229, 3309, 3346.

[35] TNA WO 208/3442; *Prisoners of war holding strong anti-Nazi views*.

[36] TNA WO 208/4200; *Special extracts from interrogation reports on German and Italian prisoners of war 1942 Dec-1945 Mar*. Extract from SR Draft No 3992 dated 29th April 1944.

[37] TNA WO 208/4149; *Interrogation Reports on German Prisoners of War 2700-3050*. SRN 2971 dated 2nd March 1944.

[38] TNA WO 208/4970; *The Story of MI19*. WO 208/3527; *Special camp for Anti-Nazi POWs: suggested transfer from No 1 Camp to No 7 Camp*.

AT CSDIC UK

Four U-593 prisoners, including the captain, were flown to Britain in time to feature in SR transcripts on 21st December and for their initial statements to be included in the NID 1/PW weekly summary of 25th. Five from U-73 were similarly flown back for priority interrogation and crop up in the eavesdroppers' reports on New Year's Eve.[1]

This was not unusual. A recurring theme of Naval Intelligence subject reviews is their anxiety to get hold of survivors before inexpert questioning could put them on their guard or give away too much information about what NID were looking for. Tiredness and the disorientation of a rapid change of scene also helped; and the contents of prisoners' pockets when they were deloused on arrival could yield useful information. U-boat and E-boat crews captured off the British coast were often housed at CSDIC within twenty-four hours.

Most prisoners passed through a sorting centre to identify those of interest to CSDIC, but NID made it clear from the start that they wanted to talk to *all* submarine crewmen.

The survivors of T-25 were in London in the small hours of 3rd January, less than three days after they were plucked from the water. The first 'M' Room transcript of one of their conversations was later the same day.

Escort Group 6 landed *Alsterufer*'s crew at Londonderry (Derry) on 3rd January 1944 before continuing its cold, wet watch on the Western Approaches. The crew were expected in London on 10th January but were actually in their cells by 8th.

The remaining seventy-four U-boat survivors left Algiers sometime on or after 19th December and travelled to the UK with convoy MKF 27, arriving on 4th January 1944.* They reached Latimer House or Wilton Park by 11th.[2]

Duke of York landed the *Scharnhorst* survivors at Scapa Flow on 2nd January 1944. *Matrosengefreiter* (Ordinary Seaman) Günter Strater was a stretcher case, handled separately. The rest were bundled blindfold aboard the *St Ninian*, a regular ferry across Pentland Firth to Scrabster, then had an uncomfortable 22-hour train ride south under guard aboard the ironically-named 'Jellicoe Express' from Thurso. Presumably they would have been in a sealed carriage so at least would have had seats, unlike many of their British fellow passengers. They arrived in London on the evening of 3rd and the first CSDIC transcript of their conversations was on 4th.

Reflecting the impact of the *Scharnhorst* news Winston Churchill met at least one of their escorts (Marine F L Shippey); and Vyacheslav Molotov, the Soviet Foreign Minister who was seldom generous in praise for his allies, offered his congratulations on a 'splendid achievement.' The *Red Star* of 31st December published a 150-line account of the battle based on an interview with Rear Admiral Archer (Senior British Naval Officer, North Russia), an exceptional compliment.[3] The treatment of the *Scharnhorst* prisoners is especially interesting because they were all ratings so their intelligence value might have been thought limited.

The scramble to clear space for the surge of new guests meant that some of them were temporarily placed in the London District Cage (6-8 Kensington Palace Gardens) where they were housed ten to a room and underwent preliminary interrogation.[4] These stragglers rejoined their shipmates by 12th January.

---

* One survivor spoke of transport to Casablanca but I believe he was mistaken. There is no corroboration and a long road journey would make no sense with Oran so near.

At CSDIC UK

So, between about 4th and 12th January 1944, a string of vehicles with blacked-out windows deposited forty-six crewmen from U-593, thirty-three from U-73, seventy-four from *Alsterufer*, sixty-two from T-25, and thirty-six from *Scharnhorst* at two Buckinghamshire country houses and their flotillas of temporary buildings. The views could have been anywhere, and at Latimer the Chess Valley road was closed for the duration to avoid giving the inmates any clues.

Figure 13: It could have been anywhere.

Most of the 251 had been questioned before and some more than once – on the rescuing ship, at the Algiers detention centre (where they left warnings about a suspected stool pigeon for their successors) and on the journey to Britain. The interrogators thus faced a disparate group of people with varying backgrounds and motivation, and who had already had practice at stonewalling curious British officers. They reported on 24th January:

'Morale of prisoners has always shown considerable variation, as has also their security consciousness. The latter has been highest in U/Boats, where fear of capture is always present in the men's minds and the effect of insecurity on the safety of their U/Boat comrades can be very easily appreciated. These facts are usually impressed on

U/Boat crews by their C.O.s on the first day at sea. Captured crews are particularly tough if they are not segregated before interrogation, and C.O.s and/or officers are able to lecture the men on the importance of security during interrogation. Lack of security consciousness, however, can never in itself be taken to imply low fighting morale.'[5]

Against that the speed with which they were brought into the system contributed to their tiredness and disorientation, and the CSDIC staff were by then old hands: fluent German speakers who knew the country well and could adapt their approach to the interviewee.

U-73

The interrogation summary for 1st January 1944 included preliminary results from the five crew members flown to the UK: *Mechanikersmaat* (Leading Torpedo Operator) Willy Zwietasch, *Maschinenmaat* (Engine Room Artificer) Walter Losch, *Matrosenobergefreiter* (Able Seaman) Kurt Wehling, *Funkobergefreiter* (Telegraphist) Joseph Stäger and *Matrose I* (Ordinary Seaman) Ude Nissen. The identities of both Mediterranean advance parties are inferred from SR reports transcribed before their shipmates arrived in the UK, in this case starting on 31st December 1943.

All had skilled roles but non-commissioned ranks, in contrast to U-593 whose commander was one of those selected.

Horst Deckert, U-73's captain, had spent much of his youth in Argentina. His crew described him as an efficient officer with a burning desire to emulate his predecessor by winning the knight's cross but suspected him of inflating his claims to that end. He certainly boasted of several successes which NID could not verify. The interrogators found him correct and tight-lipped, giving the impression of a fanatical Nazi. He was a merciless disciplinarian: several survivors had been disrated for various offences, one all the way from sub-lieutenant to ordinary seaman.

This was presumably Ude Nissen who described his truncated naval officer training to *Alsterufer's* 2nd mate, another Nissen. Interestingly the accelerated qualification seems to have started and 'peacetime' ended four years *before* the outbreak of the Second World War.

> '*N(Am)46* [*Matrose* Ude Nissen]: *At one time the training lasted a year, then six months and latterly it was four months. Then I joined the U-boat arm without knowing a thing about it; I did two patrols and then I was detailed to the U-boat officers' course. That consists of the U-boat training division at PILLAU and GDYNIA, the U-boat school, the torpedo course, the signal's course and the gunnery course. It lasts eighteen months in all.*
>
> *N 2146* [2nd Officer Johannes Nissen]: *In peacetime to become a Leutnant takes –*
>
> *N(Am)46: In peace time it takes four-and-a-half years. From 1935 on it took four years, from 1937 three years and from 1940 two-and-a-half years.*
>
> *N 2146: And probably even less now?*
>
> *N(Am)46: Well, it still takes two-and-a-half years.*
>
> *N 2146: Some of them go to the Steuermann's* [helmsman's] *school much too soon; their training has been shortened, cut down by another four months. They have a very full syllabus. They tackle nine subjects in three-and-a-half (?) years. They are: navigation, seamanship, naval law, physics, English, marine engines, naval construction and mathematics.*'[6]

Although a less than happy boat there was little sign of disaffection or disloyalty among the crew. *Funkegefreiter*

(Leading Telegraphist) Theodor Essman (N2159) may have been a limiting case but was probably not alone.

'N 1552 [a stool pigeon]: *Who do you think is to blame for the war?*
N 2159: *The English, of course!*
N 1552: *Why? How?*
N 2159: *Well, the FÜHRER warned them after all!*'[7]

In an eventful life U-73 had been badly damaged by air attack once and suffered lesser trauma on two other occasions. One of these, in port at Toulon, delayed her final sailing. She had lifted eight German army officers – presumably escapees – from the coast of North Africa in August 1943 and brought them back to Toulon. On another occasion three British airmen, rescued and confined to the forward compartment, were caught timing the boat as she dived. On her penultimate patrol U-73 landed a Corsican agent with money and explosives near Oran in Algeria. He was caught the next day.

Stool pigeons and listeners quickly discovered that preparations were under way to move the surviving Mediterranean U-boats from Toulon to new facilities at Marseilles.

'N 1552: *Are they supposed to be enlarging MARSEILLES at present?*
N(Am)45 [Maschinenmaat (Leading Stoker) Walter Losch]: *Well, it's not finished yet, but it soon will be, about February(?).*
N 1552: *Is the base to be transferred from TOULON altogether or what?*
N(Am)45: *Well, they have smashed up the base at TOULON. The shipyard is almost in ruins.*'[8]

In the meantime the rudimentary crew and non-existent boat shelters at Toulon had to do. They also filled out details of the escort routine for submarines entering and leaving port, no doubt useful for the Allied boats habitually lurking outside.

Confirmation of the remaining U-boat strength in the area was also handy.

> '*N(Am)42* [*Funkobergefreiter* Josef Stäger, U-73]: *English submarines are lying outside the harbour at TOULON. A German boat was lost there on a trial run. Two torpedoes – on a trial run.*
>
> *N 1485* [a stool pigeon]: How many boats would you say we have got left in the MEDITERRANEAN?
>
> *N(Am)42:* A few.
>
> *N 1485:* I should say thirty.
>
> *N(Am)42:* There aren't more than ten boats there now.
>
> *N 1485:* Ten boats!
>
> *N(Am)42:* Not more. When we were there, there were twelve boats left. Now DIGGINS and KELBLING have been sunk and now we. If BRÜNNING has joined them there now, there will be about ten boats – not more.'[9]

Judging by the frequency of SR intercepts most U-73 survivors were 'dumped' before the end of January 1944. Nineteen of them passed through Number Seven (Winter Quarters) Camp, Ascot before being shipped out on 1st February for embarkation to Canada.[10] *Leutnant zur See* (Junior Sub-Lieutenant) Kurt Kinkele was interesting enough to be kept at least until 25th February. He later became a successful record company executive and liked to wind up his US contacts by mentioning that he first saw America through a periscope.

Deckert was imprisoned in Arizona. He later returned to live in the United States under an anglicised name and worked as an engineer at a ball bearing plant in New Hampshire. He corresponded with and met one of the officers from his nemesis USS *Edison* who recalled that he blamed Hitler – but only for the latter's military mistakes.[11] He stayed in touch with many of his old crew for as long as possible, until he died in 2006.

It is a reasonable guess that Commodore Rushbrooke, the Director of Naval Intelligence, paid close attention to the interrogation report. In one of the curious symmetries you find in wartime his last seagoing command from May 1941 until June 1942 was the carrier HMS *Eagle*, torpedoed and sunk by U-73 under her previous commander in August 1942.

U-593

The four prisoners rushed back were the commander (*Kapitänleutnant* Gerd Kelbling), a PO Telegraphist (*Oberfunkmaat* Fritz Zimmerman), an Engine Room Artificer (ERA), and a Chief ERA (*Obermechanikersmaat* Günther Hünert). They arrived by 21st December and were described as 'extremely security conscious.'[12] The interrogators had nonetheless elicited information about the boat itself, other boats and personalities operating or expected in the Mediterranean, and U-boat tactics by Christmas.

Just five days after U-593 went to her grave the NID weekly summary of prisoner-of-war statements produced its first results, presumably from CSDIC Algiers. By then Kelbling, despite his skill, experience and security-consciousness, had supplied or confirmed the information that U-642 (Herbert Brünning) and U-450 (Kurt Böhme) had recently entered the Mediterranean, that Albrecht Brandi had escaped or been released from internment in Spain and was to get another boat, that Wolfgang Lüth (an ace commander on his way back from a long and successful patrol) was to retire from active duty, and that U-431 (Dietrich Schöneboom) was still with 29th Flotilla – apparently unaware that it had been sunk with all hands the previous October. He also gave the mistaken information that

Korvettenkapitän von Freeden, a former minesweeper captain, now had a U-boat in the Mediterranean.

His crewmates added that U-380 (Josef Röther) had been seen in Toulon (in fact when it was handed over to Brandi) and U-453 (Egon Reiner Freiherr von Schlippenbach, who had already moved on) was in the Mediterranean. All this informed the Operational Intelligence Centre's U-boat gazetteer as well as strengthening CSDIC's hand for the next interrogation.

Kelbling had commanded the boat ever since she was built and had run the perilous gauntlet of the Straits of Gibraltar in October 1942. Her penultimate patrol was a fruitless attempt to intercept an Allied submarine landing and recovering agents at the Baie de Cavalaire, near St Tropez. Kelbling was later told the agents had been captured ashore and the mission aborted.

One of his favourite tricks was to surface at night near a hospital ship while recharging his batteries, relying on the ship's large radar echo to mask his own signature from any patrolling destroyers. It was important first to check that the hospital ship was not itself equipped with radar. Destroyer captains were probably reminded to peer closely at anything wearing red crosses after this revelation.

As casualties mounted it became increasingly difficult for an adequately fit and competent seaman to avoid 'volunteering' for the U-boat arm. Training was abbreviated and promotion accelerated, which itself did nothing for the crews' life expectancy. A conversation between Kurt Kinkele of U-73 and his opposite number *Leutnant zur See* Armin Weighardt from U-593 gave some idea of the gravitational pull the service exerted on postings.

'N 2186 [Weighardt]:   *I volunteered for the U-boat arm.*
N 2185 [Kinkele]:   *I was actually talked into joining the U-boat arm by a friend of mine, although actually I wanted to go in destroyers again.*

N 2186:   Would you have been able to get in a destroyer again?
N 2185:   No. It was like this: we were asked what we wanted to go in. In my group – for instance, there were about fifteen of us – eight volunteered for the U-boat arm, but twelve were sent to the U-boat arm, and now all except one have gone to it in course of time.
N 2186:   Well, <u>now</u> it's obvious. Now <u>everyone</u> goes to the U-boat arm, all the administrative personnel etc.
N 2185:   Not all, but a large number have already been retrained for U-boats.'[13]

An unnamed able seaman from U-73 was heard in Algiers complaining that he had only volunteered for coastal service, not the Navy, but had been drafted into the U-boat arm.[14]

Leutnant zur See Kurt Heinemann described a sophisticated attack trainer at Neustadt, in which an officer under training sat in a full-size conning tower looking down through his periscope on model ships in a water tank. To pass the course each prospective captain had to make fifteen successful attacks in frighteningly realistic simulated conditions. That was the good news. Another prisoner told *Matrose* Nissen of U-73 that many captains were getting their first command without the benefit of a patrol as captain under instruction beforehand, because too many of them had been lost on seagoing familiarisation sorties.[15]

As with U-73 most of the survivors were cleared quickly. The junior officers (Kurt Heinemann, Armin Weighardt and *Leutnant (ing)* Martin Liebig) stayed longer, with Weighardt held at least until 25th February.

A formal printed report of the interrogation results was issued in February 1944. In June NID summarised and consolidated what they knew about current U-boat types, specifications, methods and tactics into a 62-page reference book (see Appendix C).[16] From then on, their attention turned to the novel technologies and tactics being thrown into the fray by an increasingly desperate Third Reich.

After interrogation Kelbling was sent to a Canadian prisoner-of-war camp along with 33 of his crew. He was eventually repatriated to Germany in September 1947. In the mid-1990s he met a survivor of HMS *Tynedale*, which he had torpedoed, who invited him to a reunion of St Nazaire veterans: the vessels had previously sparred off the coast of Brittany. He died in 2005.

Scharnhorst

Lieutenant Edward Thomas RNVR, Admiral Fraser's Staff Officer (Intelligence), was acutely conscious of the rule that interrogation should await the professionals but was overruled in his clash with the gunnery officer's anxiety to know if his salvoes had caused *Scharnhorst*'s speed reduction. His task was not helped by the fact that the only German-speaking officer on board was a young doctor. The SO(I) did his best on the way back, combining a coherent account of the battle from the fleet's perspective with the little he could extract from the prisoners.[17] The weekly report to the Director of Naval Intelligence on 3rd January observed ruefully:

> '*S.O.I. to C. in C. Home Fleet regrets to report that the morale of the SCHARNHORST prisoners appears to be extremely good.*'[18]

A week later,

> '*Preliminary report that morale was good has been fully confirmed and Captain's popularity seems to have been largely responsible for this. Very few are inclined to blame anyone for the loss of the ship. General impression amongst P/W that they would destroy convoy or be sunk themselves. Several did not expect to return.*'

The CSDIC interrogators observed plaintively that,

> *'The task of obtaining reliable technical information and an accurate account of the last action was hindered by evidence of inexpert preliminary interrogation, during which the prisoners apparently received sufficient information on the action from the British point of view to colour their own version and make the extraction of a parallel account most difficult.*
>
> *The fact that all but four of the survivors were below decks or under cover during practically the whole of the action has proved a major drawback. Most of the remainder were unable to distinguish between the explosion of torpedoes, the impact of the heavy shells and the firing of their own heavy armament. To many of them, the order to prepare to abandon ship came as a surprise, as they had no idea that "SCHARNHORST" had been damaged to that extent.'*[19]

The *Duke of York* report also commented on the prisoners' high morale and inability to distinguish between the different kinds of explosion going on around them.[†] It drew out the date and time of *Scharnhorst's* sailing, some details of the admiral and captain – both new on board – and the ship's complement and equipment. Tellingly it then focussed on matters of immediate concern to an operational officer: the hits obtained and their effect. The final point brought home both the crew's faith in their ship and the horror of her final moments:

> *'Abandon ship drill was apparently rudimentary and none of the survivors seems to have had an abandon ship station. Lifebelts were apparently not worn and were only put on if they could be found at the last moment.'*[20]

Once at CSDIC the survivors *'presented a front of tough, courteous security consciousness which, together with the limited extent of their knowledge, has presented interrogating officers with one of the most difficult problems since the war started.'*

[†] The report is reproduced in full at Appendix B – *Scharnhorst* Survivors' Interrogation aboard *Duke of York*.

At CSDIC UK

The interrogators felt hamstrung by lack of Admiralty guidance about the information required.[21] This was understandable; the convoy campaign had been an unremitting struggle since the first day of the war, Naval Intelligence was oriented toward it and several CSDIC officers had personal experience of the U-boat battle. Thanks to German protectiveness toward their major surface units there was not the same depth of experience to draw on, just anxiety about what the ships *might* do.

Nonetheless, after a fortnight they were beginning to find gaps in the prisoners' defences:

'Ps/W mostly young ardent Nazis with high morale, but subject to the temptations of youth to brag and boast and air their knowledge. This fact has made it possible to exhaust a good deal of the knowledge which they possess. There were no officers captured, and none to give a security pep talk after capture.'[22]

A number of captives disappear from the SR records within a day or two, suggesting that the most intransigent and those who knew least were quickly removed to leave their shipmates exposed to benign influence.

As their tongues loosened the emerging picture of the carnage aboard drew a sympathetic reaction from their opposite numbers. Their reports describe gun crews choking on cordite fumes after a hit disabled their turret's ventilation; shipmates putting out a magazine fire then floundering in ice-cold water up to their waists to rescue the sound ammunition; mangled bodies swilling around in a mix of blood and sea water as stretcher parties picked their way through the damage; and the bodies of the port side gun crews gradually being washed overboard. Looking back in safety provoked a shudder even in hardened seamen.

'N 2141:   *I don't want to go to sea again.*

N 2142:   It's too dangerous, especially an action-station like mine, down in the hold. Can you imagine what it was like? I was in the computing-room for the Flak and the heavy Flak, right down in the hold; if you took up the floor-plates you would see nothing but bilge-water underneath – above me were the magazines of C turret, and a bit further over to port, a bit higher up was the propeller-shaft tunnel.'[23]

At the end, the sparse to non-existent emergency drills led to many needless deaths as crewmen misused lifebelts or abandoned ship on the listing side.[24]

CSDIC issued a preliminary report on 16th January and continued with the patient erosion of the seamen's defences. On 15th February Paul Schaffrath, a stoker, was heard to remark:

'N 2175:   Our ratings would be delighted if they could live as we are doing here. We get much too much bread. We shall send back half the bread again this evening.'[25]

By late February a 96-page draft report was ready for circulation. The survivors would have been horrified. The interrogators had excavated surprising detail about *Scharnhorst*'s construction (including an almost complete map of her compartments), capability and operations; and gone on to investigate their knowledge of her bases and other *Kriegsmarine* ships. The main gap was her electronic fit, understandably since there were no radiomen or officers rescued. Comparing the report with the surviving SR transcripts it is clear that they supplied the lion's share of this intelligence unconsciously, in 'private' conversation.

Thinking of themselves as the cream of the German Navy the crew's resentment of *Tirpitz*, in particular, for queening it over the rest while hardly ever dropping her moorings and being '*run like a detention barracks*' was fruitful ground.

'In the matter of counting "Points" for the award of the Iron Cross Second Class, "TIRPITZ" was considered especially favoured, unjustly so, in view of the fact that in the Spitsbergen undertaking "SCHARNHORST" had been detailed to enter the harbour, "as if she was a minesweeper", while the "TIRPITZ" stayed outside. After the Spitsbergen raid, more than 400 of "TIRPITZ"' crew qualified for the Iron Cross, while "SCHARNHORST", which had done all the hard work and had been in service considerably longer, only received 160 Iron Crosses. "TIRPITZ" was strongly suspected of cheating in the necessary calculations.'[26]

A survivor who had been aboard *Tirpitz* at the time of the midget submarine attack gave a first-hand account of its effect. Two mines exploded and, despite failing to attach to the hull, did extensive but not fatal damage. Greatly strengthened anti-submarine defences since the attack meant that trick could not be repeated so the only feasible approach was now by air. Prisoners gave details of fixed smoke generators being installed in defended fjords at approximately 30-yard intervals and emitting a blend of green, blue, white and black smoke intended to look from the air like an open landscape.[27]

As the survivors gave up their relevant knowledge they were progressively 'dumped' to standard accommodation. At least seven were shipped to Canada in early February.

Most of the rest had gone by mid-February. *Bootsmannmaat* Heinrich Löffenholz was recorded talking to Paul Schaffrath on 26th which was also the day the latter started work as a stool pigeon. *Zimmermannobergefreiter* (Shipwright) Martin Wallek hung on at least until 11th March. Twenty-seven of them eventually found their way to camps in the USA, eight to Canada, and one (Strater) was repatriated *via* the Red Cross.

Mechanikergefreiter (Able Seaman Armourer) Horst Zaubitzer later spoke of his time as a prisoner-of-war in Canada as one of the happiest periods of his life. His post-war career culminated in twenty years' service as fire-chief in Leverkusen, North Rhine-Westphalia. He retired in 1984 and died in 2016.

One of those in Canada was on familiar territory. Johann ('Johnny') Merkle was the only fluent English speaker among them, and their spokesman aboard *Duke of York*, because his parents had moved from Yugoslavia to Windsor, Ontario when he was a young child. In 1940 his father lost his job because of his German ethnicity so the family moved back to Yugoslavia, whence young Merkle found his way to the *Kriegsmarine*.

Conspicuously cocky on the trip to Britain, his confidence wavered in the cells: the microphones logged this conversation between Merkle (N2134) and Ernst Reimann (N2133) on 4th January:

'*N 2134:   How stupid, I said I was born at STUTTGART, and that's all untrue. I was born in JUGOSLAVIA, but we are German. My parents moved to JUGOSLAVIA. Unfortunately the others know that I was in AMERICA for a long time. I have two uncles in AMERICA, but I can't say that; they are Americans. If the IOs ask me details, I will explain it all. Then I don't care. If the IOs find out all about me and that I have given false information, I shall be done for; then they won't believe me any more.*'

'*N 2133:   Where did you learn to speak German?*'

'*N 2134:   At home, from my parents.*'

'*N 2133:   In AMERICA?*'

'*N 2134:   Yes. We were not allowed to speak English at home – only German. My father lost his job in CANADA; he was dismissed from the factory. They said; "You are a German."*'[28]

He lived down the fib and a later, rather pointless escape from a camp in northern Ontario in 1946. He was repatriated to Germany, remarried, and crossed the Atlantic once more in 1953 to immigrate to the US, where he died in 2000.

The ship's *esprit de corps* outlived her: the *Kameradschaft* (Crew Association) continued meeting long after the war. In the words of an exchange between Heinrich Löffenholz (N2135) and Paul Schaffrath on 30th January,

'N 2135: *They have already forgotten the SCHARNHORST now in GERMANY.*

N 2175: *But the two thousand and forty-eight families will never forget.*'[29]

T-25

The *Elbing* class torpedo boat was not a happy ship. The ratings largely comprised men who were inexperienced and/or unsuitable for the U-boat arm or the more active life in E-boats. Acutely conscious of their low-status escort and mining duties they would have been a challenge for a better leader than *Korvettenkapitän* Wirich von Gartzen. Although a veteran of the merchant service and a first-rate seaman he publicly denigrated his junior officers and stirred resentment by bringing women aboard overnight, calling for champagne and playing music into the small hours. He was one of thirty-three survivors of the wreck picked up by U-505 on Christmas Day. After the war he published a book on torpedo boat operations.[‡] He died in 1993.

Adding injury to insult, the ship normally lay out in the roads for fear of air attack and ratings were almost never allowed a run ashore, which officers took freely. Other complaints involved cheating over rations, leave and decorations.

Unsurprisingly relations between the wardroom and the messes were not as they should have been.

'N 1552: *How many of your officers were saved?*

[‡] Von Gartzen, *Die Flottille: Aussergewöhnlicher Seekrieg deutscher Mittelmeer-Torpedoboote*, Koehlers Verlagsgesellschaft, 1982.

> *N 2092 [*Funkmaat* Hans Petersen]: Two. They sat in the lifeboat without moving or saying a word; perhaps they were afraid that we would throw them overboard. They started baling without even being asked to.'[30]*

The crew mingled disdain for the captain's selfishness and abuse of status with grudging respect for his seamanship and refusal to leave the vessel at the end. *Matrosenobergefreiter* Alois Altendorfer summed up the dichotomy:

> *'N 2107: Our captain was an awful lecherous fellow. The way he treated the officers: "You blockheads, you idiots." The captain is certainly up to the mark. We were in an engagement in the CHANNEL – there were five boats. One of our boats was on fire and the other four cleared off and we were in the centre. There were nine boats against us – they encircled us. They kept us covered and the captain kept manoeuvring around, torpedoes to the left and right, always in twin fan salvoes. We kept on firing until we ran out of ammunition, after which we made off.'[31]*

The DNI report of 10th January observed:

> *'The junior ratings showed a notable lack of security consciousness, unfortunately not always backed up by useful knowledge. P.O. survivors are proving less forthcoming. Morale on board does not seem to have been high and there is a suggestion, which has yet to be investigated, that two of the after 105 mm. (4.1") gun positions were abandoned by their crews after the first hit by the cruisers.'[32]*

Of the surviving officers First Lieutenant *Oberleutnant zur See* Cordt von Kalckreuth was a convinced Nazi whereas his colleague, gunnery officer Günter Schramm was described as 'pleasant and forthcoming.' He was cited in the opinion survey discussed earlier:

> *'Case 357 Oberleutnant zur See in a destroyer. Regular officer. Father an ex U-boat officer of the last war, now has a wholesale paper business. Father, an observing Protestant, objects to National Socialism on ethical grounds, complaining that youth is being*

corrupted by SS principles. "When our house in Hamburg was burnt down my parents went completely mad, especially my father. He kept on shouting: 'Heil, my Führer, heil, my Führer, I have you to thank for this'." P/W was a former Pfadfinder who joined the Hitler Youth but later resigned. He took a simple view of his military duties, and his political outlook was based on a mild and rather idealistic nationalism. Since capture he has come under the influence of an anti-Nazi P/W, a middle-aged schoolmaster, and is now convinced of the iniquitous tyranny of the lesser Party chiefs, although he still has respect – tinged with recently implanted doubt – for Hitler. He is glad he did not have these doubts before capture, or "he might have gone mad".[33]

The combination of his background, a deeply dispiriting wartime role, and the opportunity to look at things from a different angle had its effect. By 24th January:

'On technical questions, e.g. gunnery, those with knowledge were fairly willing to air it, and the enthusiastic gunnery officer found common ground for discussion with British gunnery experts.'

Later Schramm was almost certainly the officer claimed in CSDIC's weekly report as their first commissioned naval stool pigeon. There is no evidence of him actually working in that role, but he certainly shared his expertise in German naval gunnery capabilities and techniques.

The two midshipmen, *Oberfähnrich zur See* Heinz Hallwig and *Fähnrich zur See* Wilhelm Krüger were described as 'nonentities' but the petty officers were 'of a good type.'

One of them, *Oberbootsmannsmaat* (Acting Petty Officer) Franz Ligensa must have felt particularly hard done-by. He started the war with the pocket battleship *Admiral Graf Spee*, trapped and scuttled at Montevideo in December 1939. Along with many of his colleagues he escaped from internment and made his way back to Germany, being caught by the British and escaping again on the way. Expecting congratulations and a financial reward he instead met suspicion of being a planted spy. He survived that and returned to duty only to find himself shipwrecked, wounded and in a British hospital. Cautiously he gave his foster-parents' name instead of his own, but had his true identity given away by a shipmate in an overheard conversation.[34]

The *Elbing* class, like many small German surface combatants, packed a versatile and powerful equipment fit into their 1,295 tons' standard displacement. As well as their main armament of four 105mm guns in dual-role high and low angle mountings and two triple torpedo tubes they carried six anti-aircraft cannon and were equipped for submarine hunting, mine laying and minesweeping. With a sprint speed of 33 knots they were slightly slower than earlier classes, a fact much resented by the crew. To put this in context they were somewhat larger and faster than the British 'Hunt' class escort destroyers used in the North Sea and Mediterranean and had roughly equivalent armament apart from the extra mine-warfare capacity. Neither intended for use in the open ocean, which was problematic on a choppy afternoon in the Bay of Biscay. The *Elbings'* construction from thin, poor-grade steel was not reassuring in a daylight encounter with cruisers. If chance and visibility worked in their favour they could however be deadly. The same flotilla had surprised and sunk the cruiser HMS *Charybdis* in the Channel on the night of 22nd/23rd October 1943.

Schramm gave an interesting insight to the torpedo-boat flotilla's defensive mindset in one conversation. He described being taken to task for concentrating on his recruits' operational and combat training rather than their political education, and was told:

'…the Americans are not interested in EUROPE, they have got to stand their ground in EAST ASIA, which is at the same time their

> largest sphere of interest. At the present moment they have no interests in EUROPE and they won't want to risk anything there for that reason. The English, that is to say, the Home Fleet, are tied down for the present by our two capital ships in NORWAY, and the remainder is occupied mainly in EAST ASIA and in the MEDITERRANEAN, with the result that, if we had to reckon with any contact with the enemy at all there, it would only be the RAF or destroyer units, etc. That was his train of thought. He then came to speak about our having to make the best of the task entrusted to us here, which was first and foremost a defensive one. Our main job was to escort U-boats in and out of port and to fetch blockade-runners in; that wasn't the usual task of a destroyer in wartime, but the task of some smaller unit, at the most of torpedo-boats or minesweepers; but, on account of the strong enemy opposition, we had to put up with the fact that destroyers had to be used nowadays.'[35]

Under the circumstance this sounds like heroically convoluted self-deception.

Viewed as torpedo-boats rather than escorts the speed issue comes into focus. To attack with a short-range weapon like a torpedo needs some combination of stealth, speed and agility; the *Elbing* class didn't have the stealth of a U-boat or the speed and agility of an E-boat. Worse again, although their radar could direct the fire of their 105mm guns, it could only look forward and to the beam. They could not cover their withdrawal by firing through their own smoke screen. This combination of shortcomings condemned their crews to – as they saw it – a charisma-free life of escort and mining duties compared to the glamorous world of the U-boat and E-boat stars.

This came out very strongly in a consolidated report on German naval gunnery assembled from cell conversation transcripts, put together by CSDIC staff with the help of RN gunnery experts who provided commentary when needed. The contributors were mostly T-25 crew plus a *Scharnhorst* survivor, a naval shore battery gunner and a couple of enthusiastic but naive prisoners who filled the role of interested laymen. This was published at about the same time as the formal printed report on T-25 in February 1944.[36]

Discussion of anti-submarine tactics did nothing to enhance T-25's reputation:

'If a submarine contact was obtained while out alone, "T 25's" tactics were quite openly stated by one officer to consist of "putting on full speed and getting away as fast as possible, dropping depth-charges as they went."

Should a contact be obtained while the Flotilla was out, the procedure would be to circle the contact at a decreasing range, firing depth-charges from the throwers, which had a maximum range of 70 yards, and dropping them over the side aft. This would never be attempted with less than three T-Boats. The German Asdic on board had a maximum range of 3,000 yards.

Asked whether any danger existed of a T-Boat being inadvertently torpedoed out in the Bay of Biscay by a U-Boat, one of the officer survivors stated that this was possible, as the U-Boats would not expect to find their own destroyers out so far.

The First Lieutenant of "U 593" [Kurt Heinemann] *stated that his idea of a U-Boat officer's heaven would be to command a German U-Boat under the British flag and have German A/S methods to deal with.'*[37]

His view is understandable. While being inside a shrinking ring of explosions (a First World War tactic) must have been alarming enough, the noise and churn of the depth charge detonations made the attacking ships' sonar all but useless and created its own opportunities. In contrast, the cold-blooded efficiency of the British 'creeping attack,' where one ship held sonar contact while directing another onto the target, gave the victim very little warning or chance of escape.[§]

Most survivors were eased out by mid- to late-January 1944. At least forty found themselves at Number Seven (Winter Quarters) Camp, Ascot, from which they were despatched to Canada at the beginning of February. The unrepentant von Kalckreuth was sent to Number Fifteen Camp at Shap Wells, Cumbria, then out to Canada with the same convoy as his shipmates. *Matrosengefreiter* Heinz Gessler and *Oberbootsmanns-maat* Franz Ligensa were held at least until 8th February, and *Oberleutnant zur See* Günter Schramm until 25th February.

In an intriguing footnote the DNI's weekly overview for 24th January included the following paragraph:

'*SURVIVORS FROM EIRE SHIP KERLOGUE*

These men have been interrogated by an Army officer. There were 5 officers, and all appear to have been very worried for fear of being charged with cowardice on return to Germany. This was probably the reason why they did not attempt to seize the ship and take her to Germany. Their morale is generally low. They will shortly be allowed out on parole.'[38]

This must refer to officers from one of the other ships sunk in the Biscay engagement as the six T-25 survivors rescued by MV *Kerlogue* were all ratings. If the interviewers had been from the Irish Army the report would presumably have said, so it does suggest that the Irish, normally scrupulous observers of neutrality, allowed British authorities to interview some of the interned seamen.

Captain Donohue of *Kerlogue* considered the number of survivors aboard, their poor condition and his dearth of supplies, and made directly for Cobh ignoring both his passengers' request to be taken to La Rochelle or Brest and

---

[§] The tactic, now called vectored attack or VECTAC, is still used.

British orders to put into Fishguard. His decision may have left the Irish government vulnerable to diplomatic pressure. This remains speculation for now.

Alsterufer

'M' Room transcripts are surprisingly thin on the ground for *Alsterufer's* crew. Just five personalities feature: *Oberfunkmeister* Friedrich Warscheid, *Oberfunkmaat* Hermann Hahn, *Matrosenobergefreiter* Heinz Vogt, 1st Officer Ernst Lemke and 2nd Officer Johannes Nissen (the first three from the naval and the last two from the merchant crew). The first transcript was on 8th January 1944 and the last on 26th, suggesting that they were questioned with some despatch and the warships had priority call on the resources available. The formal report was written in early February and published in March. Unlike the *Scharnhorst* report it contains much more information than the covert recordings, which implies that direct interrogation was a fruitful approach with this crew.

Captain Piatek was an old-school merchant master: capable, physically powerful, fearless but superstitious, a harsh disciplinarian caring nothing for politics or any authority but his own. His crew of 77, all but three of whom survived, were observed to be a cut above those from other blockade-runners in ability, intelligence and security-consciousness. They had put up a good fight but the sinking so close to home, twenty-four hours drifting in the cold, the thought of 6,000 bottles of beer reserved for a Christmas celebration and their personal contraband at the bottom of the bay took their toll. The Japanese emperor had presented the ship with enough coffee and sugar in recognition of their journey for each man to receive fifty pounds of each, and they were carrying enough extra coffee to make that up to one hundredweight (112 pounds). At 200-300 Reichsmarks per pound on the black market the coffee was worth at least 22,000 RM. The sugar was nearly six months' personal ration and at post-war Hamburg prices would have been worth about 4,000 RM. Compared with a seaman's war bonus of 55-60 marks per month (up to 540 for the whole trip) all this was riches indeed.

First Officer Lemke had lost a 24-piece dinner service, fifty pounds each of tea and cocoa, three hundred pounds of coffee and two boxes of soap.[39] His coffee alone would have fetched over 60,000 RM.

The captain and others in the know were incensed at the evaporation of the promised air support. Friedrich Warscheid, a naval CPO telegraphist, told stool pigeon Meyer about his conversation with the skipper:

'N 2173: *I told the captain, too: "All right, it's all over, they've caught us." Then he said: "But there's one thing I don't like, and that is the way the affair was handled by our Admiralty. For, on the one hand, it is of such vital importance to the war that they even take those small U-boats and jam them full with wolfram and latex, and use even the smallest ships, like ours, three thousand tons – of course ours was a fast ship, she did fifteen knots – but then on the other hand they leave us in the lurch like that."'*

Three weeks after his rescue he was still trying to work out what had gone wrong.

'N 2173: *At eight o'clock German tine, that's to say probably just as it was getting light in GERMANY, there came a WT signal saying that reconnaissance aircraft had taken off; simultaneously with the report of the take-off you are given the wavelength, so-and-so many kilocycles. So we worked out, if they took off at eight o'clock, assuming a distance of 300 or 210 km. to fly, we should have heard something on that wave-length by two or three o'clock in the afternoon. Of course I don't know if they transmit at all. It may be*

> that they maintain a wireless silence, and the aircraft only transmit if
> they have sighted something or want to report anything.
>
> N 1878: At what time was your ship sunk?
> N 2173: At two o'clock German time.
> N 1878: They should have just arrived then.
> N 2173: Yes, if they really hadn't arrived by then we should
> have been bound to see them immediately afterwards.'[40]

The later capture of one of the aircrew looking for them revealed that the crews had been given different frequencies, probably owing to the dysfunctional relationship between *Luftwaffe* and *Kriegsmarine*.

The interrogators were not at first encouraged:

> 'The 74 prisoners have not yet been interrogated in detail, but the
> initial impression is that the merchant seamen are in general
> unintelligent, boorish and apathetic; while the naval ratings, who
> comprise about half the total complement, are not talkative.'[41]

Things improved as they dried out and began to relax into their new surroundings.

> 'The crew had a low dispirited morale, but the discipline on board
> had been strict, so that they were very security conscious until the
> lessons given by their officers faded in their minds, and good food and
> gentle handling had their effect.'[42]

By the time the formal interrogation report was published in March 1944 the description had become almost complimentary.

> 'The remaining Merchant seamen and Naval ratings appeared to be
> of higher intelligence and ability than those interrogated from other
> blockade runners. Similarly their security-consciousness was more
> developed. This may be explained by the fact that "Alsterufer"
> belonged to the Naval Supply Ship Organisation and was above the
> common blockade runner status.'[43]

Alsterufer was built in 1939 as a fast fruit freighter but never took up that role before being adopted in 1940 by the *Trossschiff Verband* (Naval Supply Ship Organisation). The *Kriegsmarine*, unlike the Royal Navy, could not rely on a worldwide network of bases to support its ships so had to develop replenishment at sea techniques. Its support vessels stalked the oceans, keeping remote trysts with surface raiders (heavily armed merchant ships) and U-boats until, one by one, the bare minimum radio traffic needed to arrange their rendezvous gave them away.

In June 1940 she did a supply trip from Oslo to Hammerfest, landing troops and supplies at various points on the way to consolidate Germany's hold on newly conquered Norway. After refitting at Hamburg there was a four-month deployment to the South Atlantic in 1941 during which she supplied two raiders, the pocket battleship *Admiral von Scheer*, and a U-boat, returning with prisoners. Piatek then took over for the ill-fated blockade run.

The ship's eastern adventure included a three-month stay at Kobe during which her masts were fitted with electrical hoists allowing either or both to be telescopically lowered into the hull, changing her appearance. Only one was retracted at a time to preserve a lookout point while denying any other ship the clue to her course given by the sight of both masts. There is no record of false deckhouses being used to change her profile or frequent repainting – both ruses used by other German raiders and supply ships.

Alsterufer was preparing for the run home when the Italian government signed an armistice with the Allies and switched sides. Most Italian armed forces, including the unfortunate crews of three submarines and a raider in Singapore harbour, were caught by surprise. The Japanese quickly forestalled an incompetent attempt to scuttle the raider by opening the seacocks but the submariners thoroughly sabotaged the interior fittings of their vessels before being interned. In a lavish ceremony the Japanese presented the Germans with the hulks – and a serious challenge. As the blockade-runner left Singapore

Italian prisoners were being coerced into helping repair their boats, which were then due to take supplies back with crews scraped together locally.

N 2173 [*Oberfunkmeister* Friedrich Warscheid, *Alsterufer*]:
> *They all went to the submarines. But apart from that there was Willi ZELLER, for instance a GAF Leutnant who always wore mufti in TOKIO etc; he became a U-boat engineer officer. POHL, the engineer, also sailed with us to JAPAN; he came from the HEINKEL works and made new experiment, etc. there ...... got lots of presents from a Japanese admiral. As for the submarines themselves: nothing in them was intact! Dilapidated things: it was frightful! Oberleutnant BARTSCH clasped his head in his hands and said: "I haven't a single diagram! I've got only one receiver in three boats! Only one of the boats has a transmitter which is more or less in order, but I haven't the faintest idea where the current comes from or how it works. There aren't any tuning tables or anything. How on earth can we get it working?" All these boats were to be loaded with rubber, etc. and then proceed home. On top of that they were all men who had never sailed in a U-boat before! DOMNES released some, but only enough for one on each boat. SCHNEEWIND was one – that's the SCHNEEWIND pack. Kapitänleutnant SCHNEEWIND has one boat.*

Experienced U-boat men would have found the heavily laden craft tricky to handle. The chances of a scratch crew of non-submariners in a foreign boat with makeshift repairs on a long voyage through hostile waters did not bear thinking about.[44]

Once CSDIC had finished with them the *Alsterufer* officers appear to have been sent to Camp 15 at Shap Wells in the Lake District, the other ranks to Number Seven (Winter Quarters) Camp, Ascot. From there thirty-one of them including the captain were put on the west-bound convoy to Canada in early February.

At CSDIC UK

1. TNA ADM 223/141; *Summary of statements by German prisoners of war (April-June 1943)*. The record actually runs to the end of 1943. TNA ADM 223/144; *Summary of statements by German prisoners of war (January-March 1944)*, summary for week ending 1st January 1944. TNA WO 208/4148; *Interrogation Reports on German Prisoners of War, SRN 2451-2699 (November 1943-January 1944)*. The five U-73 crewmen flown back interestingly included none of the four surviving officers.

2. Actual and estimated arrival times are based on The National Archives records ADM 199/2190 (convoy records) and ADM 223/354; *DNI Notes Volume 1, 1944 Jan-Mar*.

3. TNA WO 208/4200; *Special extracts from interrogation reports on German and Italian prisoners of war*. Extracts from SR Drafts No's WG12, WG15 and WG24. Personal correspondence with Lance Shippey, son of Marine Frank Shippey. TNA ADM 223/354 *DNI Notes Vol 1 1944 Jan-Mar*; Notes for 3/1/44 and 10/1/44.

4. ibid. Extracts from SR Drafts No's 186, 188, 198.

5. TNA ADM 223/354; *DNI Notes Volume 1, 1944 Jan-Mar*. Briefing paper for 24th January 1944.

6. TNA WO 208/4148; *Interrogation Reports on German Prisoners of War 2451-2699*. SRN 2682 dated 9th January 1944.

7. TNA WO 208/4149; *Interrogation Reports on German Prisoners of War 2700-3050*. SRN 2476 dated 13th January 1944.

8. TNA WO 208/4148; *Interrogation Reports on German Prisoners of War, SRN 2451-2699 (November 1943-January 1944)*. SRN 2565 dated 31st December 1943.

9. ibid. SRN 2590 dated 31st December 1943.

10. TNA WO 208/3553; *Shipment of POWs to Canada* is the source for this and following references to prisoners being sent to Canada in February 1944. The prisoners travelled with convoy TA87 (departed Clyde 5th February, arrived Halifax 12th, aboard SS *Île de France*).

11. *U-73 speaks from the depths of the Mediterranean*; http://www.daileyint.com/seawar/aphjtwas.htm and personal correspondence with Franklyn E Dailey Jnr.

12. TNA ADM 223/141; *Summary of statements by German prisoners of war (April-June 1943)*.

13. TNA WO 208/4149; *Interrogation Reports on German Prisoners of War 2700-3050*. SRN 2914 dated 19th February 1944.

[14] TNA WO 208/5508; *Interrogation reports on German and Italian prisoners of war: AFHQ 1-107.*

[15] TNA ADM 186/809; *Interrogation of German naval survivors.* WO 208/4149; *Interrogation Reports on German Prisoners of War 2700-3050.* SRN 2896 dated 5th February 1944. WO 208/4148; *Interrogation Reports on German Prisoners of War, SRN 2451-2699 (November 1943-January 1944).* SRN 2594 dated 1st January 1944.

[16] TNA ADM 186/809; *Interrogation of German naval survivors.* BR 1907(97) P.14.

[17] Donald McLachlan; *Room 39 – Naval Intelligence in Action 1939-45* (Weidenfeld & Nicholson, 1968). P.165. Fritz-Otto Busch; *The Drama of the Scharnhorst* (Robert Hale, 1991). P.171

[18] TNA ADM 223/354; *DNI Notes Volume 1, 1944 Jan-Mar.*

[19] TNA ADM 199/913; *Sinking of SCHARNHORST.*

[20] ibid, PP 100-101.

[21] Imperial War Museum oral history collection, Catalogue No 18777; *Interview with Donald Burkewood Welbourn.* Reel 4.

[22] TNA ADM 223/354; *DNI Notes Volume 1, 1944 Jan-Mar.* Briefing paper for 24th January 1944. TNA ADM 223/144; *Summary of statements by German prisoners of war 1944 Jan-Mar.* Summary No 57 for the week ending 8th January 1944.

[23] TNA WO 208/4148; *Interrogation Reports on German Prisoners of War, SRN 2451-2699 (November 1943-January 1944).* SRN 2627 dated 5th January 1944.

[24] TNA ADM 199/913; *Sinking of SCHARNHORST.*

[25] TNA WO 208/4200; *Special extracts from interrogation reports on German and Italian prisoners of war 1942 Dec-1945 Mar.* Extract from SR Draft No WG450.

[26] TNA ADM 199/913; *Sinking of SCHARNHORST.* CB04051(98) P.67.

[27] TNA ADM 223/144; *Summary of statements by German prisoners of war 1944 Jan-Mar.* Report for week ending 12th February 1944, P.5. WO 208/4149; *Interrogation Reports on German Prisoners of War 2700-3050.* SRN 2894 dated 5th February 1944.

[28] TNA WO 208/4200; *Special extracts from interrogation reports on German and Italian prisoners of war 1942 Dec-1945 Mar.* Extract from SR Drafts Nos WG12, WG15 & WG24 dated 4th January 1944. I am indebted to Lance Shippey's research for the details of Merkle's pre- and post-war life.

29. TNA WO 208/4149; *Interrogation Reports on German Prisoners of War 2700-3050*. SRN 2879 dated 30th January 1944.
30. TNA WO 208/4148; *Interrogation Reports on German Prisoners of War, SRN 2451-2699 (November 1943-January 1944)*. SRN 2649 dated 7th January 1944.
31. ibid. SRN 2603 dated 3rd January 1944.
32. TNA ADM 223/354; *DNI Notes Volume 1, 1944 Jan-Mar*. Briefing paper for 10th January 1944.
33. TNA WO 208/5522; *Interrogation reports on German prisoners of war: GRS 1-11*. GRS 10 P.9.
34. TNA WO 208/4200; *Special extracts from interrogation reports on German and Italian prisoners of war December 1942 – March 1945*. Special Extract from S.R. Draft No. W.G. 75 dated 5th January 1944. TNA WO 208/4149; *Interrogation Reports on German Prisoners of War 2700-3050*. SRN 2482 dated 24th January 1944.
35. TNA WO 208/4163; *Interrogation Reports on German Prisoners of War 1731-1949*. SRN 1920 dated 1st February 1944.
36. TNA WO 208/5551; *Consolidated report on German Naval gunnery; SR 1, 1944 Feb 05*. ADM 186/809; *Interrogation of German naval survivors, 1944*.
37. TNA ADM 186/809; *Interrogation of German naval survivors*. CB 04051(96): German Destroyer "T 25" Interrogation of Survivors" February, 1944.
38. TNA ADM 223-353; *DNI Notes*. 24.1.44.
39. TNA WO 208/4149; *Interrogation Reports on German Prisoners of War 2700-3050*. SRN 2852 dated 25th January 1944.
40. ibid. SRN 2796 dated 20th and 2815 dated 22nd January 1944.
41. TNA ADM 223/877; *NID UC Reports: Nos 315-500 (incomplete) 1943 Apr 01 - 1944 Jun 28*. NID UC Report No 415 dated 8th January 1944.
42. TNA ADM 223/354; *DNI Notes Volume 1, 1944 Jan-Mar*. Briefing paper for 24th January 1944.
43. TNA ADM 186/809; *Interrogation of German naval survivors*. CB 04051 (97) German Blockade Runner "Alsterufer" Interrogation of Survivors March, 1944.
44. TNA WO 208/4149; *Interrogation Reports on German Prisoners of War 2700-3050*. SRN 2793 dated 20th January 1944. It is unlikely that any of the ex-Italian boats ever left port. *Kapitänleutnant* Fritz

Schneewind died in 1945 trying to bring the Type IXC U-183 home.

"That Which Changes Us"

Gregory Bateson's 1972 definition of information is still illuminating. To paraphrase, if data does not affect my behaviour then, for me, it has no information content.

It would be naive to suggest that interrogations from five coincidental sinkings, on their own, affected the course or outcome of the war. Intelligence is the art of piecing together disparate fragments of data to make a coherent story, then testing that story for truth. Only then does it become information.

It is still worth looking at these fragments to see where in hindsight they fit into the developing picture and how that picture affected Allied behaviour. Captured equipment and documents, signals intelligence, spies and reconnaissance all help to build a picture of the enemy's capabilities and intentions but only the operator of the equipment can tell you how well or badly it works in practice. He can provide valuable insight into tactics, morale and rumour, and tell reconnaissance teams where to look.

How to Sink a Battleship?

Even as the war tilted in the Allies' favour during 1943 Germany's surviving capital ships remained a potent threat to the sea lanes, tying up much of the Royal Navy's strength just in case they should sortie. *Blücher*, *Königsberg*, *Karlsruhe*, *Admiral Graf Spee*, *Bismarck* and now *Scharnhorst* were at the bottom of the sea, but the last two had cost a lot of effort to sink – and *Scharnhorst*'s sister ship *Gneisenau* was still afloat, although largely dismantled. So were four heavy, four light cruisers and the lurking grey elephant in the room – *Tirpitz,* still under repair after the midget submarine attack the previous September. The Royal Navy's assessment was that it would take three of their latest *King George V* class battleships to subdue her if she ever gave battle.

In 1942 Admiral Godfrey, Director of Naval Intelligence, invited ideas for dealing with *Tirpitz* from the whole of his domain. They came; from all levels, skills and areas. They ranged from almost-practical to beyond-bizarre, and generally involved either sinking her at her moorings or luring her out to sea where she could be ambushed. Most would have been near-suicidal for the poor souls tasked to carry them out, but a couple bore a startling likeness to the pitfall dug for *Scharnhorst* the following year. Each received a polite reply and serious – if not always lengthy – consideration.[1] The experience was positive enough for Godfrey to suggest setting up a permanent channel to hear and review suggestions from the floor.

As it happened the Battle of North Cape was the last capital ship fight of the European war, but no-one could have known that. The first page of the Top Secret weekly NID 1 (Germany and Northern Europe) briefing was devoted to the location and readiness of Germany's remaining heavy ships.

It was thus a matter of urgency to find out just how *Scharnhorst* had stood up to such a battering for so long.

She was classed by the *Kriegsmarine* as a *Schlachtschiff* or battleship and designed for fifteen-inch (380 mm) main armament. For political reasons she and her sister-ship *Gneisenau* were completed with eleven-inch (280 mm) guns instead. This led the Royal Navy to call them battle-cruisers rather than battleships. The term is however deceptive: to the British it meant a ship which sacrificed armour protection for speed and firepower. *Scharnhorst* and *Gneisenau*, on the other

"That Which Changes Us"

hand, were built to survive an encounter with a heavy unit long enough to use their high speed for escape. At North Cape it almost worked.

By this time, it was clear that the Germans had quite simply lied about the size of their surface warships. They consistently broke the displacement limits set in the Anglo-German Naval Treaty of June 1935 across all classes of vessel, in the case of *Bismarck* and *Tirpitz* by an extraordinary 10,000 tons (the equivalent of bolting on a 'treaty' heavy cruiser). Despite the occasional voice crying in the wilderness the Naval Constructors' Department had looked at the length and beam of the *Bismarck* class and concluded that they must be very shallow draft to stay within treaty limits – therefore designed for use in the Baltic, so no threat to us.

The Admiralty, having complied with the earlier Washington Naval Treaty (1922) and the London Naval Treaties of 1930 and 1936, now found its new fourteen-inch armed battleships relatively under-gunned.

Completion of *Tirpitz'* repairs at the end of March 1944 triggered a remorseless procession of air raids to stop her being made ready for sea: six attacks by Fleet Air Arm carrier aircraft and three by RAF heavy bombers repeatedly damaged the ship and eventually completed the job by sinking her in November.

So the answer to the question posed above remained 'with great difficulty.' Post-war comment tends glibly to write off capital ships as hopelessly vulnerable to air attack since the 1941 sinking of HMS *Prince of Wales* and *Repulse*. That was however a limiting case: they had nowhere to run, no support and faced land-based bombers who could keep flying sorties until the job was done. In less favourable circumstances the task still demanded a concentration of force to limit the target's room for manoeuvre, disable her fighting ability and do catastrophic damage below the waterline.

Naval Tactics

U-boats were signalled in port or under escort by their number, once on patrol by their captain's name. The Submarine Tracking Room therefore needed to know who was driving which boat in order to make sense of the intercepts they were getting from Bletchley Park. Checking this information and filling in the gaps was one of the interrogators' key interests. It was also important to know where they were and what new tricks they were getting up to.

In the Atlantic BdU and OIC played a constant, deadly chess-game with one trying to throw a U-boat patrol line across a convoy's expected path and the other diverting merchantmen around the trap or, if all else failed, trying to punch through with a concentration of escorts. By contrast there was no attempt to co-ordinate U-boat action in the Mediterranean: each commander was given a general patrol area and left largely to his own devices. This much reduced the need for communication, which unfortunately limited the scope for Bletchley Park's cryptologists to look into their minds. U-73 survivors did however furnish information about the new prefix groups and transmission schedules in use.

The Mediterranean's shallower, clearer water also affected tactics. Under air attack a U-boat would fight it out on the surface unless there was at least 60 to 80 metres depth under her keel, a policy reinforced by the perception that Allied airmen there were much less efficient than those in the Atlantic. It may simply be that the Middle East squadrons were at the back of the queue for centimetre-band radar, but recall that U-593 beat off and seriously damaged a searchlight-equipped Wellington before her own demise.

Surface attackers were a different matter. Given enough warning the only thing to do was to go as deep as possible and stay as quiet as possible – a 'silent running' speed of one knot or 50-60 rpm was given. If forced to the surface the sensible thing was to abandon ship and scuttle. Kelbling saved his whole crew that way whereas Deckert of U-73 opened fire in a futile act of defiance and lost nearly a third of his.

The relatively short distances in the Mediterranean seriously affected a submarine's daily routine. Skippers surfaced only long enough to charge their batteries, typically four hours a day, whereas the vast tracts of the Atlantic gave them much more leeway. The effect on conditions inside the boat cannot have been pleasant.[2]

Many boats came to grief attempting the perilous run through the Straits of Gibraltar. The standard tactic was to drift through submerged, hugging the African coast as closely as they dared. Despite pioneering German work on mapping the complex sub-surface currents (of great value to the Royal Navy after the war), even an experienced skipper could find himself somewhere completely unexpected. Some claimed to have made the passage on the surface at night in the radar shadow of a Spanish merchant ship. All knew that it was in effect a one-way trip, and the density of anti-submarine forces made them feel like 'lost souls.'

Depth charges were a matter of personal and professional interest to both sides. An experienced U-boat crewman reckoned that at 50 metres' depth they needed to explode within 20 metres of the boat to be lethal or very damaging; at 150 to 200 metres' depth this reduced to five metres. An officer from T-25 gave the lethal radius as eight metres without specifying depth. The most vulnerable part of the boat was the stern – both U-73 and U-593 were crippled by damage to the water inlets for their Diesel cooling system.

Prisoners who had served aboard UJ-boats (submarine-chasers) or minesweepers contributed a little extra knowledge about German active (*S-Gerät*) and passive (KDB) sonar, its frequency range, sensitivity and associated tactics.

Scary Submarines

The workhorse Type VII (500-ton, medium range) and Type IX (750-ton, long range) U-boats in their various versions served the *Kriegsmarine* well for much of the war. Soaring losses in the second half of 1943 told their own tale however: the technological pendulum as well as the intelligence advantage was swinging the Allies' way. Microwave radar, long range aircraft and escort carriers, in particular, had closed the Atlantic 'air gap' and made surfacing perilous at any time. In Italy, and soon in France, there was a new imperative to disrupt supplies on the short sea crossing to beachheads on Germany's doorstep.

The new arrivals added a couple of fragments to the steadily building body of evidence about innovations on the stocks. A UC report in November 1943 had summarised and clarified the garbled and conflicting reports to date, suggesting up to four classes of small coastal submarine were in development with displacement from 140 to 250 tons and length from 65 to 110 feet. Rubber covering was mentioned, as was very high submerged speed.[3]

The second lieutenant of U-536 had recently mentioned a U-boat under development with underwater speed of up to twenty-five knots.[4] By early March 1944 hard information was beginning to coalesce about these craft. Known as W-boats (because their propulsion units were the brainchild of *Hellmuth Walter Werke* of Kiel) they were intended *'as a surprise weapon for use during an Allied invasion of the Continent ... probably to operate against coastal shipping ..., but possibly also against unprotected anchorages.*' A succession of UC reports gave a detailed analysis of their construction, capabilities, armament, building yards, programme and likely tactics – and had to counter incipient alarm by stressing that they were *not* yet operational.[5]

This was the Type XVIIA U-boat, of which only four examples were built, and none achieved anything. Only three of the follow-on Type XVIIB and none of the larger Type XVIII were completed. They were powered by HTP (high test peroxide, a solution of hydrogen peroxide in water) which gives the dual advantages of air independence and high energy density. It is also very tricky to handle. The Royal Navy's experimental post-war HTP-fuelled submarines HMS *Explorer* and *Excalibur* were nicknamed *Exploder* and *Excruciator* by their crews, and not just for the convenient wordplay. Accidents with HTP torpedoes led to the loss of HMS *Sidon* in 1955 and the Russian submarine *Kursk* in 2000. The other downside was noise, both from the fizzing power-plant and the hull cutting through the water. Kurt Böhme of U-450 put it graphically:

'Seven knots, three-quarters speed or maximum speed, and you can't hear yourself speak in the conning-tower because there's such a noise set up outside by conning-tower fairing and all those things, guns and 2 cm. – the flak that's standing up there and all that sort of thing, it all vibrates. The protective plates on the quadruple mounting move to and fro, the vibration is terrific. Just imagine what it would be like when doing twelve knots submerged! A cod is streamlined, and a U-boat must be likewise. Nothing should protrude, there must be no corners.'[6]

Nonetheless, as a product of desperate ingenuity to which the anti-submarine forces of the day would have had no counter, the threat was worrying enough.

Prisoners told of a rubber-covered '*schwarzes*' (black) U-boat impervious to radar and sonar. This was a blind alley as the rubber covering didn't work too well and peeled off at sea. An alternative trial, covering the boat's upper surfaces with netting stretched over outriggers to mask its profile made it unmanageable.*

A U-593 survivor stated that small, 150-ton U-boats were being sent south overland, which appeared to confirm earlier reports of their presence in the western Mediterranean.

A prisoner from U-73 mentioned Mediterranean tests of underwater diesel propulsion using the *schnorkel* – a pre-war Dutch invention which allowed fresh air to be piped into a submerged submarine and exhaust gases ejected through flexible trunks. It had been shelved as an unnecessary complication until the realities at sea made it vital to explore any way of improving a submarine's survivability. It wasn't perfect. The inlet dipping under water caused wild pressure fluctuations inside the boat and the exhaust gave out a tell-tale plume, but it allowed U-boats to operate much closer to the British coast than otherwise possible. The discovery prompted an urgent NID alert in the form of a UC report. A later report gave a refined technical description and the critical information that it was only suitable for fair weather use, in sea states 3-4 (slight to moderate) and speeds up to 2.3 knots. *Leutnant zur See* Schager of U-450 was unimpressed.

> *'We never used the 'Schnorkel'. What's the point? It's only of value when there's a full moon and we can proceed at periscope depth and keep a look out. But there's an Admiralty order to the effect that all boats are to be equipped with it as quickly as possible.'*[7]

At around this time the first hints surfaced of the most troubling development of all. A June UC report first gave it a name: Type XXI. This ocean-going boat was a conceptual step-change in several respects. Conventionally diesel-electric

---

* A few boats were successfully fitted with rubber coating ('*Alberich*') at the build stage. See my *Castaways in Question* for details.

powered it had clean lines, powerful motors and huge battery capacity to give high underwater speed and endurance: a true submarine rather than a submersible. It was built in sections at factories inland and could be assembled on the slipway in six weeks or so, reducing its vulnerability to air raids while building.[8] What the interrogators did not yet realise was that its advanced quieting, sonar and fire control would allow it to attack without showing even a periscope above the surface. 118 boats were commissioned but design and production issues plagued the class. Only two made operational patrols, both without effect. If those boats had been available and working a couple of years earlier the Battle of the Atlantic might have worked out differently.

The smaller 250-ton Type XXIII was based on the same principles. Six boats of the 61 commissioned did operate around the British Isles while another seven were lost to various causes. Although technically advanced they were so cramped they could carry only two torpedoes each so, although they had some success, their impact was limited.

The Type XXI design was the basis of the post-war Russian 'Whiskey' class (NATO designation) and its successors, and informed both US and British submarine development.

Less dramatically but still significant, there were reports of new Type VII variants, one lengthened for torpedo transport to resupply Far Eastern bases and one strengthened for increased diving depth.

The first clue to these developments came from prisoner interrogation. The information they gave was often garbled, partial and contradictory but countered the reconnaissance evidence of reduced conventional U-boat building, which might otherwise have led to false complacency.

Castaways of the *Kriegsmarine*

Torpedoes, and how to dodge them

At about 0500 hours on 20th September 1943 U-270 torpedoed HMS *Lagan*, a River class frigate escorting convoy ON 202 in the Atlantic. The badly damaged ship was towed to the Mersey where she was deemed beyond repair and eventually broken up for scrap. One officer and 28 ratings were killed or missing. In the torrid few days that followed the escorts HMCS *St Croix*, HMS *Polyanthus* and HMS *Itchen* were sunk along with six merchant vessels at a total cost of over 440 lives.[9]

The unfortunate *Lagan* was the first ship lost to the new T5 *Zaunkönig* (Wren) acoustic homing torpedo, itself derived from the T4 *Falke* (Falcon), of which only about 100 were made and 30 used. It was one of a number of developments facilitated by German adoption of electric propulsion which, though slow, reduced production cost and eliminated the weapon's tell-tale wake. It also opened a new tactical option – to go after the escorts first and leave the convoy defenceless.

Thanks to earlier interrogations this development, though unwelcome, was no surprise. NID already knew that T5 – known to the Allies as GNAT for German Naval Acoustic Torpedo – was to be deployed imminently. The message hadn't reached the Assistant Chief of the Naval Staff (U-boat Warfare and Trade), Sir John Edelsten, who penned the following memo to the DNI:

'On the 23rd October I received the Interrogation of U.607. (C.B.04051/74). The U-boat was sunk on 13th July and an officer prisoner gives accurate details of the GNAT. The LAGAN was sunk on 20th September by a GNAT.
I should like to be assured that such vital information has not taken from the 13th July to the 23rd October to reach our technical experts. Also please inform me if such information is transmitted to

Commanders-in-Chief without delay, including A.O.C. in C., Coastal Command.'

Rushbrooke pointed out by return that the Directorate of Torpedoes and Mining had been kept up to date with data as it accumulated since 1942, and that the document Edelsten was reacting to was actually a reprint of one issued the previous August. In the meantime, the Admiralty had issued general messages on 22nd, 24th and 27th September giving a reasonably accurate description of the torpedo, its capabilities and limitations.[10] Ships could defeat the weapon's homing by slowing down so that they were too quiet for it to acquire or by outrunning it – self-noise limited the torpedo's speed to 25 knots. There had also been enough warning to develop decoys codenamed FOXER (UK) and FXR (US), which were promptly deployed. The Royal Navy used a single noisemaker, the US Navy preferred two towed abeam. The development puzzled *Funkgefreiter* Hansen of U-744.

> 'N 2536: (re Foxers): *They have some sort of peculiar apparatus there. I don't know what it is for. We heard sounds like 'kch, kch' in the multiple hydrophone, and then up on board the destroyer I saw a sort of buoy. They were towing it at a distance of about 200 m and it was making the same sound, something like a crow's 'caw'. The artificer from the SPATZ ..... I was once with him. He thought that it was something to counteract the T5. I don't think so.'*[11]

That was not the end of the story. Significant uncertainties remained: what frequency did the torpedoes respond to, over what arc and how did they respond? What further developments were likely? What were the tactics for their use? Without complete understanding we could not know whether a torpedo that overran the decoy would circle to attack it again or run on to find the towing ship. Moreover, the decoys had to broadcast over the entire spectrum of naval and merchant ship propulsion noise, interfering with the escorts' own sonar performance.

The interrogators struck lucky with U-73 and U-593. A Torpedo Petty Officer from each boat (Willy Zwietasch and Günther Hünert) had recently attended a short course on the T5 at Gdynia, and was able to fill in some of the missing detail.

They gave the weapon's speed and range as 24½ knots and 5,000m – both slight underestimates but near enough – and the safety run-out before the homing mechanism was enabled as 300 to 400m. It was claimed to detect sounds within an arc ±45° of straight ahead in the 'supersonic' band (NID doubted this as it was also said to be impervious to Asdic transmission). It steered toward the loudest noise using full left or right helm, or straight ahead. There were separate settings to attack an approaching or receding target, along with one to disable homing when it was not required or not working, and a safety mode for maintenance. With the torpedo nose now occupied by the homing system's hydrophones a different way of triggering the warhead had to be found from the previous impact pistol. A combined inertia and magnetic fuze was set into the top of the weapon, which created the option of detonating under the target's keel – far deadlier than a direct hit against the ship's side.

Maintenance was finicky: T5s needed regular greasing like all torpedoes but with much greater care: the nose and a strip along the top had to be kept clean and polished. Scratches and dents were to be avoided at all costs and the nose and screws were extremely delicate.

In use the torpedo was fired from periscope depth as normal and had to approach within 300 to 400m of the target to detect it. In the meantime the firing submarine had to proceed for one minute at 'dead slow' (and Kelbling of U-593 kept to 'slow' for a further minute) to avoid the risk of the weapon being attracted back to the U-boat.[12]

Post-war analysis showed that of 640 T5 torpedoes fired operationally just 6% hit their targets. Over 2,500 were fired in development, an extraordinary technical achievement for the time, again presaging the direction of later research.[13] But for the timeliness and detail of the information provided by CSDIC the butcher's bill would certainly have been far higher. The weapon's psychological impact was nearly as significant as its tactical value. Several U-boat prisoners subsequently reported escorts turning away from them despite their blatantly showing a couple of feet of periscope.

Prisoners also mentioned trials carried out in the Baltic of blind firing acoustic torpedoes against sonar bearings (in fact related to the development of the Type XXI U-boat) and an improved homing weapon, they thought faster. In fact, the T11, as it became, embodied several improvements including reduced self-noise, variable enabling range, better counter-measure resistance and the ability to launch from greater depths. It arrived too late to make any difference.

U-boats also carried conventional thermal-powered straight-running torpedoes and another electrically driven design: T3, known as Curly. This was a pattern-running weapon designed to attack a convoy's merchantmen. After launch it turned onto a pre-set course to port or starboard (so the submarine did not have to point directly at its target) and could then be set to proceed in weaving series of linked semicircles or circle continuously to port – the circle in either case having a diameter of 75m. The idea was to maximise the chance of it hitting something when let loose among the stately, regular lines of a freighters. At a convoy's rate of advance the electric torpedo's relatively low speed was not a drawback whereas its wakelessness and cheapness were positive benefits.

On occasion the torpedo's rudder failed to centre after the initial course change, so that the weapon circled unnervingly over the submariners' heads. This happened to U-73 on her last patrol.

The Germans studied or developed over fifty torpedo types including wire-guided, hydrogen-peroxide fuelled, alternative homing technologies and some frankly weird physical configurations. They did not however feature in the conversations we are interested in.

Electronic Warfare

The invention of electronic warfare (EW) is usually credited to an unknown Russian radio operator at Port Arthur in 1904. He held down the key of his spark-gap transmitter, producing steady noise to disrupt the attacking Japanese fleet's shell-spotting communications.

Things had come a long way by 1943.

During 1941 the Allies had started to fit radar to aircraft in the form of Anti-Submarine Visualiser (ASV) Marks I and II (176 MHz), and to British and Canadian ships as the Type 286 (later Type 291) radar. Although limited in performance they were good enough for U-boat skippers to experience planes and destroyers appearing suddenly out of the black night while they were preparing a convoy attack, leaving or approaching port, or vulnerably charging their batteries. Submarine losses began to rise.

Inevitably it was not long before a crashed Wellington bomber with ASV Mk 2 on board gave the game away. The Germans hastily adapted an existing French receiver, dubbed Metox after the firm that made it, to detect these radars. Because it only had to detect the signal on arrival, not after it had been degraded by reflection, two-way path loss, and 'sea clutter' it could in principle 'hear' an approaching radar long before the radar could detect the submarine. It betrayed its rushed development by its unreliability, fragile antenna, and inability to take a bearing or pick up short transmissions. It was easily confused by non-radar signals and, worst of all, emitted a strong and potentially detectable signal itself. Still, it was better than nothing and worked well enough to tilt the technological seesaw back a little, helped by further evolutionary improvements over the next few months. It and its successors were known to the Admiralty as GSR – German Search Receiver.

Early in 1943 new microwave radars operating in the 3,000 MHz range (ASV Mk III and Type 27x) began to find their way into service, the former in the face of intense competition between RAF Bomber and Coastal Commands for the precious sets. Surprise attacks began to rise again. *Kriegsmarine* confusion was helped by a captured RAF officer who, with great presence of mind, claimed in his interrogation that they could home on Metox emissions from a great distance. Improved search receivers – Wanze G1 and G2 followed by Borkum – solved the emissions problem but still didn't detect the new radars.

Finally, in September 1943, the German navy learned what it was up against. The news came after a long delay, presumably due to the dysfunctional relationship between the services, from analysis of equipment the *Luftwaffe* had found in a bomber shot down over Rotterdam in March. A new receiver (Naxos) was quickly developed to detect the higher frequencies. It had the drawback of needing a man on the bridge to rotate the fragile antenna had by hand, unscrew it and pass down through the conning tower hatch before the submarine could dive. Unsurprisingly this chore was often missed in the heat of the moment.

Allied crews had already learnt to observe partial or complete radar silence with their older, low-frequency sets. They now evolved a range of tricks to cope with the new development, such as leaving their radar in 'search' mode rather than 'track' and reducing power as they approached to avoid alerting the U-boat's radio operator to his peril. Some overreacted and reverted to visual search, no doubt giving many U-boats a stay of execution.

How had these technological developments filtered through to the crews staggering through the door in January 1944, and how were they using them? We can summarise their physical outfit in the following table:

	f (MHz)	U-73	U-593	T-25	*Alsterufer*
Metox	120–240				
Wanze G1	200–250				
Wanze G2	200–250	✓	✓		
Borkum	100–400	✓			
Samos	90–470			✓	✓
Naxos	2,500–3,750	✓	✓		

Table 1: GSR Fit
(f – Range of frequencies the equipment could detect)

None of the *Scharnhorst* survivors were in the right specialties to comment.

A stool pigeon who was himself a radio technician eagerly pumped *Funkmaat* Gerhard Rachel of U-73 for current thinking on the different equipment. The number of blanks and queries suggests the listeners had trouble keeping up with the jargon, so the final report must have relied heavily on the stool pigeon's feedback.

'N 1878:   *Did you have the 'Borkum-Gerät'?*

N 2152:   *Hm.*

N 1878:   *What wave-band does it work on?*

N 2152:   *From 30 cm. to 3 m. ...... You bring the detector into operation and there are two coils(?) on it and then you go on to low frequency amplification, i.e. 'Naxor'(?). Of course, the WT rays(?) are not as good as with the 'Wanze 2' ...... 'Wanze 1' is said to radiate too.*

N 1878:   *Yes, and so you have 'Wanze 2' ......*

N 2152:   *'Wanze 2' is said not to radiate. The 'Borkum' has been kept on as reserve apparatus. Originally the 'Borkum' was only developed because 'Wanze 1' radiates.*

N 1878:   *Is the 'Wanze 2' 100% perfect then?*

N 2152:   *It's very good indeed.'*[14]

U-boat crews were at the front of the queue for the new equipment. U-406 sunk on 18th February 1944 and U-473 sunk on 6th May carried a full range of experimental GSR equipment, their survivors were thus able to give CSDIC a good view of current German thinking. *Alsterufer* had been away for nine months and the torpedo-boat flotilla's usual inshore escort duties did not qualify them for an urgent upgrade.

After a period of near-paranoid fear that Allied ships and aircraft could home onto GSR, U-boat crews were beginning to trust the newer equipment. Their difficulty was that the Mediterranean was such a 'noisy' electronic environment that it was tricky to distinguish an imminent threat from the background clutter.

T-25 had four masthead aerials connected to her GSR set giving a rough indication of bearing. At night, the strength of any signals received was assessed on a scale of one to five: at five the ship put up barrage fire in the quarter with the strongest reading. She also carried an Identification Friend or Foe (IFF) set which was switched on only when the GSR picked up a contact.

Alsterufer, with the same equipment, had been ordered on no account to use it during the journey home because of fears that its emissions could be detected. This barely mattered because tropical heat had affected the set making it almost useless. Canvas squares were used to camouflage the aerials.

The apparently 'silent' approach of aircraft fitted with centimetre-band radar had created suspicion that the Allies were using some form of infra-red detection. The anti-infra-red paint used in response actually made vessels *more* conspicuous to radar.

This fear was made more credible because some U-boats were issued with the *Seehund* (Seal) infra-red telescope, which crews had mixed feelings about. It was fragile and added to the bridge clutter having to be removed before crash-dive.[15]

U-boats also carried Radar Decoy Balloon (RDB or *Aphrodite*) floats, each of which flew a balloon trailing several foil reflectors and could be thrown overboard to distract radar-equipped aircraft or ships when the submarine dived. This must have looked like a great idea from a desk on shore. Like most of their colleagues, Deckert deployed them seldom and Kelbling never. Some crews used the balloons as footballs.[16] A captain whose stock-in-trade is stealth and unpredictability tends to have trouble putting up a big, shiny sign saying, 'I was here.'

Another innovation of doubtful value was the Radar Decoy Spar-Buoy (RDS), a floating timber construction about 27 feet long by 12 feet high with reflecting metal strips attached. They were supposed to be laid in large numbers across the Biscay killing ground to confuse Allied aircraft. There is no record of this being done, probably because a U-boat would have to stop on the surface while assembling them and they didn't look enough like a submarine to be worth the risk.

Finally an officer from U-593 mentioned having seen trials with wire netting stretched around submarine conning-towers to break up their radar signatures. Several configurations were tried with towers mounted on rafts. None worked: if the netting was stretched far enough away from the structure to help it made the boat unwieldy and threatened to tear away in the first heavy sea.[17]

Neither U-73 nor U-593 was fitted with radar but prisoners indicated that, in a revival of interest, modified aircraft sets operating in the 50 cm. waveband were being fitted to U-boats. One telegraphist from U-73 had attended a course on the equipment. Only the most brazen skippers had any interest in using it.

T-25 carried an eighty-centimetre radar set with the antenna on the foremast. With a range of 12 km. in good conditions against surface targets and low-flying aircraft it was useful for gun and torpedo aiming – with one critical flaw. The antenna could only be trained port and starboard 90° through forward; it could not look aft. In the words of her gunnery officer:

'Absurd. With a torpedo-boat especially it is a question of making off after firing your torpedoes, and of making a short attack with your guns, and of covering your retreat when turning off. A torpedo-boat never has to fight a head-on engagement.'[18]

Despite complaints new craft were still being built with the same flaw, yet another factor in the flotilla's dismal morale.

Although *Scharnhorst* had efficient radar she had just two (compared to *Duke of York's* thirteen for various functions). Losing her forward antenna left her more than half blind.

Defensive Dodges

A submerged U-boat was invulnerable to radar or (usually) visual detection but could be found by the analogous Asdic (active sonar) in which the hunting vessel fired a directional sound 'ping' and listened for its reflection from the submarine, or by passive sonar where the operator listened for the submarine's own noise. The Admiralty's pre-war expectation that Asdic would solve the U-boat problem proved well short of the truth but, in experienced hands, it was a deadly tool.

Such a threat demanded a countermeasure, which the British called Submarine Bubble Target (SBT). This was first deployed by the *Kriegsmarine* in 1942 and comprised a launcher to eject small chemical containers through the submarine's hull. They reacted on contact with water to produce clouds of bubbles, lasting about fifteen minutes, and giving a sonar echo about the same size as a U-boat. The tactic was to deploy several while making sharp turns in alternate directions between each one.

As with RDB this was a trick that worked better in theory than in practice. Previous CSDIC interrogations had yielded enough information about the technique to ensure that anti-submarine forces were prepared for it. Like RDB it had the drawback of confirming the presence and recent location of a submarine, and it needed time to deploy, time that a skipper with a destroyer on his case seldom had. Critically the bubble target gave no Doppler shift – it did not move – and hovered at 80 to 100 feet depth. U-73 and U-593 both carried SBT. One of Deckert's stokers complained that it had failed when he tried to use it and the U-593 interrogation report is clear that it was 'never used.'

There were also unconfirmed reports of a miniature electric torpedo intended to mimic a submarine's propeller noise, and an oil charge to create a slick on the surface and give the impression that the submarine had been sunk. Apart from the last – which would never have convinced a cynical, war-weary sub-hunter – it is striking how many of these presage modern techniques.

The large U-boats patrolling the remote reaches of the South Atlantic and Indian Oceans tried yet another innovation:

helicopter observation kites towed above and behind the boat on the surface, with the pilot reporting back to the boat by radio. In the event of a crash dive the kite and hapless pilot were 'of course' abandoned.[19]

Is There A Doctor Aboard?

Medical officers aboard ship were technically non-combatants and thus exempt from interrogation. By the same token their job was to look after the health of the crew on a deployment sometimes lasting months, but NOT to assist with warlike duties. Their core role could be challenging enough.

'N 2173 [Oberfunkmeister Friedrich Warscheid, Alsterufer]: On board we were weighed once a month. I was the only one not to lose weight. All the time we were down there (FAR EAST) they all lost weight.'[20]

Opinions varied in U-boats about the value of a medic aboard a submarine whose crew was the physical pick of the *Kriegsmarine*. There was little he could do about the health cost of tinned food, canned air and no daylight over a long patrol. Rheumatism, kidney disorders and bone softening were common ailments only partly mitigated by vitamin supplements. By early 1944 Dönitz' order to stay up and fight it out with aircraft unless there was ample time to dive had made casualties from air attack so common that a medic was universally carried.[21] There was a strong temptation for the officer concerned to earn his keep by mucking in with general duties.

Maschinengefreiter (Stoker 1st Class) Josef Better of U-845 didn't realise he was undermining his medical officer's claim to privileged status when he told a stool pigeon,

> 'N 2370: Our ship's surgeon had the job of ejecting the SBT ('Bolde' gear): that's why we called him 'Dr. Bolde' in fun.'[22]

Equally *Funkgefreiter* Hasbach of the E-boat S-147 cheerfully told a stool pigeon that the flotilla surgeon sailed every patrol, on a different boat, manning the starboard machine gun.

> 'N 1485: It is a bad look-out if he is taken prisoner.
> N 2453: He doesn't have to say that he ...... Our 'Obermaat' said; "I sailed as a member of the watch." If he had had any gumption he would have said immediately: "I mean as sick-bay attendant." Then he would have had a chance of being repatriated, if he had been put down here as being on the sick-bay staff.
> N 1485: It's a lousy job being on the sick-bay staff.
> N 2458: Not with us. Ours go on all the operations and everything, they can prove their worth. Bui it is rather a dead end: you can become a 'Sanitätsoberfeldwebel' and that is the end of it.'[23]

The distinction was a matter of life and death for *Oberstabsarzt* Walter Weispfennig, medical officer of U-852 when he took part in the machine-gunning of survivors from SS *Peleus* on 13th March 1944.

> 'N 1878: The IO said that someone from your boat had thrown hand grenades at the survivors.
> N 2531: Yes, I told the IO in CAIRO that HOFFMAN (PW) fired and threw a hand grenade and that the ship's surgeon fired.'[24]

In November 1945 he was convicted of war crimes and joined his skipper, *Kapitänleutnant* Heinz Eck and *Leutnant zur See* August Hoffmann in front of a firing squad.

Weispfennig doesn't seem to have been much appreciated for his medical contribution either, though it is not certain that the following refers either to him or to U-852.

> 'N 2531: …Once a seaman died on board. The ship's doctor was told (that he was dying) and he said: "I can't do anything", and

didn't go down to see him. He didn't behave at all well. He never bothered about the wounded at all.'[25]

Weapons of Mass Destruction

There had been rumours for some time of German preparations for gas warfare. Back in May 1943 *Fähnrich* (Midshipman) Karl Völker of U-175 described going on a gas course, anti-gas capes issued to troops and vast dumps of shells ready for use.[26]

Günter Schramm told a stool pigeon how ordnance officers he knew well would clam up when gas ammunition was mentioned, leading him to believe it was planned for deployment. A three-way conversation with a coastal artillery gunner mentioned empty shells from 10.5 cm upwards, bombs and sprays from tanks or aircraft – the last being impractical because of the immense number of planes needed to contaminate an area. His T-25 shipmate *Feldwebel* Diessel admitted the possibility of gas shells but said he had never seen any.[27]

A common theme was that Germany would never stoop to first use, not least because of the immense resource disparity between the two sides. *Matrosengefreiter* Wolfgang Blumenberg of U-386 put it in a nutshell.

'N 2189:   *I know for certain that preparations for gas warfare have been made, not defensive ones, but offensive. But I don't believe the Germans will do it as they haven't an air force left and the English would be able to retaliate a thousandfold, and they know it.'*[28]

Allied troops preparing for D-Day still had to have unpleasantly realistic anti-gas training.

Blumenberg was also susceptible to some of the wilder tales about new weapons. A mix of half-knowledge, distortion and wishful thinking produced a blizzard of snowballing rumours: a wall of noise from which analysts had to pick out the music of genuine intelligence.

'N 2189: (Re new gas-bombs): There is a liquid in then which is ejected on impact and the moment it touches human or animal flesh it produces an effect of boiling liquid and if it touches the ground it turns into a gas. The heat of the body doesn't turn it into gas, it's [sic] effect is similar to 'Lost'(?). When it touches the ground it turns into gas and sweeps along the ground and wherever it comes – grass turns black, everything is burnt up. And that ground can never again be cultivated. It is the same as if you were to burn some field, the ash is completely useless. If a human being is sprayed by it, the effect is the same as if you had held him in boiling water and pulled him out again. You could peel of [sic] his skin, just like that. That is the effect of that stuff. Wherever it touches, nothing more will grow. The amount they have in readiness is enough to make a whole section of the earth practically disappear. However, the man who told me this said that, on <u>express</u> orders of the FÜHRER, it was kept in readiness <u>only</u> in case the other side should start with it first.'[29]

This and stories of 'liquid air' bombs that could ravage vast areas were pure imagination but Schramm's conversation above contained a tantalising clue to the German nuclear project.

'N 2074: On the other hand, although I really don't know, there must be some fantastic plans in existence; I heard from an old school friend of mine who, after he had passed his 'Abitur', went in for chemical research and whom I met again quite recently on leave in HAMBURG. He told me some really interesting things about modern developments in splitting the atom – goodness knows, he gave me a very lengthy talk, of which, of course I understood very little. He was also very careful how he expressed himself, so he certainly didn't go to the root of the matter, but all the same it's a

question of the minutest bodies. Probably atomic weights of the order of those described in that novel by DOMINIK: 'Atomic Weight 500' ('Atomgewight 500'), which can be steered from great distances and after a quite definite time, i.e. after a time which can also be controlled – can cause destruction at the chosen spot; (it is likely) that experiments were being carried out all over the place, i.e. in his own district, and that he was taking part in those developments.'

The allied atom bomb project was itself so closely guarded a secret that the implications of this snippet may well have been missed.

A more urgent concern was the gradually coalescing information about the approaching V-weapon assault. Conflicting, imprecise and garbled reports of powerful new weapons had been received from a number of sources, including prisoners-of-war, since early 1943. The muddle was hardly surprising since it was easy to confuse multiple programmes including pilotless aircraft (V1), guided glider bombs, long-range rockets (V2), multi-barrel mortar (*Nebelwerfer*), and long-range guns (V3). Any or all of the reports could have been mistaken or deliberate misinformation. By March 1943 eavesdropped conversations between generals at Trent Park had cleared up any doubt that something sinister was going on. Accumulated evidence justified a heavy air raid on the Peenemünde research centre in August, which delayed the development programme and prompted the dispersal of work to other sites.

As speculation started to appear in the British press at the end of 1943 there was still significant debate about what exactly the threat was, and when it would materialise. 'M' Room ears were alert for any clues from every new batch of arrivals. They proved as contradictory as always, but *Bootsmannmaat* (Leading Seaman) Heinrich Löffenholz (N2135) of *Scharnhorst* seemed to know something.

'N 2135: A cadet told me about it. "Herr Bootsmaat," he said, "if I hadn't seen it for myself, I shouldn't tell you about it. We were sent from the school at MURWIK on demolition work on the BALTIC coast. One of those things came down there. Somehow or other it came down prematurely. Not a window-pane remained intact within a radius of a couple of km." Trees uprooted, he said. And one of the engineers, who was there at the time, said it was an apparatus some metres long and ...... diameter – they are like rockets. It made a 14m. deep crater.'

Although he had no idea of the distinction between V1 and V2 he came up with a surprisingly accurate timing for the assault, which began on 13th June 1944.

'?N 2135: It's to be ready this spring and if it isn't ready there will be a lot of trouble in GERMANY. The thought of reprisals is the only thing that keeps the people of GERMANY going. They all look forward to revenge.'[30]

He may also have had an uneasy premonition of the reaction the weapons would provoke. Their robotic, indiscriminate killing hardened British public opinion and led many to express hatred toward Germany for the first time. This reflected the hardening of civilian resistance in German cities worst affected by allied bombing, and often discussed by prisoners.

'N 2135: I believe that if the German people were consulted they would rather make peace with ENGLAND than wait for the reprisals.

N 2166 [Maschinenhauptgefreiter Rolf Zanger, Scharnhorst]: The Germans are not as peace-loving as all that, that they can forgive the English their terror air-raids!

N 2135: But at least the Germans are humane!'[31]

Others saw the approaching onslaught in terms of its effect on their personal fate. Löffenholz' crewmate Matrosenobergefreiter Willi Alsen believed enough tales of its awesome destructive power to want to be well out of the way.

"That Which Changes Us"

> 'N 2130: *I'd rather go to CANADA. If the reprisals start – they'll come over here and smash everything to bits. No damn joke. It would be better to be in CANADA. The war has ended for us. I should like to have been in it longer.'*[32]

Whereas *Funkobergefreiter* Josef Stäger of U-73 thought the confusion might create an opportunity for escape.

> 'N(Am)42: *It's easier to get back to GERMANY from ENGLAND than from AMERICA. We may also have a chance when reprisals against ENGLAND start.*
> N 1485: *The secret weapon?*
> N(Am)42: *Yes.*'[33]

The one-ton warheads carried by the V weapons were destructive enough but some of the impressions in prisoners' heads were so wildly exaggerated that we have to wonder if they had come across stories of the nuclear research being carried out.

> 'N 2254 [*Funkobergefreiter* Hans Ewald, U-264]: *(Re Dödel); It will come like a flash of lightning. I heard that they intend firing only four of those rockets on LONDON. That will destroy the whole town.'*[34]

If so, their sources were living in a fantasy world. The post-war internment of German nuclear researchers at Farm Hall in Essex revealed that they were a long way from achieving a practical bomb.[35] Nonetheless the imminent wonder-weapons seemed to offer the only prospect of salvation in a bleak military outlook and may help explain the rallying spirits noted earlier. Franz Ligensa of T-25 seemed to oscillate between hope and despair like a spinning coin.

> 'N 2178: *Well, the only thing to do is to be radical. When you see how they send us so senselessly to our death, you lose all respect towards the leaders.*

----oOo-----

N 2178: It's still a toss-up. The English haven't won the war yet. The Germans have already achieved miracles. Just you wait until we start using the rockets.'[36]

Leutnant zur See Kurt Heinemann of U-593 was keen to convince First Officer Lemke of *Alsterufer*, or perhaps himself, that *this* time the technology was going to deliver as promised.

'*N 2182:* The new weapon will certainly work. That'll shake them. If that were not so, then things would be quite different in the GAF [German Air Force]. After all, we haven't been sleeping for two years. The new weapon is going to win the war! I believe in it.'

★ ★ ★

'*N 2182:* DÖNITZ himself told us in the mess that the new weapon is definitely coming.

I heard about the new weapon from a GAF general in WIESBADEN. He said it wouldn't come in January but in April, and a General like him wouldn't be taken in. He wouldn't go around asking for trouble. I shouldn't like to be in LONDON when that happens.'[37]

Interrogators and stool pigeons kept their ears open for any clarity in the matter of guns, rockets or pilotless aircraft. Unfortunately, few prisoners had anything concrete to add to the constant eddy of rumour and exaggeration. While Hans Ewald's description could have applied either to V1 or V2 it at least seemed to eliminate guns for the time being.

'*N 2254:* They want to wipe out the whole of ENGLAND; not with aircraft, but with rockets, 'Dödel'. The things are said to weigh twenty tons.

N 1485: Have you ever seen one?

N 2254: No, you can't get near them. They fly under their own power; there's some sort of substance inside them, and they keep flying as long as that burns, it works somehow like that. They are not fired off, but are released electrically by a short-circuit.'[38]

A stool pigeon report the next day made it clear that Ewald was reporting hearsay.

> 'He had heard from a friend of his who was stationed near CHERBOURG that there are emplacements there for secret weapons. These weigh 20 tons and work on the 'Nebel System'. They are fired electrically. It is considered that four will be enough to flatten LONDON.'[39]

The other key question was where were they made? Peenemünde had been flattened once and was under continued observation; intensive reconnaissance sought out potential assembly and launch sites in France but that could not be the whole story. As a matter of urgent interest to all Germans it was a natural subject for a stool pigeon to broach with *Matrosengefreiter* Heinz Gessler (N2177) of T 25.

> 'N 2177: (Re reprisal weapon). I know that where we were at FRIEDRICHSHAFEN there is a factory where they build the whole damned thing. Let's get away from here as soon as possible, because they are going to take reprisals, we are sure of that. HITLER will not capitulate.
>
> N 1552: (Re Rocket producing factory at MARKDORF near FRIEDRICHSHAFEN). How many people do they employ?
>
> N 2177: I don't know. No one either enters or leaves there.
>
> N 1552: How long has the thing been there?
>
> N 2177: Six months to a year at the most.'[40]

Leutnant Schürmann, a *Luftwaffe* bomber pilot, told Günther Schramm:

> 'A 1459: GÖRING visited us at RIGA; he made a very agreeable impression on me. What he said then was still very full of promise. He said that he could say with absolute certainly [sic], that the weapon which they had got up their sleeves would be a hundred percent successful. They would never again undertake anything which involved the use of a not fully tried weapon. This time the weapon would be fully developed and would prove a success. I was

also just recently at ...... where the people are working. Thirty thousand convicts and workers etc. work there. They've been working there for two years now, they don't leave the place. That's where the secret weapon is being produced. That's why the English know so little about it.'[41]

They know now.

Bigotry and Atrocity

We have seen that captivity gave some CSDIC guests welcome relief from the tension between their ethical views and their obligation to the Nazi state. For others, the system simply sanctioned, directed and amplified their baser instincts. *Oberleutnant zur See* Cordt von Kalckreuth from T-25 posed a stark contrast to his colleague Günter Schramm.

'N 2075: *At the time when they shot von RATH*[†] *we should have exterminated the whole bunch of Jewish swine. Now ENGLAND and AMERICA are infested with them. If they weren't over here the war would probably have been over by now. They've all left (GERMANY). They are doing well here.*
N 2146 [2nd Officer Nissen, MV *Alsterufer*]: *Oh, the English and Americans are no friends of the Jews either.*
N 2075: *But they don't kill them and that's bad enough. They want a Jewish world plutocracy and the English want that too. A great many English are completely permeated by Jewish influence.*'[42]

Unguarded conversations threw disturbing light on the prisoners' widespread awareness of and acquiescence with the Nazis' programme of extermination. Most tried to distance

---

[†] The 1938 assassination of Ernst vom Rath, a German diplomat in Paris, by a Jewish teenager provided the pretext for *Kristallnacht*, an orgiastic night of murder, destruction and arrest against Nazi Germany's Jewish population.

themselves from the events they had witnessed. Franz Ligensa (N2178, the *Graf Spee* veteran) and Heinz Gessler of T-25 compared experiences:

'N 2178:   I saw in the east(?) how the Germans shot the Jews ...... I never said anything about it.
N 2177:   I knew all about the persecution of Jews in VIENNA (?). In 1930 when they ...... all the Jews there, when they rounded them up and fetched them out of their houses! They beat them up, stole their jewellery, and if a ring couldn't be taken off a finger easily, they just broke that finger, or cut it off.
N 2178:   God will not let <u>that</u> go unpunished! What the Russians are doing over there – well, they are Asiatics. That is riff-raff!
N 2177:   But <u>we</u>, the cultured people!
N 2178:   It isn't my fault if those people commit such sins. You can't hold me responsible for them!'[43]

Many had an uncomfortably growing awareness of a reckoning due. *Alsterufer's* Second Officer Nissen (N2146) discussed the topic with a *Luftwaffe* captain Dette.

'A 1442:   We're lucky to be here and not to have to be present when the collapse comes. It will be frightful when the mob is let loose against the Nazis. The SS will fight down to the last man. The worst thing we could have done was that Jewish business.
N 2146:   Yes, I was going to say that too. We shall have to pay for that. That didn't originate with the people; no one can tell me that. STREICHER did us a frightful amount of harm abroad. Up to 1937 everything was going <u>so</u> well.'[44]

Several prisoners knew of the massacres in Libau (Liepāja), Latvia, but *Maschinengefreiter* Kurt Liedtke of U-845 revelled in the vicious reprisals after a heavy brothel mirror fell on German customers below.

'N 2398:   Then we killed a hundred-and-eighty Jews, also Letts, we dragged everybody we could get hold of out of the houses, *even children and so on, it was a hell of a business! They all started wailing! Because they weren't to blame! We didn't catch the actual culprits. Three 'Kompanien' marched through LIBAU and then smoked everybody out. They took the women out of the shops. Then, when we had a hundred-and-eighty of them, RETTER (?) ...... was an Oberleutnant, in command of 1 "Kompanie" said: "We have got enough!" We formed them all up and we marched to ...... There are several different races in LATVIA; Jews are in the majority and there are others, the ...... The real Letts were unimportant people, we didn't do anything to them, but the Lachudas (?) were the ones. If there was the slightest suspicion about any of those, we said: "Come along with us." – a hundred-and-eighty of them. The Oberleutnant wanted to make it two hundred, but that was too much, LIBAU would have been almost empty then. One fellow was riding along the street on his bicycle and he was immediately pulled to the ground; he can't have had any idea of what was happening. A hundred-and-fifty of them would have been Jews; children and women were separated, we didn't touch the Latvian women, but we took all the Jewish women. The English made a terrible fuss in their newspapers about it.*

N 2383: *Well, let them write!*

N 2398: *They toppled over like ninepins. We formed them up in a row of fifty at a time. A burst of fire and they were gone. They were piled up so high that you couldn't see over them. The next ones that came shovelled earth over them, in this way making another hole, and the next ones stood in that. They were trodden down and then covered up and then it was the turn of the next ones. We covered up the next row. The ones who were still alive suffocated in the sand."*[45]

Very few of Libau's Jewish population survived the war.

Gefreiter (Private) Pfaffenberger, captured toward the end of 1944, had done time in Buchenwald for insulting a Party official and gave a detailed inmate's view of conditions there.

CSDIC verified parts of his account with pre-war refugees serving in the British Army but felt compelled to note, '*Some of PW PFAFFENBERGER's statements appear fantastic, but they are given for what they are worth.*'[46] Sadly the infernal pictures of prisoners with interesting tattoos selected for death so that their skins could be made into lampshades, and repeated hangings to prolong suffering, proved only too accurate.

If anti-Semitism was the bigotry of the moment, it had no claim to exclusivity. Holocaust scholarship reminds us how easy it was to fall foul of Nazi racial and cultural doctrine or simply to be seen as a useless stomach.

Some of the servicemen passing through CSDIC clung to their Christian faith as the single fixed moral point in a mad, turbulent universe but others sharply illustrated Martin Niemöller's point: '*First they came for the Socialists, and I did not speak out — Because I was not a Socialist. ... Then they came for me — and there was no one left to speak for me.*'

The following exchange is noteworthy both for the participants' total absorption of the National Socialist world view and their complete isolation from reality at the start of 1944. Aged nineteen and twenty-four they had little concept of anything else.

'*N 2140 [Matrosengefreiter Hans Hager, Scharnhorst]: A clean sweep must be made of the Catholics too.*

N 2166 [Maschinenhauptgefreiter Rolf Zanger, Scharnhorst]: Not now, but when we have won the war we will do so.'[47]

Evidence obtained from covert eavesdropping was carefully preserved but never used at war-crimes trials because of concern for the security of the source and the safety of former stool pigeons. Consequently, some convictions which might otherwise have been obtained were missed.[48]

Not all data led to change.

1. TNA ADM 223/473; *NID memoranda: training and administration 1933-1948* appears to include all the suggestions received.
2. TNA WO 208/4149; *Interrogation Reports on German Prisoners of War 2700-3050*. SRN 2851 dated 25th January 1944. WO 208/4148; *Interrogation Reports on German Prisoners of War, SRN 2451-2699 (November 1943-January 1944)*. SRN 2562, 31st December 1943.
3. TNA ADM 223/877; *NID UC Reports: Nos 315-500 (incomplete) 1943 Apr 01 - 1944 Jun 28*. NID UC Report No 401, 26th November 1943.
4. TNA ADM 186/809; *Interrogation of German naval survivors*. CB 04051 (94) "U 593" Interrogation of Survivors, and CB 04051 (95) "U 73" Interrogation of Survivors.
5. TNA ADM 223/877; *NID UC Reports: Nos 315-500 (incomplete) 1943 Apr 01 - 1944 Jun 28*. NID UC Reports No's 445 dated 10th March 1944, 447 dated 11th March 1944 and 495 dated 7th June 1944.
6. TNA WO 208/4150; *Interrogation Reports on German Prisoners of War 3051-3359*. SRN 3338 dated 12th April 1944.
7. TNA ADM 223/877; *NID UC Reports: Nos 315-500 (incomplete) 1943 Apr 01 - 1944 Jun 28*. NID UC Reports No's 432 dated 24th February 1944 and 458 dated 30th March 1944.
8. TNA ADM 223/120; *Naval Intelligence Division Reports UC 251-500 1942 Sept – 1944 June*. Report No 472 dated 1st May 1944. TNA ADM 223/877; *NID UC Reports: Nos 315-500 (incomplete) 1943 Apr 01 - 1944 Jun 28*. NID UC Report No 495 dated 7th June 1944.
9. TNA ADM 223/475; *Intelligence collection methods*: Memo from ACNS (UT) to Commodore Rushbrooke (DNI) dated 23rd October 1943 and Godfrey's reply dated 28th October. Ed Offley; *Turning the Tide* (Basic Books, 2011), P.378.
10. TNA ADM 223/475; *Intelligence collection methods*. Memo from ACNS(UT to DNI dated 23rd October 1943 and DNI's reply dated 28th October.
11. TNA WO 208/4150; *Interrogation Reports on German Prisoners of War 3051-3359*. SRN 3212 dated 22nd March 1944.
12. TNA ADM 223/809; *Interrogation of German naval survivors*. CB 04051(94) "U 593" Interrogation of Survivors.

[13] G. J. Kirby, B.Sc, F.R.A.S., R.N.S.S.; *A History of the Torpedo Part 3* in *Journal of the Royal Naval Scientific Service*, Volume 27 No 2, March 1972. P.85.

[14] TNA WO 208/4149; *Interrogation Reports on German Prisoners of War 2700-3050*. SRN 2753 dated 15th January 1944.

[15] ibid. SRN 2985 dated 28th February 1944.

[16] TNA ADM 223/142; *Summary of statements by German prisoners of war, 1943 July-Sept*. Summary No 42 for week ending 19th September 1943.

[17] TNA WO 208/4149; *Interrogation Reports on German Prisoners of War 2700-3050*. SRN 2895 dated 4th February 1944.

[18] TNA WO 208/5551; *Consolidated report on German Naval gunnery; SR 1, 1944 Feb 05*. P.4.

[19] TNA ADM 223/877; *NID UC Reports: Nos 315-500 (incomplete) 1943 Apr 01 - 1944 Jun 28*. NID UC Report No 423 dated 28th January 1944.

[20] TNA WO 208/4149; *Interrogation Reports on German Prisoners of War 2700-3050*. SRN 2816 dated 22nd January 1944.

[21] ibid. SRN 2995 dated 4th March 1944.

[22] TNA WO 208/4150; *Interrogation Reports on German Prisoners of War 3051-3359*. SRN 3206 dated 21st March 1944.

[23] TNA WO 208/4151; *Interrogation Reports on German Prisoners of War No's 3360-3650*. SRN 3555 dated 30th April 1944.

[24] TNA WO 208/4200; *Special extracts from interrogation reports on German and Italian prisoners of war December 1942 – March 1945*. Extract from S.R. Draft No. WG 1407 dated 5th June 1944.

[25] ibid.

[26] TNA WO 208/4196; *Interrogation Reports on German and Italian Prisoners of War SP/F 1-142*. SP/F/116 dated 6th May 1943, SP/F/117 and SP/F/118 dated 8th May 1943.

[27] TNA WO 208/4149; *Interrogation Reports on German Prisoners of War 2700-3050*. SRN 2781 dated 17th January 1944, 2722 date 11th January 1944. WO 208/4163; *Interrogation Reports on German Prisoners of War 1731-1949*. SRX 1897 dated 10th January 1944.

[28] TNA WO 208/4149; *Interrogation Reports on German Prisoners of War 2700-3050*. SRN 2979 dated 3rd March 1944.

[29] ibid. SRN 2965 dated 3rd March 1944.

[30] ibid. SRN 2708 dated 10th January 1944.

31. ibid. SRN 2868 dated 28th January 1944.
32. TNA WO 208/4148; TNA WO 208/4148; *Interrogation Reports on German Prisoners of War 2451-2699*. SRN 2636 dated 4th January 1944.
33. ibid. SRN 2591 dated 1st January 1944.
34. TNA WO 208/4149; *Interrogation Reports on German Prisoners of War 2700-3050*. SRN 2989 dated 3rd March 1944.
35. Jeremy Bernstein; *Hitler's Uranium Club: The Secret Recordings at Farm Hall* (American Institute of Physics, 1996).
36. TNA WO 208/4149; *Interrogation Reports on German Prisoners of War 2700-3050*. SRN 2905 dated 8th February 1944.
37. ibid. SRN 2851, 2853 dated 25th January 1944.
38. ibid. SRN 3014 dated 3rd March 1944.
39. TNA WO 208/4196; *Interrogation Reports on German and Italian Prisoners of War SP/F 1-142*. SP/F/135 dated 4th March 1944.
40. TNA WO 208/4149; *Interrogation Reports on German Prisoners of War 2700-3050*. SRN 2902 dated 5th February 1944.
41. TNA WO 208/4163; *Interrogation Reports on German Prisoners of War 1731-1949*. SRX 1933 dated 1st February 1944.
42. TNA WO 208/4149; *Interrogation Reports on German Prisoners of War 2700-3050*. SRN 2727 dated 13th January 1944.
43. ibid. SRN 2884 dated 2nd February 1944.
44. TNA WO 208/4163; *Interrogation Reports on German Prisoners of War 1731-1949*. SRX 1914 dated 22nd January 1944.
45. TNA WO 208/4150; *Interrogation Reports on German Prisoners of War 3051-3359*. SRN 3319 dated 5th April 1944.
46. TNA WO 208/4140; *Interrogation Reports on German Prisoners of War 1111-1264*. SRM 1144 dated 30th December 1944 and 1153 dated 1st January 1945.
47. TNA WO 208/4149; *Interrogation Reports on German Prisoners of War 2700-3050*. SRN 2912 dated 10th February 1944.
48. Helen Fry; *The Walls Have Ears*. Chapter 14.

INTERNATIONAL RELATIONS

The relationships between the Third Reich and its allies, neutral trading partners and occupied territories were a matter of keen interest to the British Ministry of Economic Warfare and Political Warfare Executive. What follows is inevitably partial and distorted, based on the testimony of people whose experience of the world outside was largely confined to the bases, bars, bordellos and prisons of garrison towns across the unholy Axis empire. Nonetheless it provided valuable pieces for the intelligence jigsaw which the analysts were constantly trying to fit together.

France

Sabotage was a constant low-level worry. *Funkegefreiter* Theodor Essman of U-73 described a harrowing experience on the way back to base.

'*N 2159: I came back from the course. In FRANCE the train I was in was attacked during the night.*
N 1552: Where was that?
N 2159: DIJON-LYON, on the stretch between MULHOUSE and TOULON. The train was ten hours late as a result. The front coaches were destroyed, the rear ones were pulled away again. It was like this: a goods train approached from the side. An explosive charge had been placed underneath it. They worked it out so that the goods train arrived at the same time as our express train. Actually the goods train got there rather earlier ...... explosion ...... flew round about behind.

The engine fell into some dip – you could see the steam coming out – and we were lying on the other side. It only tore up one rail. We went crashing down a steep slope. What a row! Everything came down. One fellow was lying like this and all the luggage fell down on his head. He was badly hurt. Gasmasks, rifles everything that was up there came down.

N 1552:   When was this?

N 2159:   When did I come back? On 23rd November.'[1]

At Marseilles things had reached such a pitch that it was standard practice to send a train ahead with French crew and coaches to test the line. The warren of interconnecting buildings in the *Vieux-Port* became supposedly so dangerous for Germans that it was blown up, making about 20,000 people homeless.[2]

Young men rushing ashore with one thing on their mind too often found that their imagination, or service brothels, would have to do. This observation by *Zimmermannobergefreiter* (Shipwright Able Seaman) Martin Wallek of *Scharnhorst* neatly encapsulates the dual standards they often applied.

'*N 2129:   At BREST the French girls didn't dare have much to do with us, because they were afraid of being knifed in the back in the dark. It ought to be like that with us in AUSTRIA. Our girls go with all the Italians and Frenchmen who come to work for us.*'[3]

Much of the gossip picked up by CSDIC secret listeners found its way back via the 'black' propaganda radio station *Atlantiksender*. Inevitably this led to a paranoid fear of espionage, some but not all of which may have been justified. St Nazaire in Brittany was particularly affected.

'*N 2333* [Leutnant zur See Hellmuth Jonas, U-744]: *(Re. espionage at ST. NAZAIRE): The English wireless station used to broadcast the strangest things, things which German U-boat officers had said in the U-boat bar, in the wardroom and so on.*

N 2328 [Oberleutnant zur See *Rolf Albrecht, U-386*]: *Were there girls there?*
N 2333: *Yes.*
N 2328: *Then it's no wonder, because the girls are all spying for the enemy. We have found that out now. Eighty per cent of all the girls there were spying for the enemy. ST. NAZAIRE was the worst spy centre in the whole of FRANCE. They have cleaned it up now. The number of women they arrested there! The main thing was that they closed all the bars. It was a pity – but the right thing to do. The officers' bar was a nest of spies. They knew the gossip which went on at ST. NAZAIRE and the transmitter broadcast everything. If an officer was punished, the girls knew it the next day. If a U-boat captain was locked up, which does happen sometimes on account of some stupid business at home, they knew about it the next day. ST. NAZAIRE was supposed to be closed now as a U-boat base, on account of espionage. Our camp was at LA BAULE, a hutment camp. Now with feverish energy they are –*
N 2333: *Building huts?*
N 2328: *Hm.'*

The toxic blend of spy and invasion fever saw at least one French woman well-known around the naval base executed.[4] It affected La Baule, just west of the port, where the local *madame* was suspected but never caught.

'*N2254:* *There are continual police raids at LA BAULE. The town is full of spies.*'[5]

St Nazaire fortress held out until the end of the war although it was toothless without its submarines and ships. If it was a miserable time for the Germans posted there it was doubly so for the Breton population. Repeated RAF raids had barely scratched the U-boat pens but shattered the town. According to *Funkobergefreiter* Franz Rossmeissl of U-406,

'*N 2223:* *What a sight ST. NAZAIRE is: not a house is undamaged! There's not a single pub left at ST. NAZAIRE. Under* the wreckage which was still standing, they set up planks and sold a little wine there. The whole of ST. NAZAIRE has been evacuated now. There are no longer any French there. But they have re-opened one brothel now for the people living at the hostel. They've smashed up everything – everything. Not a house is left standing right out to the outskirts.'[6]

Nor was Toulon immune from paranoia. One conversation suggests that the loss of U-73 may have come just in time to save a probably innocent staff officer from lynching.

'N 2079 [*Matrosenobergefreiter* Alfred Vogt, T-25]: Spies – those can only be staff officers.

N 2158 [*Maschinenobergefreiter* Gerhard Pohl, U-73]: I suspected a Korvettenkapitän at the base, an Austrian. We all discussed it amongst ourselves in the crew. Each one of us in the crew suspected him. The fellow ought to be beaten to death.'[7]

Scharnhorst crew remembered little consideration for the local population from their sojourn at Brest. A dummy battleship had been constructed from two merchant ships welded together and was towed around the harbour as a decoy whenever an air raid threatened. The anti-aircraft guns aboard were perfectly genuine. The real ships held their fire unless things got too warm, in which case they blazed away with everything available.

'N 2142: We had no regard for the French. The HIPPER shot up the whole harbour area. They fired their 10.5 at all houses showing a light. The French are a beastly race. Believe it or not, there were guns posted all over the place with the sole job of keeping an eye on the French. As soon as they showed a light it was fired on. A '3.7' mounting and a 2 cm. had the sole job of watching for French lights. Their own police, French police, unearthed a French transmitter which was in the service of the English, at BREST. The police even got German decorations.'[8]

International Relations

The Netherlands

The crew of T-25 admired the speed and firepower of the large ex-Dutch destroyer ZH-1 (formerly *Gerard Callenburg*) which had been salvaged and taken over by the Germans in 1940. They had plenty of leisure to do so, having been detailed to tow her in after she suffered an engine failure during the *Osorno* mission. ZH-1 was sunk in a battle with British destroyers shortly after D-Day.

Nazi ideology allowed for a degree of racial affinity with the Dutch. Intermarriage was actively promoted at first.

'N 2301 [*Mechanikersmaat* Günther Radder, U-472]: *The state encourages us to marry Dutch girls. They're the right stuff. You get an extra RM 1000 from the state on top of that.*'[9]

His information may have been out of date by the time he was captured. An E-boat seaman rescued in October 1943 observed,

'*The C.O. said: "You won't get permission to marry a Dutch girl even if she is expecting a child. So you had better be a cad for five minutes and say it wasn't you."*'[10]

Some Dutch took the Führer's mark willingly enough. There were Dutch volunteers in the *Kriegsmarine* and a local SS battalion was among the defenders of Arnhem when it finally fell in 1945. Others were driven to compliance by desperation.

'N 2110 [*Obermechanikersmaat* Heinrich Raithel, T-25]: *We wore side arms, when we went ashore in HOLLAND. The women from the town used to turn up in front of the shelter. As soon as they found out that they could sell themselves for a loaf of bread and so on, they came along. With an army loaf you could –*
N 2175 [*Maschinenobergefreiter* Paul Schaffrath, *Scharnhorst*]: *It wasn't like that with us. They still had enough to eat. The louts used to come along the pavement, three or four of them beside each other, when we had no side arms. They simply ran you down. But once we had side arms, then we just went like this and they disappeared.*'[11]

E-boat crews stationed permanently in the country had plenty of opportunity to observe the effect of petty, vindictive German rule. Dutch workers were kept on lower rations than their German colleagues, which did nothing for their mood or productivity. An *Obermaschinenmaat* from S-88 complained,

> '*Why do they provoke them through the N.S.B. (Dutch Nazi Party)? … Do they think it has helped, or done any good at all, taking their radios away from the Dutch? They get the news they want just the same without radios. It'll get in just the same as before. But a great many respectable Dutchmen, who have so far stood up for us, are now annoyed not to have any music and not to hear anything.*'[12]

A crewman from S-96 explained the reality of life under Nazi administration to a colleague, presumably a newcomer.

> '*N 1913:   (Re his superior officer's interpretation of an order by General CHRISTIANSEN): "If you come to blows I shall always back you, so if you are going along the street and a Dutchman comes towards you, don't make way for him at all," he said. And of course that was grist to our mill.*
>
> *N 1921:   What do you mean?*
>
> *N 1913:   It started immediately. Three men came back from GERMANY and then a Dutchman got into the tram, which was absolutely crammed full; he got half inside and then went back again. He couldn't manage all his parcels, and then one of the Germans said to the Dutchman; "What are you up to?" And he answered: "Shut up." The next moment the German had hit him, and drew blood; his whole coat was messed up; and then they threw him out of the tram. And that sort of thing went on all the time. Afterwards whenever ZWINGE (?) saw a Dutchman standing there and looking askance at him, he used to say: "Have you got anything against the Germans?" and if he didn't immediately answer "No", he hit him. That's how it was all the time.*'[13]

Ethnic cousins or no, the brutality of the 1940 invasion and the arrogance of German occupation left no opportunity for the occupiers to relax.

> 'N 2140 [*Matrosengefreiter* Hans Hager, *Scharnhorst*]: ... *Where we were they shot a Blitzmädel. I was going home one evening by tram with the Gruppenführer. Suddenly there was a bang – two holes in the windows and two Blitzmädels were hit; one of them was killed. There's a cord and when you pull it the tram stops. Some soldiers pulled it, jumped out and rushed out into the house. They thrashed the swine to death. The number of soldiers who got bumped off when they were drunk! There are any number of those canals in AMSTERDAM; in the morning our people used to fish the fellows out – in the Jewish quarter. They've sent them all to POLAND. The recruits weren't allowed to go out at all. Anyone who wanted to go out was allowed out only if armed with a pistol. It was a bad time.*
>
> N 2167:   *When was that?*
>
> N 2140:   *In March 1942.*
>
> N 2167:   *I was at DEN HAAG(?) in 1941 and a few of the coastal gunnery people disappeared; we then got orders that if there was any trouble in the town, or if we were attacked or anything, we were to beat the other fellow to death – not merely wound him; we were to give him such a blow – we carried side-arms as well – that he would be killed on the spot. We were either to stab him or –*
>
> N 2140:   *When we went out our CPO always said: "If they attack you and you come back with a hiding, bring the fellow with you, dead or alive."*
>
> N 2177:   *Kill him immediately.*'[14]

As the Dutch resistance gained confidence the cycle of violence intensified. *Maschinenobergefreiter* Schaffrath of *Scharnhorst*, by then well embedded in his stool pigeon role, drew out the following admission from U-boat survivor *Funkgefreiter* Tudass:

'N 2463: A short time ago the Dutch killed two of our fellows at ROTTERDAM. So we set out with tommy-guns and killed them right and left. The Dutch are treacherous swine.'[15]

Denmark

The surprise, near-bloodless 1940 invasion of Denmark in defiance of the previous year's non-aggression treaty was over in a matter of hours when the Danish government chose surrender over futile slaughter. Co-operation meant the country was left largely to run itself for three years while Danish Jews escaped the ravages inflicted on their co-religionists elsewhere in Europe. Underground newspapers flourished, passive resistance was commonplace and small-scale acts of sabotage began to grow as the reality of arms-length occupation dawned.

'N 2146 [2nd Officer Johannes Nissen, MV Alsterufer]: An order was once issued in DENMARK, permitting every German soldier to take as much stuff out of the country as he could carry. You should have seen them, each one with several porters following him.'[16]

Unsurprisingly the habit of systematic, barefaced pillage and high-handed arrogance provoked a reaction. As in other occupied countries the currency was pegged at an artificially low level against the Reichsmark, making goods incredibly cheap. Luxuries such as cake were not only cheap but readily available long after they had become a distant memory in Germany.

'N 2397 [Maschinenmaat Werner Wiezorek, U-744]: We had a few fellows who were in DENMARK. They kept beating up the Danes, they did it intentionally. They would walk along a street and if one of then approached – the street is very slippery – they would

*slide along it and knock into the Danish fellow and beat him up ......
(laughs). They did all sorts of things like that. There was a hell of a
lot of trouble in DENMARK. The Danes were always trying to
organise some sort of rebellion.'*[17]

Things came to a head at the end of August 1943 when the Germans declared martial law and the Danish government ceased functioning but refused to resign. The Danish Navy scuttled 32 of its ships while another thirteen managed to escape to Sweden.

'*N 2175* [Maschinenobergefreiter *Paul Schaffrath,* Scharnhorst]: *Was there no army in DENMARK, no infantry?*
N 2371 [Matrosengefreiter *Rudolf Voigt, U-845*]: *There were a few Navy men there; there were a few hutments where U-boat men could spend the night.*
N 2175: But DENMARK is occupied, isn't she?
N 2371: Yes, but not in sufficient strength. They were scared stiff every day. They thought the Danes would come along some time and smash their heads in.'[18]

The fleeing ships brought news of the revolt, which quickly reached Britain and prompted cheerfully disparaging newspaper articles about the Nazi empire cracking up. In retrospect they were fractionally premature.

An attempt to round up Danish Jews at the beginning of October was frustrated when a disillusioned German maritime attaché Georg F. Duckwitz leaked the plan. Most were quickly sheltered by civilians and later smuggled out of the country.

Norway

Northern Norway was a bleak, inhospitable posting made more so by the inactivity of the capital ships stationed there. Most of the entertainment had to be found from the ships' own resources though several prisoners mentioned a 'Strength through Joy' ship (effectively a floating brothel), and there was talk of 'hunting' trips to the interior where there was much drink consumed and ammunition spent for little trouble to the wildlife.

Among the sparse population of the Finnmark there were a few almost insanely brave resistance workers operating two clandestine radios (codenamed Ida and Lyra) and occasionally taking direct action. Wilhelm Kruse, who had transferred from *Tirpitz* to *Scharnhorst* with Admiral Bey's staff on Christmas Day, saw a sentry shot by a sniper and was narrowly missed himself. The man was later caught and beheaded.[19]

Further south, life could be even more adventurous. Kruse, again, had an epic journey to Germany and back on leave.

'N 2141:   North of NARVIK you can only start leave-journeys once a week. You've no idea how lucky I was that nothing happened to me at OSLO, and that I came through the whole journey so well. And was I happy when I was back on board! When I travelled down we didn't leave from OSLO but from MOSS, which is a sort of suburb of OSLO, there was a train there; there were blood-stained clothes lying on the platform! As I got into the train I asked: "What's happened here?" "Well, I'm not really supposed to say. A train was attacked. It was a Norwegian train travelling from ANDALSNES to OSLO and behind were two coaches for members of the German armed forces. They placed mines inside them and exploded them on the journey. There was a mine in each coach."'[20]

★ ★ ★

'N 2141:   I was at OSLO for nine days. They blew up railway lines and that sort of thing. They had set fire to the university there. It blazed like a torch. What excitement there was everywhere!
N 2138:   In OSLO?
N 2141:   Yes. There were riots and acts of sabotage, all carried out at one fell swoop. All at once all the rail-communications round

about OSLO were severed; one night they were all blown up. And now, before Christmas, on the 20th December, there was a great explosion. That was in the English papers too. In the German newspaper, the 'arzeitung', it said: "A severe explosion occured [sic] in OSLO harbour on the Sunday before Christmas during trans-shipment of ammunition. Considerable damage was caused to buildings. Several conflagrations broke out, large residential areas were destroyed. The casualties among the civilian population cannot yet be estimated."'[21]

As the tide of war turned against Germany the relatively free passage of men and materials it had previously enjoyed to Norway *via* Sweden became much more restricted. This forcibly increased the use of the route through Denmark, perhaps helping to harden the Danes' attitude toward Germany.

Italy

U-73 was based at La Spezia over a year and a half, during which she underwent two major overhauls. After the second, two attempts at sea trials were cut short by engine room explosions. Sabotage was suspected. Continual air raids and a hostile population ensured it was not a happy time.

'N 2061 [*Matrosenobergefreiter* Kurt Wehling]: *The French population behaved wonderfully towards us, as though nothing had happened, although they had had so many killed. When we were at SPEZIA – they bombed the whole town and the shipyard to blazes – we hardly dared go out any more .... they stoned us and spat at us.*

A 881 [a stool pigeon]: *The Italians?*

N 2061: *Yes.*

A 881: *When was that?*

N 2061: *In May.*'[22]

Things only got worse. When the armistice was signed the remains of the Italian fleet at La Spezia ran for Malta, provoking furious retribution against the unfortunate officers left behind. The switch from uneasy ally to occupied territory made the streets actively dangerous for Germans. *Funkobergefreiter* Joseph Stäger recalled,

> '*N(Am)42: We couldn't go on shore at all when the business (MUSSOLINI and Italian armistice) started. The Wops threw stones at us. We had a hell of a time!*'[23]

If Toulon was an improvement La Spezia must have been a fearsome billet.

Japan

The smartness and discipline of Japanese crews visiting Brest and Danzig (Gdansk) left a favourable impression despite their paranoid secrecy. Germans seeing them on their home or occupied territory however came away with a very different view as two deeply and incompatibly racist outlooks met nose to nose.

> '*N 2174* [1st Officer Ernst Lemke, *Alsterufer*]: *I can't stand the Japs. They are a lousy lot. They can't bear us, they make it quite obvious, too. We are whites, too. It is a disgrace to civilisation that we are their allies, they are holy terrors. It is a necessity brought about by the war, but it is contrary to our racial policy. They are 'monkeys'.*'[24]

Consistent themes were Japanese arrogance and their expectation of full access to German technology with not the slightest thought of reciprocating. First Officer Lemke of *Alsterufer* gave examples to Günther Schramm.[25]

> '*N 2174: There's an airman over in JAPAN with whom I got on very friendly terms. You are sure to have heard his name – STÖHR. He used to be the German stunt-flying champion at the*

same time as UDET. He's now a test pilot with MESSER-
SCHMITT in GERMANY and he was then sent over (to
JAPAN). We send everything to JAPAN - the newest types of
aircraft and anything else we may have.

N 2074:   Do we get anything from JAPAN?

N 2174:   Good God, no! We send them aircraft engineers etc.
and we build them aircraft factories taking the latest models over, the
latest materials and aluminium. When the aircraft are there
STÖHR tests them over there. When he climbs out of the aircraft
he's not allowed to go near it again. It goes into the factory where
some slight alteration is made to it, a smaller wing perhaps or a new
bracing is added, and then it's a Japanese aircraft. He's not allowed
to see the aircraft any more.

Then there was the German auxiliary cruiser which was based on
JAPAN. Japanese experts and so on were all over the ship, looking it
over from top to bottom. It was obvious that the captain didn't like it,
he didn't want to give the show away, he had E-boats and all sorts of
things on board. They had flaps and torpedo tubes etc., which was no
concern of theirs. So he refused to let them see it. When he got definite
instructions from the admiral that he was to show everything, to hold
nothing back. Whereupon he shut himself in his cabin and said:
"They can go to hell!" The Japanese went right over the whole ship,
they wormed their way into every nook and cranny, they
photographed and made sketches of everything. Afterwards, the
officers on the auxiliary cruiser wanted to look over something
Japanese too so they were fetched and taken to see an ironclad ship
which had lain near PORT ARTHUR as a floating fortress!
(laughter) They made a dreadful fuss about that and there was a hell
of a row afterwards, so they were taken to see an aircraft-carrier.'

Systematic, petty humiliations such as being spat on in the street were routine. During *Alsterufer's* visit a dockyard trip, arranged after much negotiation, got no further than the manager's office.

An earlier survivor of SS *Regensburg* had similar views.

'N 1566 [*Maschinengefreiter* Heisch]: *Those yellow monkeys aren't human beings; they are still animals.*

The Japanese always say that one Japanese soldier is worth two German, three English, five French or twenty Italian soldiers. When the war is once finished, the white races, GERMANY and ENGLAND, will march against the yellow peril. Then I shall enlist again voluntarily.

When the Japanese came on board, they always wanted to photograph everything.'[26]

Seamen making harbour after a long, tense voyage were frustrated by delays in getting ashore, and when they finally got there found themselves in the unaccustomed role of second-class citizens. One party thought they had overcome the language difficulty, explained what they wanted to a local guide, and were ushered into a private room where they were decorously served – tea. Others quickly discovered that women regarded as higher status were reserved for their hosts. *Oberfunkmeister* Friedrich Warscheid summed up the situation.

'N 2173: *There were some marvellous half-caste women in SINGAPORE, mixtures between Filipinos and Europeans, Filipinos and Japanese, Filipinos and Jews. But we weren't allowed to have anything to do with them. There would have been trouble with the Japanese authorities immediately.*'[27]

In the Dutch East Indies (now Indonesia) there were stories of German and Dutch women who had stayed behind, had their property confiscated and were confined to internment camps. There the alternatives were starvation, prostitution or 'bar work.' *Alsterufer's* First Officer Ernst Lemke fulminated,

'*If they don't behave as the Japanese wish, they slap their face, or hit them on the mouth. The Japanese place most value on having a white woman, a German or Dutch woman for instance, as his mistress; it satisfies his racial pride to have humiliated the woman to such an extent that she becomes his mistress. Japanese officers go in and out of the camp and keep a woman there. For fifty yen etc. ...... a white woman, a German woman. For the women in the town are left without a penny to support themselves, until they are so weary and have reached such a pitch that they ...... themselves in order not to starve. They don't get any work. Well, they can work, they can go into the bars, and that means the same as becoming a prostitute. When you, as a German, hear that sort of thing, it makes you mad.*'[28]

They also realised they had blundered into a police state beyond even their imagining. German crew were strictly warned to obey the injunction against going ashore armed. Five men from *Michel*, a German raider, had been apprehended in uniform and beaten almost to death. It seemed almost any pretext would do. Lemke again, in the same conversation:

'JAPAN has more police than any other country in the world, it's worse than RUSSIA, worse than GERMANY – there are three police stations at every corner.

N 2182 [Leutnant zur See Kurt Heinemann, U-593]: *Do they need them because something is always happening?*

N 2174: No, not for that reason, but for the greatest spy and informer system you could imagine. Everyone knows all about everyone else. Then those ratings were hauled off to the police station – in uniform – and thrashed, beaten up with truncheons, given a hiding, because the Japanese had caught a white man. With absolute sadism.'

Racism, paranoia and internal politics made a toxic cocktail. When *Alsterufer* arrived at Batavia (Jakarta) the Japanese authorities demanded a plain text version of the coded signal announcing the ship's arrival and the crew were at first confined to the ship. The signal stipulation was from fear of espionage, and the petty inconvenience because the town was under Japanese Army control; their own naval officers had to go cap-in-hand to the army for permission to move around the port![29]

Piling on the humiliation, German ships were ordered to strike their own flag in port and fly the Japanese ensign instead. Piatek furiously elected to leave his mast bare.

Watching British and American prisoners of war doing heavy forced labour in Singapore harbour elicited sympathy even from the hard-boiled seamen of *Alsterufer*.

Germans in Tokyo were required to give up their tram seats to Japanese and bow low as they passed the Emperor's palace. That is, until Italy's surrender brought at least a temporary sense of vulnerability.

'N 1878 [a stool pigeon]: *If GERMANY loses the war; then Japan is done for as well.*

N 2173 [*Oberfunkmeister* Friedrich Warscheid, *Alsterufer*]: *Yes, they know that too. You noticed that all right when ITALY fell. All of a sudden it was – "Germans, Germans," and in TOKYO they demonstrated etc.; advertisements, newspapers, neon advertisements at night etc.: and when the DUCE was liberated, my God, what a hullabaloo, everything decorated with flags etc. GERMANY, HITLER – German prestige rose tremendously then. They were all wildly enthusiastic. The day after the fall of ITALY we returned from NARA(?), and for the first time the people in the train stood up for us and offered us their 2nd class seats in the express so that we could sit down. The national emblem was on our khaki shirts too, and we heard how whispered to each: "Germans!" They stood up and made room for us.'*[30]

All *Alsterufer* survivors were scandalised by the treatment they had endured in the Far East. Second Office Johannes Nissen (N2146) managed the most balanced view.

'N(Am)46 [*Matrose I* Ude Nissen, U-73]: *I've heard peculiar things about the Japanese treating nearly all Germans as internees.*

N 2146: Oh no, it's not as bad as that, but the Japanese are suspicious by nature and are terribly afraid of espionage, and to be quite truthful, they hate anyone who is white.[31]

The formal NID report came to the conclusion that *'The more intelligent and responsible officers, such as Captain Piatek, Lemke, the First Mate, and Oberfunkmeister Warscheid, had no illusions on the subject and said that it was quite clear that German residents in Japan and visiting German sailors were there merely on suffrance [sic] and that, in fact, the Japanese considered themselves at war with all the white races.'*[32]

Lemke put it pithily:

'N 2174: Those apes – you should just have a look at the fellows – the great majority of them. There's nothing I hate so much as the Japanese. They hate us regardless of the fact whether we are Russian or English or French or German. They are white men and the Japanese hate them.'[33]

Matrosengefreiter Hans Hager of *Scharnhorst*, with no known direct experience, nevertheless summed up the feelings of many.

'N 2140: The Japanese are the Jews of the east.'[34]

---

[1] TNA WO 208/4149; *Interrogation Reports on German Prisoners of War 2700-3050*. SRN 2747 dated 12th January 1944.

[2] TNA WO 208/4148; *Interrogation Reports on German Prisoners of War 2451-2699*. SRN 2589 dated 31st December 1943.

[3] TNA WO 208/4149; *Interrogation Reports on German Prisoners of War 2700-3050*. SRN 2834 dated 25th January 1944.

[4] TNA WO 208/4150; *Interrogation Reports on German Prisoners of War 3051-3359*. SRN 3087 dated 14th March 1944. WO 208/4196; *Interrogation Reports on German and Italian Prisoners of War SP/F 1-142*. SP/F 134 dated 4th March 1944.

[5] TNA WO 208/4149; *Interrogation Reports on German Prisoners of War 2700-3050*. SRN 2990 dated 4th March 1944. WO 208/4148; *Interrogation Reports on German Prisoners of War 2451-2699*. SRN 2534 dated 21st December 1943.

[6] ibid. SRN 2988 dated 29th February 1944.

7. ibid. SRN 2764 dated 14th January 1944.
8. TNA WO 208/4148; *Interrogation Reports on German Prisoners of War 2451-2699*. SRN 2626 dated 5th January 1944.
9. TNA WO 208/4150; *Interrogation Reports on German Prisoners of War 3051-3359*. SRN 3165 dated 20th March 1944.
10. TNA WO 208/4147; *Interrogation Reports on German Prisoners of War 2200-2450*. SRN 2385 dated 2nd November 1943.
11. TNA WO 208/4149; *Interrogation Reports on German Prisoners of War 2700-3050*. SRN 2829 dated 20th January 1944.
12. TNA WO 208/4147; *Interrogation Reports on German Prisoners of War 2200-2450*. SRN 2377 dated 30th October 1943.
13. ibid. SRN 2284 dated 9th October 1943.
14. TNA WO 208/4149; *Interrogation Reports on German Prisoners of War 2700-3050*. SRN 2867 dated 28th January 1944.
15. TNA WO 208/4151; *Interrogation Reports on German Prisoners of War 3360-3650*. SRN 3478 dated 27th April 1944.
16. TNA WO 208/4149; *Interrogation Reports on German Prisoners of War 2700-3050*. SRN 2731 dated 13th January 1944.
17. TNA WO 208/4150; *Interrogation Reports on German Prisoners of War 3051-3359*. SRN 3321 dated 6th April 1944.
18. ibid. SRN 3245 dated 24th March 1944.
19. TNA WO 208/4149; *Interrogation Reports on German Prisoners of War 2700-3050*. SRN 2836 dated 23rd January 1944.
20. ibid. SRN 2818 dated 21st January 1944.
21. ibid. SRN 2837 dated 23rd January 1944.
22. TNA WO 208/4148; *Interrogation Reports on German Prisoners of War 2451-2699*. SRN 2558 dated 31st December 1943.
23. ibid. SRN 2589 dated 31st December 1943.
24. TNA WO 208/4149; *Interrogation Reports on German Prisoners of War 2700-3050*. SRN 2853 dated 25th January 1944.
25. TNA WO 208/4163; *Interrogation Reports on German Prisoners of War 1731-1949*. SRX 1907 dated 19th January 1944.
26. TNA WO 208/4145; *Interrogation Reports on German Prisoners of War 1489-1900*. SRN 1617 dated 12th April 1943.
27. TNA WO 208/4149; *Interrogation Reports on German Prisoners of War 2700-3050*. SRN 2789 dated 20th January 1944.
28. ibid. SRN 2855 dated 26th January 1944.

[29] ibid. SRN 2788 dated 20th January 1944.
[30] ibid. SRN 2803 dated 20th January 1944.
[31] TNA WO 208/4148; TNA WO 208/4148; *Interrogation Reports on German Prisoners of War 2451-2699.* SRN 2668 dated 9th January 1944.
[32] TNA ADM 186/809; *Interrogation of German naval survivors (1944).* B
[33] TNA WO 208/4149; *Interrogation Reports on German Prisoners of War 2700-3050.* SRN 2855 dated 26th January 1944.
[34] ibid. SRN 2912 dated 10th February 1944.

Prelude to Götterdämmerung

With the Allies fighting their way up Italy and men and supplies pouring almost uninterrupted into Britain it was obvious to the most casual observer that a second front in Europe was imminent. The question was, where and when? Seldom has it been as urgent and as vital for each side in a conflict to divine the other's thoughts.

For the naval team at CSDIC the problem narrowed down to finding out what their guests had been led to expect and how they had been briefed to react.

Mediterranean

The Allied advance in Italy was bogged down between Naples and Anzio but the bulk of the U-boat force had already retreated from its previous home at La Spezia to Toulon. The French Mediterranean coast looked worryingly vulnerable to *Funkobergefreiter* Kälsch (N2361) of U-450.

'N 2361:   (re fortifications on the French MEDITERRANEAN Coast): *At our place they always reckoned on being invaded. If the enemy want to come, they'll certainly come down there, too.*
N 2189:   *What makes you think that? Aren't the coastal fortifications there up to much, or what?*
N 2361:   *For one thing I don't believe that they are, and besides, if they make a surprise landing there, there are so many places where they would get a foothold. Of course it's guarded ...... The whole coastline is mountainous – We went on mountain tours there – and*

these fortifications are built into the mountains. They have built in kind of dug-outs, with large telescopes. You can sweep everywhere with them. That is their only purpose. A watch is kept up there continually, by one Unteroffizier and a few men .... constantly relieve ...... then those observation numbers (?) – point such-and-such, which has a certain code number and a certain code name, and also telephone connections. They can also observe aircraft. But I'm convinced that they can get a foothold there.'[1]

Toulon was an uncomfortable posting for submarine crews. Its unprotected docks left their boats vulnerable to the constant procession of air raids, one of which on 24th November 1943 had toppled a crane and caused enough damage to delay Deckert's last departure. Port facilities were so badly knocked about that their time ashore was barely more comfortable than on patrol. U-73 and U-593 survivors, among others, spoke of plans to move the force to new fortified bunkers being built at Marseilles.

'N 2182 [*Leutnant zur See* Kurt Heinemann, U-593]:
MARSEILLES is going to be set up as a base. I don't know exactly when that's going to be.'[2]

This was disturbing. The RAF had missed the chance to destroy pens on the French Atlantic coast while they were being built and they had since proved impervious to attack. No-one was about to make that mistake again. A stool pigeon chatting with a U-450 survivor rescued on 10th March 1944 asked:

'N 1878: *I thought you were to be transferred down to MARSEILLES?*
N 2344: *That's what they wanted, too. The shelters at MARSEILLES were to be ready by 1945 and they probably stuck up notices about that all over the place and one of these notices, of course, got to the 'HQ of the Royal Army Air Force'. Whereupon they dropped a whole day's production of bombs on the whole works.*

As a result, the plan to have the shelters ready by the spring of 1945 was immediately ditched again.[3]

After this the US Fifteenth Air Force bombed Marseilles on 27th May in a raid that killed more than 1,800 French civilians, the single most costly of the war for the local population. Allied landings under the codename Operation *Dragoon* began on 15th August, Toulon and Marseilles fell on 26th and 28th respectively. The U-boat pens at Marseilles were never completed.

Norway

One of Hitler's obsessions was a possible Allied attempt to retake Norway. It was a conversational highlight for *Scharnhorst* survivors *Steursmannsgefreiter* (Navigator's Yeoman) Wilhelm Kruse (N2141) and *Matrosengefreiter* (Ordinary Seaman) Rudi Birke (N2142).

'N 2142:   ...*If the English intend to land in NORWAY I can't promise then any rosy future. They are particularly interested in NORWAY. What I told him (IO) about the 38 cm guns is not true. They are not there at all.*
N 2141:   *I am sure that ADOLF intends holding NORWAY. Otherwise they wouldn't have fortified it so strongly.*'[4]

CSDIC staff knew no more than their subjects about Operation *Overlord*, the increasingly imminent Normandy landings, and so kept probing. *Scharnhorst* crewmen were a fruitful source. For example, Birke went on to boast about a fortified farm near the ship's anchorage.

'N 2142:   (re Battery near SOPNES): *Then he (IO) asked me again whether there is another 'Batterie' as well. They (the English) will soon see, when firing starts from all sides.*'[5]

Similarly *Obergefreiter* Martin Wallek and *Matrosenobergefreiter* Willi Alsen discussed the Norwegian fortifications at length.[6]

This was all to the good. Guns and troops tied up there were effectively out of the game until they performed a 'scorched earth' retreat from the Finnmark at the end of the war.

Northern France

The rapidly strengthening defences of the Channel and North Sea coasts were a different matter. Since August 1943 there had been a call for knowledgeable captives with previous postings on the French coast to be passed back to the UK for in-depth interrogation.

'Hellfire Corner' of Kent had long been subject to shelling from enormous gun emplacements on the Pas de Calais. This was not news, but any extra information was always welcome. This was provided by *Matrosenobergefreiter* Kurt Close of U-73.

'N 2157:   *The railway guns on the French coast load automatically. Everything works automatically and they've been set up all over the place. Firstly they fire a great distance and then the ammunition has tremendous explosive power. They used them at SEBASTOPOL; it's an enormous gun, you can move them around on two lines but when you want to fire them you have to set them on four lines. They are those huge railway guns. We have got railway guns which stand on a single line, but this gun has to be assembled. When it is travelling, when you want to move them around you do it on two lines but when you want to fire it then you have to use four lines. Nowadays they are not only used as railway guns, they have also been built into emplacements and those are the enormous guns you sometimes see at the cinema. The fortifications are not near PARIS at all, but on the coast. If the Allies want to get to GERMANY then they must first break through the belt of fortifications on the coast and then the belt of fortifications along the 'West Wall'.*'[7]

Prelude to *Götterdämmerung*

A U-340 crewman described the impressive defences of Brest to *Obermechanikersmaat* Hünert of U-593.

> '*N 1980: How the cliffs on the ATLANTIC WALL were fortified! If anyone tries to attack it, he will pay for it with his life. In that part where we were stationed, they would be shot down to the last man. No-one can get in there. If it is fortified everywhere as heavily as it is near BREST, then it's lilies for them! They've got a hard nut to crack, if they want to get in there.*
>
> *Men who had fought in AFRICA arrived at BREST. All the tanks belonging to the Afrikakorps are around ST. NAZAIRE; they are all distributed about the district. There must be some reason for concentrating everything like that. They are concentrating everything there and waiting for the enemy to come.*
>
> *N 2048: My opinion is that the English won't give us any peace until they have seen that they can't gain a foothold on the mainland of EUROPE. When they realise that they are being thrown out everywhere, then they will leave us in peace.*'[8]

Despite the wall of steel facing outward and intermittent sabotage in the occupied territories (see International Relations above) base security could be astonishingly lax. *Oberleutnant zur See* Cordt von Kalckreuth of T-25 let slip the following:

> '*A Leutnant was once sent to ST NAZAIRE on a security mission to check up …… He arrived wearing an overcoat with two stars on it, making him a Kapitänleutnant. His tunic underneath was that of a Leutnant. He arrived without identity card or pay book. He made himself a sort of pass, on a piece of crumpled blue paper, and wrote on it: "Kapitänleutnant so-and-so is permitted to go everywhere, Admiralty," and some sort of signature and then what looked like the imprint of some sort of stamp. He went up to the sentry …… was allowed through at once. He visited absolutely everything. He went inside the torpedo depot, where all the torpedo heads were lying …… Then he got one of the officials to explain the whole thing to him, the main switchboard …… then he laid a whole lot of explosive charges*

and everything. No one noticed anything. Then he changed and went back to the sentry – where one hour before he had gone through – and asked whether a Kapitänleutnant had just gone in and was told "Yes" ...... and then there was a tremendous to-do about it.

An administrative officer was sent to a U-boat base in BREST, to the secret registry of the Flotilla in order to ...... a very secret plan. No one was allowed to know anything about it, only a Flottillenchef and a few Kommandanten. He arrived as an administrative officer: when he wanted the documents they said they weren't allowed to part with them ...... long discussion ...... he stole the documents and went off with them under his arm. Now it's all tightened up; when a ship puts in and ties up near the U-boat shelters there and you go ashore, the sentries check the ...... immediately.'[9]

St Nazaire had been subject to a daring and successful raid in March 1942, which disabled the only battleship-sized dry-dock on the French Atlantic coast. The catastrophic Dieppe raid the following August had however convinced allied planners there was no point trying to take an existing port from the sea. For their part, in the mounting invasion fever the Germans did not intend to be caught again.

This stool pigeon report stressed the level of nerves running at St Nazaire, and gave more information about the extent to which the already bomb-proof U-boat shelters had been fortified.

'N 2261 [Mechanikerobergefreiter Karl Heinz Stadtler, U-264] states that:-
Invasion fever is rife in ST. NAZAIRE and elsewhere. PW had been in LA PALLICE when two British cruisers were announced. All U-boats were immediately ordered to be got ready to sail and even boats which were not in a condition to dive were equipped with torpedoes. Instructions were given that all boats must go out and fight. Defences of the harbour and U-boat shelters largely rests with the workmen who are being trained as soldiers, and use of MGs is

Prelude to *Götterdämmerung*

included in their course. Shelters in ST. NAZAIRE have been strengthened by the addition of turrets taken from French tanks, of which one has been built in at each corner of the shelters and a larger one on top. All the quadruple 2 cm. guns removed from U-boats have been mounted on the roofs of the shelters. When the shelters' doors are shut, they form casemates for 37 mm and 20 mm guns and also type 81 MGs. Two erections have been built, one on either side of the shelters as forts with protection consisting of two 3" steel plates supported by 6" of concrete. The telephone exchange has been built into one of the shelters.

Security exercises have been carried out recently in the shelters and on several occasions the officers taking part have been able to reach their objectives in the U-boats. As a result security measures in ST. NAZAIRE have now been made much stricter.

Army regiments in ST. NAZAIRE consist chiefly of Dutch, Cossack and Indian troops, with practically no Germans at all. There is continual brawling going on between these foreign troops and the German Naval Personnel.'[10]

Inevitably, when it came to facing the actual landings, Plan A involved a Wagnerian death-ride.

'N 2199 [Oberleutnant (Ing) Heinz Weitz, U-406] states that:- Standing orders in the event of invasion are that all U-boats which can should go out and fight. Those that cannot should remain in their shelters with a large enough crew to deal with scuttling charges etc. The remainder of the crew will be turned into troops for land defence.'

Another crewman from the same boat gave the impression of order, counter-order, disorder:

'N 2200 [Maschinenobergefreiter Herbert Breuker] has given the following information in addition to that given in C.S.D.I.C. (U.K.) Report S.R.N.2931.

The following procedure in case of invasion has been made to U-boat personnel everywhere:

Seaworthy U-boats in harbour to be manned immediately and endeavour to make their way to another unattacked base. They are not to attack the invasion fleet unless they receive specific orders. All U-boats in shelters which cannot be moved owing to damage to be blown up.

Personel [sic] *to report at once to base and if unable to man outgoing U-boats to be drafted to the interior and not to bear arms repelling invaders.'*[11]

Matrosengefreiter Wolfgang Blumenberg of U-386, captured in February 1944, may have felt that a submarine crewman's lot, however short his life expectancy, was better that that of the 'poor bloody infantry' in the face of the expected onslaught.

'*N 2189 states that:-*

St Nazaire

It was previously intended that in case of invasion U-boats' crews were to be taken away from the base in a motor bus, which had been placed at their disposal. This order has now been changed and U-boat personnel will be issued with green infantry uniforms, rifles and hand grenades, and are to fight as infantry.'[12]

He and two of his companions believed that ordinary operational U-boats would not be used between Cherbourg and Rotterdam but small 'Walter' boats would be sent to French bases by road or rail to engage the invasion fleet.[13] He worked as a stool pigeon almost to the end of the war.

In contrast to U-boat crews' hair-trigger readiness the Biscay torpedo-boat flotillas seemed to live in a bubble of denial. Günter Schramm, chatting with seasoned stool pigeon A713, drew a picture of startling fatalism.

'N 2074:   *Two months ago WESERMÜNDE was made our home port. We were supposed to go there in July, I believe, for a refit.*
A 713:   *The invasion will have started long before July. Have you been preparing for the invasion in any way?*
N 2074:   *Not at all.*

Prelude to *Götterdämmerung*

A 713: No naval preparations as far as you are concerned?
N 2074: None at all.
A 713: You didn't carry out any exercises?
N 2074: Absolutely nothing, we never thought of it!
A 713: Didn't you do any invasion exercises at all?
N 2074: What exercises can you do on board!
A 713: Didn't you do any landing exercises?
N 2074: We did one landing exercise, but it had nothing to do with any invasion.
A 713: Didn't you have any orders what you were to do in the event of invasion taking place?
N 2074: Nothing at all!'[14]

As ever, *Scharnhorst's* crew had the most positive take on the situation.

'? *N 2166* [*Maschinenhauptgefreiter* Rolf Zanger]: *If they come with battleships and that sort of thing, with heavy long-range (?) artillery and that sort of thing, I certainly think that they will get through. They may have heavy losses, but they will get there; but they will be thrown out again.*'[15]

On the afternoon of D-Day, with Allied troops already pouring into the beachheads, thirty-five U-boats left their Brittany bases with orders to attack the cross-Channel supply routes regardless of risk. They met an impenetrable wall of anti-submarine ships and aircraft. Just five returned for a net score of two frigates between them. U-boats based in the Channel ports had a little more success but the *Kriegsmarine* was increasingly forced to resort to near suicidal missions by 'small battle units:' human torpedoes, one- or two-man submarines and motor boats.

---

[1] TNA WO 208/4150; *Interrogation Reports on German Prisoners of War 3051-3359*. SRN 3163 dated 20th March 1944.

[2] TNA WO 208/4149; *Interrogation Reports on German Prisoners of War 2700-3050*. SRN 2900 dated 6th February 1944.

[3] TNA WO 208/4151; *Interrogation Reports on German Prisoners of War 3360-3650*. SRN 3364 dated 14th April 1944.
[4] TNA WO 208/4149; *Interrogation Reports on German Prisoners of War 2700-3050*. SRN 2732 dated 10th January 1944.
[5] ibid. SRN 2913 dated 10th February 1944.
[6] ibid. SRN 2707 dated 9th January 1944.
[7] ibid. SRN 2742 dated 13th January 1944.
[8] TNA WO 208/4148; *Interrogation Reports on German Prisoners of War 2451-2699*. SRN 2544 dated 25th December 1943.
[9] *TNA WO 208/4149; Interrogation Reports on German Prisoners of War 2700-3050*. SRN 2730 dated 12th January 1944.
[10] TNA WO 208/4196; *Interrogation Reports on German and Italian Prisoners of War SP/F 1-142*. SP/F/136 dated 18th March 1944.
[11] ibid. SP/F/133 and SP/F/132 dated 10th March 1944.
[12] ibid. SP/F/137 dated 1st April 1944.
[13] ibid. SP/F/138 dated 8th April 1944.
[14] TNA WO 208/4163; *Interrogation Reports on German Prisoners of War 1731-1949*. SRN 1901 dated 11th January 1944.
[15] TNA WO 208/4149; *Interrogation Reports on German Prisoners of War 2700-3050*. SRN 2740 dated 14th January 1944.

Conclusion

Early 1944 saw both the ultimate development and the last hurrah of the CSDIC model hastily set up at the start of the war. The three legs of the service – direct interrogation, microphones and stool pigeons – supported each other in a finely-tuned system running a model of inter-service co-operation completely alien to the fascist dictatorships they opposed.

A key goal for the interrogators up to the period we have examined was to understand enemy engineering advances in an increasingly technology-led war and pre-empt any nasty surprises. This they largely achieved, though often struggling to interpret the mangled half-knowledge of their subjects and shake their customers' disbelief. The belief that 'If we can't do it they can't either' was rudely shaken more than once.

The T4 and T5 homing torpedoes, for instance, were the result of a programme started in the mid 'thirties, building on electrical propulsion development that never stopped after 1918, and involving thousands of test firings. British and American technology stood no chance of catching up until years after the war, though tactical and technical counter-measures were rapidly deployed.

Other ideas such as the *schnorkel* and even more advanced torpedo concepts had been left on the shelf in the expectation that they would be too late for use in a short war. By the time they were dusted off in desperation they served only to distract and dilute the engineering effort available.

Seemingly trivial gossip was anything but. It fed the interrogators' act, the impression of omniscience which was their most powerful weapon. It helped keep the bleary-eyed troglodytes of Operational Intelligence Centre and the Submarine Tracking Room up to date on who had which boat, where they were and what they were doing (if they were still alive). Not least, it and the psychologists' efforts helped focus and give weight to the sustained propaganda effort directed at German citizens at home and in captivity, and to lever open the cracks appearing in the Axis alliance and the 'Thousand-Year Reich.'

Sadly, some of the lessons there to be learnt, such as the counter-productive effect of the 'unconditional surrender' declaration and of the bombing campaign on civilian morale, seem to have been missed or ignored.

Other authors have looked in much more detail at the light cast on the Holocaust and other atrocities by prisoners' unguarded conversations. It would be futile to repeat their work but wrong to pass by without mentioning the much wider knowledge of and participation in these activities than some post-war mythmaking would have us believe.

The garbled, conflicting rumours coming through just a few months before the start of the V1 assault arouse sympathy for the 'Crossbow' intelligence analysts trying to make sense of the whole thing.

D-Day, the long-awaited second front, was also at the forefront of both sides' thinking. News of the resources poured into the fortification of Norway must have provoked a chuckle from those in the know, the constant strengthening of the Atlantic Wall in France less so. The strategic choice to land over beaches and bring temporary harbours along avoided the need to attack fortress-ports frontally but created a logistics headache for allied armies until Antwerp opened for business in November 1944. Although Dieppe and Calais surrendered relatively willingly Boulogne and Le Havre took a lot of work,

Conclusion

and St Nazaire lasted almost to the end. All needed a lot of repair and clearance before they could be used.

Although many of the German crews themselves seemed confused about what was expected of them the emerging picture of naval opposition to the landings was that U-boats and perhaps the remaining surface ships would try to interfere from Biscay ports while the Channel itself was left to light forces. In the event a wall of steel across the Western Approaches made that a futile hope.

The surge of naval prisoners in January 1944 stressed the CSDIC system to its limit and may well have highlighted the need for redesign to cope with the massively increased flow of captives expected after D-Day. The expanded process envisaged a much larger role for preliminary interrogation at the Command Cages.

Moreover, there had already been talk of stripping experienced staff from CSDIC to mobilise the forward intelligence units needed for liberation and occupation. This only increased in volume and urgency.

Finally, the capture of intact equipment and documents was a rare treat before the landings but increasingly common afterward. This with the change in naval focus from blue water to coastal combat changed the nature of intelligence required.

In parallel Naval Intelligence was preparing the initial target list for Assault Unit 30. This composite band of intelligence technical officers with Royal Marine Commandos providing muscle and a Forward Interrogation Unit team integrated for the relationship aspects was the brainchild of Ian Fleming, and was briefed to go with (or sometimes ahead of) front line troops and grab anything or anyone of naval intelligence interest. It is very likely that prisoners' off-the-cuff comments about their home ports provided some of the information for that target list.

Perhaps Commodore Rushbrooke, DNI, should have the final word in his parting tribute when Lieutenant-Commander Cope moved on to his next posting:

'During five years of war the interrogation of prisoners of war has been developed from an incidental source of Intelligence to one of unique value; the Royal Navy and other Services have become reliant upon it; and this result is largely due to the persistent and imaginative effort of yourself and your team at Cockfosters and Latimer.'[1]

---

[1] Original document in the author's possession.

Appendix A – Eavesdropping Timeline

The chart on the next page plots the frequency of 'M' Room intercepts (ovals), intelligence mentions in weekly reports (triangles) and formal reports issued (stars) for the five vessels we have focussed on.

The heavy concentration of marks against *Scharnhorst* and T-25 may reflect a particularly strong effort prompted by the unusual capture of crewmen from large surface warships. On the other hand it may partly be explained by U-boat crews' better security awareness. The relatively low level of apparent interest in *Alsterufer* is surprising, though perhaps by the end of January they had nothing left to add to the story of the few blockade-runners left at sea.

U-593 first features in weekly reports before the advance party's likely arrival in the UK, so this must be based on information gleaned from CSDIC Middle East.

31 out of 71 *Alsterufer* survivors, seven from 36 *Scharnhorst*, 41 of 61 from T-25, 34 from 48 U-593 and 19 from 32 U-73 crew were shipped to Canada on 5th February 1944 aboard the liner SS *Île de France* with convoy TA87, arriving Halifax on 12th. Most or all would have been transferred to their temporary holding camps by 20th January.

T-25 continued featuring in weekly summaries until 25th March, entirely owing to the continued co-operation of Günther Schramm.

Formal reports on T-25, U-73 and U-593 were issued in February 1944, *Alsterufer* in March, and *Scharnhorst* in April.[1]

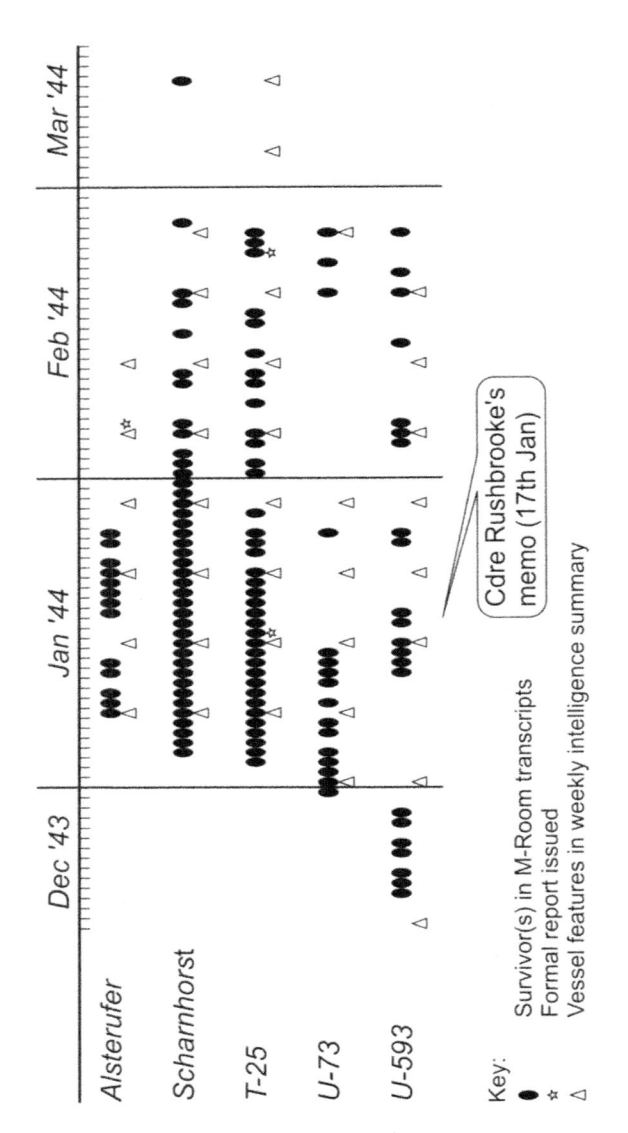

Figure 14: Eavesdropping and Reporting Timeline.

---

[1] TNA ADM 223/809; *Interrogation of German naval survivors*.

APPENDIX B – *SCHARNHORST* SURVIVORS' INTERROGATION ABOARD *DUKE OF YORK*

Commander (N) E H Thomas DSC & Bar was the SO(I) aboard Duke of York. Survivors were interviewed by a 'young doctor,' the only officer who spoke German. This was most likely Temporary Surgeon Lieutenant D C Galloway MB CLM. The interrogation report was signed off by RNVR Temporary Lieutenant (Special Branch) William Walker Stevenson, a junior gunnery officer.

★ ★ ★

SECRET

APPENDIX IX

SUMMARY OF INTELLIGENCE OBTAINED FROM PRISONERS AND NOT ALREADY INCLUDED IN THE DESPATCH.

The following main points of interest concerning the action which have not already been included in the despatch were obtained from the 36 prisoners during their preliminary interrogations onboard DUKE OF YORK and in the United Kingdom. The most senior survivor was of the equivalent rating of Acting Petty Officer.

(i) The morale of the prisoners was high. Interrogation was difficult, owing to their security consciousness and the fact that all but four were between decks where they saw little of the action and were unable to distinguish between the explosion of torpedoes, the impact of heavy shells and the concussion of their own guns.

(ii) "Scharnhorst" had left Langfiord at 1900 on 25th December with the destroyers Z.28, Z.31 and Z.34 in company.

(iii) "Scharnhorst" flew the flag of Rear Admiral Bey, Admiral Commanding Destroyers, who was taking the place of Admiral Kummetz, away on leave. The Admiral and his staff of 30 joined just before the ship left Langfiord. He was not well known to the Ship's Company.

(iv) "Scharnhorst's" Captain was Hintz *[sic]*, formerly Captain of the "Leipzig", who took over command in October from Captain Hoffmeier. This was his first operational sortie in the ship. He seems to have been popular onboard but was criticised by all survivors for his handling of the ship.

(v) She carried 40 cadets onboard who were under training.

(vi) Her normal complement was 1,903 officers and men.

(vii) It was stated that she could attain a maximum speed of 33 knots.

(viii) She carried three above water torpedo tubes each side but did not fire them during the action.

(ix) She carried three Arado aircraft on this occasion, two in the hangar abaft the funnel and one on the catapult. None of them was used and all were destroyed when a shell hit the hangar during the second engagement with the DUKE OP YORK.

(x) Prisoners state that she was designed to withstand 14 torpedo hits without being sunk. They ascribed her loss to the fact that nearly all the torpedo hits (they believed 8 in all) were on the starboard tide. (N.B. The probable

Appendix "B"

hits are assessed as 6 port side, 5 starboard side.) They were also emphatic that she was sunk by torpedoes and that DUKE OF YORK would never have sunk her by gunfire.

(xi) The following ten hits during the second engagement with DUKE OF YORK were confirmed, although their order is unknown :-

    (a) On the forward port 150 mm twin turret, putting the gun and ammunition hoist out of action.

    (b) On the aircraft hangar, destroying both planes and causing a fierce fire which was apparently put out in ten minutes.

    (c) On the forward 105 mm. mounting on the starboard side.

    (d) On the starboard side near the funnel,

    (e) In the tween deck on the port side in compartment 10.

    (f) In the battery deck on the port side in compartment 9.

    (g) On the forward starboard 150 mm. turret, immediately before the final torpedo attack.

    (h) On the starboard after single 150 mm. gun.

    (i) On one quadruple 20 mm. mounting on the starboard side which flew through the air and crashed on the deck.

    (j) A hit somewhere on 'B' turret causing the ventilation system to fail and the turret to fill with smoke every time the breeches were opened.

(xii) Survivors insist that no shells penetrated the armoured deck, though a large number penetrated the decks above it and exploded on contact with the armour causing great havoc and many casualties.

(xiii) Abandon ship drill was apparently rudimentary and none of the survivors seems to have had an abandon ship station. Lifebelts were apparently not worn and were only put on if they could be found at the last moment.

Appendix C – Contents of NID U-boat Compendium, June 1944

This book has been prepared from interrogation of survivors and other information available to N.I.D. as a handbook on the types, equipment and habits of German U-boats. It is designed to be a convenient manual for easy reference by those who are continually reviewing U-boat information; and to give a conspectus of the subject for the benefit of those who have not had access to the volume of material that has accumulated during the war.[*]

2. It summarizes basic information on U-boats contained in the C.B. 04051 series.

3. Every effort has been made to make it as accurate and balanced as possible. It is emphasized, however, that it does not claim to be exhaustive or definitive, and it does not supersede technical and other Admiralty publications on the subject.

4. U-boat design, equipment and habits are continually changing, and this summary, which has been written historically, does not necessarily give information on the current situation.

5. Statements are graded, where possible, according to the system described on the back page of every W.I.R.

6. The Secret nature of this summary should be carefully preserved.

---

[*] The full text of the report is available online at www.uboatarchive.net/CumulativeEdition.htm.

CONTENTS
CHAPTER
- I.— U-BOAT TYPES AND SPECIFICATIONS.
- II.— U-BOAT GUN ARMAMENT.
- III.— STANDARD U-BOAT EQUIPMENT.
- IV.— DIVING.
- V.— WORKING UP AND PREPARING FOR SEA.
- VI.— FIRST OPERATIONAL PATROL.
- VII.— DURATION OF PATROL—TIME IN HARBOUR.
- VIII.— ROUTINE IN HARBOUR.
- IX.— SAILING AND PASSAGE TO PATROL AREA.
- X.— LOOK-OUT ROUTINE.
- XI.— U-BOAT STRATEGY AND TACTICS
- XII.— U-BOAT ORGANISATION.
- XIII.— U-BOAT BASES IN GERMANY AND OCCUPIED COUNTRIES.
- XIV.— GERMAN U-BOAT TORPEDOES AND MINES.
- XV.— TRAINING FOR THE U-BOAT SERVICE IN THE GERMAN NAVY.
- XVI.— U-BOAT BUILDING YARDS.
- APPENDIX.—ELEMENTARY NOTES ON U-BOATS.

Chapter I.—U-BOAT TYPES AND GENERAL SPECIFICATIONS.
(i) Summary of U-boat types and foreign submarines in German Service 1
(ii) General 1
(iii) Type I 2
(iv) Type II A, B, C, D 7
(v) Type VIIB, C 8
(vi) Type VII C/42 9

Appendix "C"

(vii) Type VIID 9
(viii) Type VIIF 10
(ix) Type IX C 11
(x) Type IX D 11
(xi) Type IX D2 12
(xii) Type X B 13
(xiii) TypeXIV 14
(xiv) Recent U-boat Building Developments 15

Chapter II.—U-BOAT GUN ARMAMENT.
(i) Types of gun fitted 16
(ii) Arrangements of armament 16
(iii) Flak U-boats 18
(iv) Performance and Ammunition 18
(v) Armour 19
(vi) Rocket projectors 19
(vii) Triple Bandstands 19
(viii) 3 mm. gun 19

Chapter III.—STANDARD U-BOAT EQUIPMENT.
SECTION I.—Propulsion.
(i) Diesel Engines 20
    (a) Types and manufacturers 20
    (b) Superchargers 20
    (c) Short bursts of high speed on the surface 20
    (d) Speeds when surfaced 20
(ii) Electric motors 20
    (a) Manufacturers 20
    (b) Details 20
    (c) Speeds submerged 21
(iii) Switchboards 21
(iv) Batteries 21
(v) Schnorkel (Extensible Exhaust and Air-intake) .. 21
(vi) Single-unit propulsion in U-boats 21
SECTION II.—German U-boat communications.

(i) Anglo-German equivalent wave ranges 22
(ii) W/T Equipment 22
    (a) W/T Transmission 22
    (b) W/T Reception 22
(iii) Manufacturers 22
(iv) Arrangement of sets 22
    (a) General 22
    (b) Contents of cabin 1 22
    (c) Contents of cabin 2 22
    (d) Miscellaneous 22
    (e) Diagram 23
(v) Operational performance 23
    (a) HF/WT 23
    (b) VL/F 23
(vi) Intercommunication between U-boats 23
    (a) General 23
    (b) Funkschlüssel gespräch 23
    (c) M/F Beacon Signals 23
    (d) D/F 23
    (e) S/T 23
    (f) VH/F 24
    (g) V.S 24
    (h) Infra-Red 24
(vii) Aerials 24
    (a) W/T 24
    (b) D/F 24
    (c) VH/F 24
(viii) Manning 24
(ix) Interception of Allied Communications 24
(x) Trend of Development 24
SECTION III.—Radar.
(i) Use of Radar 25
(ii) Radar set types 25

Appendix "C"

(iii) Aerial Arrays 25
(iv) Azimuth Accuracy 25
(v) Range of sets 23
    (a) Gema 25
    (b) Seetakt Hohentwiel 25
SECTION IV. — G.S.R. (German Search Receiver).
(i) Purpose 26
(ii) Types 26
    (a) Rohde and Schwarz 26
    (b) Metox R600 26
    (c) Wanz 26
    (d) Wanz II 26
    (e) Borkum 26
    (f) Naxos 26
    (g) Manufacturers 26
(iii) G.S.R. Aerials 27
    (a) Southern Cross Type 27
    (b) Drum type Aerial 27
    (c) Figure and Aerial 27
    (d) Naxos 27
(iv) G.S.R. Watch 27
(v) Range of G.S.R. 27
(vi) Recent Developments 27
SECTION V.—Miscellaneous.
(i) Decoys 28
    (a) Radar Decoy Balloons 28
    (b) Radar Decoy Spar-buoy 28
    (c) Submarine bubble target 28
(ii) Echo Sounder 29
(iii) Elektrolot 29
(iv) Welding equipment 29
(v) Hydrophones 29
    (a) G.H.G. 29

(b) K.D.B 29
(vi) German Asdic 29
   (a) U.S.G. 29
   (b) A.E.G. 29
(vii) Collapsible look-out masts 29
(viii) Rotor-Kite 29
(ix) Aircraft 30
(x) Paint and Camouflage 30
(xi) Air Purification 30
(xii) Scuttling Charges 30
(xiii) Booby Traps 30
(xiv) Compasses 31
(xv) Gyro Sextant 31
(xvi) Depth charge plotting gear 31
(xvii) Buoys 31
   (a) Shadowers Pyrotechnic Buoys 31
   (b) Aircraft Beaconing Buoy 31
   (c) Meteorological Buoy 31
(xviii) Electric Distillers 31
(xix) Bathythermograph and thermometer 31
(xx) Voigt Schneider auxiliary propellor 31

Chapter IV.—DIVING.
(i) Diving Depths 32
(ii) Crash Diving Times 32
(iii) Diving Angles 32
(iv) References 32

Chapter V.—WORKING UP AND PREPARING FOR SEA.
(i) Building and fitting out 33
(ii) Commissioning 33
(iii) Acceptance Trials 33
(iv) Wiping 33
(v) Silent running Tests 33
(vi) U-boats Ausbildungs Gruppe 33

Appendix "C"

(vii) Torpedo Firing Trials 33
(viii) Agru-Front 34
(ix) Commanding Officers Torpedo-firing 34
(x) Gunnery exercises 34
(xi) Tactical exercises 34
(xii) Independent exercising 34
(xiii) Theoretical Tactical Training 34
(xiv) Final overhaul 34
(xv) Preparations for first patrol 34

Chapter VI.—FIRST OPERATIONAL PATROL.
(i) Departure 35
(ii) Escort 35
(iii) Kiel to Norway 35
(iv) At Kristiansand S. 35
(v) Departure from Kristiansand S. 35
(vi) Course up Norwegian Coast into Atlantic 35
(vii) Passage of "Rosengarten" 35
(viii) In Atlantic 35
(ix) Return to Base 35
(x) Arctic Patrols 35

Chapter VII. — DURATION OF PATROL—
TIME IN HARBOUR 36

Chapter VIII. — ROUTINE IN HARBOUR.
(i) Arrival from Patrol 37
(ii) Entry into Shelters 37
(iii) Guard Routine, Accommodation and Leave 37
(iv) Medical Examination 37
(v) Refits 37
(vi) Overhaul at Base 37
(vii) Authorities on Shore 37
(viii) Preparations for Patrol 37

Chapter IX. — SAILING AND PASSAGE TO PATROL AREA.

(i) Escorts leaving Harbour 38
(ii) Diving Policy 38
(iii) Speed on passage 38
(iv) Supplies for U-boats at sea 38
    (a) Supply U-boats 38
    (b) Another operational U-boat 38
    (c) Surface ships 38
    (d) From shore 38
    (e) Present day situation 38

Chapter X. — LOOK-OUT ROUTINE.
(i) Watches 39
(ii) Bridge Watch Routine 39
    (a) Cruising watches 39
    (b) Dangerous areas 39
    (c) Shadowing for attack 39
    (d) Responsibilities of look-outs 39
(iii) Crash-diving 39
(iv) Binoculars 39
(v) Anti-Dazzle Glasses 39

Chapter XI. — U-BOAT STRATEGY AND TACTICS
(i) Types of Operation 40
(ii) Attacks on convoys 40
    (a) Detection 40
    (b) Procedure on detection 40
    (c) Duties of contact-keepers 40
    (d) The attack 40
(iii) Attacking positions in general 41
    (a) Tactics 41
    (b) Direction of Attack 41
(iv) The abandonment of Pack attacks on convoys
    in summer 1943 41
(v) Attacks on distant areas 41
(vi) Intercommunication between attacks 41

Appendix "C"

(vii) Tactics against surface craft 41
    (a) When attacked in daylight 41
    (b) When attacked at night 41
    (c) Asdics 41
    (d) Covering other U-boats 41
    (e) U-boat Countermeasures 41
(viii) Tactics against aircraft 41
    (a) General 41
    (b) Previous tactics 42
    (c) Present tactics 42
    (d) Use of armament 42
    (e) Detection 42
(ix) Deception 42
    (a) (i) S.B.T. 42
        (ii) R.D.B. 42
        (iii) R.D.S. 42
    (b) (i) Oil charges 42
        (ii) Dummy H.E. 42
        (iii) Wreckage 42
(xi) U-boats as escorts 42
(xii) Trend of U-boat offensive 42

Chapter XII. — U-BOAT ORGANISATION.
(i) Organisation 43
(ii) Flotillas 43
(iii) Flotilla Badges 43

Chapter XIII. — U-BOAT BASES IN GERMANY, OCCUPIED AND AXIS COUNTRIES.
(i) Germany 44
    (a) North Sea 44
    (b) Baltic 44
(ii) France 45
    (a) Operational Bases 45
    (b) Potential Bases 47

(c) Potential Bases for small U-boats 47
(iii) Norway 47
    (a) Operational Bases 47
    (b) Subsidiary Bases 48
    (c) Possible Bases 48
(iv) Holland } Potential Bases 49
(v) Belgium   }
(vi) Italy—Operational Bases 49
(vii) Greece 49
(viii) Far East 49

Chapter XIV. — GERMAN U-BOAT TORPEDOES AND MINES.

(A) Torpedoes:
(i) Introductory 50
(ii) "Gnat" Torpedo 50
(iii) 21" Electric Torpedo 51
(iv) Improved Electric Torpedo 51
(v) 21" Air Torpedo 51
(vi) "Curly" 52
(vii) "Fat 1" 52
(viii) "Fat 2" 52
(ix) "Lut" 52
(x) Pistols 53
(xi) General information on U-boat Torpedoes and Mines ... 53
(xii) Torpedo Tubes 53

(B) Mines:
(i) Torpedo mines 53
(ii) Type "GO" mines 53

Chapter XV. — TRAINING FOR THE U-BOAT SERVICE IN THE GERMAN NAVY.

(i) General Remarks 54
(ii) Training for Commissioned rank 54
    (a) New Entry Training 54

Appendix "C"

  (b) Initial Sea-time 54
  (c) General Naval Training Course 54
  (d) Second Sea-time 54
(iii) Provision of U-boat Officers 54
  (a) General 54
  (b) Training of U-boat Commanding Officers 54
  (c) U-boat Schools 55
  (d) U-boat Torpedo firing course 55
  (e) Convoy attack teacher for Commanding Officers 55
  (f) U-boat Torpedo firing flotilla 55
  (g) U-boat Commanders training course 55
(iv) Training of New Entries 55
  (a) General 55
  (b) Manning Depots 55
    (i) Germany 55
    (ii) Belgium 56
    (iii) Holland 56
    (iv) France 56
  (c) Drafting Depots 56
(v) Specialised Training 56
  (a) Telegraphists 56
  (b) Signalmen 56
  (c) Stokers 56
  (d) Torpedo ratings 56
  (e) U-boat personnel 56
(vi) Training of Petty Officers 56
  (a) Seaman Petty Officers 56
  (b) Petty Officer Telegraphists 56
  (c) Stoker Petty Officers 56
  (d) Torpedo Gunners Mates 56
  (e) Schools 56
(vii) Training of Chief Petty Officers 56
  (a) Torpedo and Telegraphist P.O's

  (b) Chief Stoker Petty Officers 56
(viii) Special Courses 57
  (a) Gunnery 57
  (b) Gunnery Schools 57
  (c) Divers Course 57
  (d) Mining Course 57
  (e) Torpedo recovery 57
  (f) Torpedo control 57
  (g) Radar and G.S.R. Operators 57
  (h) Hydrophone Listening 57
  (i) Electric Welders 57
  (j) Navigation 57
  (k) Ships Cooks 57
  (l) Sick Bay Attendants 57
Chapter XVI. — U-BOAT BUILDING YARDS.
(i) Hamburg 58
  (a) Blohm and Voss 58
  (b) Deutche Werft, Finkenwärder 58
  (c) Howaltswerke A.G 58
  (d) Stülkenwerft 59
(ii) Kiel 59
  (a) Germania 59
  (b) Deutsche Werke 59
  (c) Howaltswerke A.G 59
(iii) Danzig 59
  (a) Schichau 59
  (b) Danziger Werft 59
(iv) Bremen and Vegesack 59
  (a) Deschimag Bremen 59
  (b) Vulkan Vegesack 59
(v) Lübeck 60
  Flenderwerke 60
(vi) Wilhelmshaven 60

Appendix "C"

Marinewerft 60
(vii) Flensburg 60
    Schiffbau 60
(viii) Emden 60
    Nordseewerke 60
(ix) Rostock 60
    Neptune 60
(x) Bremerhaven 60
    Deschimag (Seebeck) 60
    (a) Slips in Industrie Haven 60
    (b) Dry docks 60
    (c) Nord Deutsche Werft 60
(xi) Stettin 60
    (a) Stettiner Oderwerke A.G. 60
    (b) Stettiner Vulkanwerke 60
Appendix. — ELEMENTARY NOTES ON U-BOATS.
(i) Construction 61
(ii) Fuel tanks 61
(iii) Periscopes 61
(iv) Machinery 62
(v) Seaworthiness 62
(vi) Effect of machine-gun fire 62
(vii) Diving 62

APPENDIX D – STOOL PIGEONS

Extracted from WO 208/4970; *The story of MI19* at the National Archives, Kew.

★ ★ ★
S.P. Control and P/W Welfare Section

The refugee S.Ps. described below were paid out of a Special Fund provided by D.D.M.I.(P/W) and they were also in receipt of family allowance on the same scale as 'other ranks' in the British Army – the I.O. Welfare Officer whose duty it was to look after them saw to their pay and allowances and maintained constant touch with them in order to prevent ennui, a danger ever-present after long spells of nerve-racking communion with prisoners, to whom in the large majority they harboured intense dislike, if not hatred.

The Welfare Officer's policy vis-a-vis Ps/W was to disassociate himself completely from the Interrogating Officers and the Intelligence aspects of the camp generally. This proved to be sound as it quickly spread and was believed, with the result that Ps/W often confided in him seeking his sympathy. This enabled the Welfare Officer to exercise subtle persuasion which often resulted in facilitating the work of the Interrogating Officers. There are a number of noteworthy instances of tough and fractious Ps/W becoming amenable to interrogation. The Welfare Officer must be patient, sympathetic by character, wide awake and a good actor.

On 30 October 1940 what appeared to be a German Air Force P/W arrived at Cockfosters Camp together with three other Ps/W who were collected at various places. He wore the correct uniform and an identity disc and was in possession of unimportant trifles usually found on Ps/W. He seemed resigned to his fate and gave the ordinary particulars associated with P/W personalis [sic].

After reception, medical inspection etc. being completed, he was assigned to a P/W room.

This latest arrival was a pre-war refugee from Germany, who had placed his services at our disposal. He had been interviewed and investigated from every possible angle and finally vetted before he arrived at Cockfosters, and supplied with the uniform etc. he was wearing.

The refugee soon after arrival was visited by a British officer, who with the assistance of an officer from A.D.I.K. (the Air component of C.S.D.I.C.(U.K.)) arranged details regarding name, past history, rank and career befitting his physique, accent and personality etc. He had to learn his part as a soldier in the G.A.F., literature dealing with aerial activity had to be absorbed, drawings and photographs of German planes had to he studied and visits organised to depots where a German machine could be seen and explained. When he felt sufficiently confident he was placed in a room with a P/W after being briefed as to what was required.

Few people were aware that there was an S.P. in the camp. He lived under exactly the same conditions as ordinary Ps/W except that he had a daily walk with a British officer, to whom he reported progress. Facilities existed which enabled all conversations to be checked. If the S.P. got into difficulties, ways and means had to be found to relieve the situation. In the same way, when he was finished with his man, the S.P. had to be removed in such a way that no suspicion remained. It was generally arranged that the P/W left the S.P., the former usually expressing regret at losing such a pleasant companion.

The first experiment was eminently successful and with experience and constant coaching more subtle methods were applied and with ever-increasing knowledge of German

Appendix "D"

mentality in war-time, and additional details of flying, training, tactics and strategy it was seldom found that a P/W could withstand a well-trained S.P., if of the right type and personality. The garrulous would be allowed to 'run on' and, if suspicious, the S.P. pretended to be security-minded and was hurt by his companion's boorishness and lack of trust. In these circumstances, the S.P. would often suggest a game of chess in the course of which a question skilfully put would often produce good results.

In 1940 more and more S.Ps. were introduced selected from amongst refugees in the U.K. Incidentally, 93 persons were interviewed and only 4 selected as great difficulty was experienced in finding people possessing the proper personality, intelligence, courage, outlook and memory. It was also required that S.Ps. should be good judges of people and have some knowledge of the world outside Germany and Austria.

The training of these refugee S.Ps. followed the course already described and after a remarkably short period of training they were able to pose as a member of any arm of the German Armed forces. Wherever possible they posed as a member of a different arm to that to which their victim belonged.

Here it might be mentioned that all movements of S.Ps. had to be worked out beforehand with infinite care. S.Ps. had to be exercised in such a way that they never came within sight of any point from which they might be observed.

Then again walks had to be carefully timed so that the S.Ps. did not meet Ps/W when leaving or entering the building. The Camp Interpreter and certain reliable warders who came into contact with the S.Ps. had to be brought into the picture. They had to remember never to address an S.P. by name or pretend that they had ever seen him before. Addressing him by the wrong name or appearing to know him when he was supposed to be a new arrival might have ruined everything.

S.Ps. were entitled to buy certain goods from the canteen. These goods were entered up on an account card in the same way as genuine Ps/W and signed for by him in a P/Ws presence. Care had to be taken that this card corresponded with his temporary name, rank and supposed time of arrival. The detailed work was very exacting. A somewhat ill-fitting uniform might pass muster if an S.P. was playing the role of an O.R. but as an officer he had to have a uniform that fitted well and corresponded with the time he was supposed to have worn it.

Any decorations he wore had to have a convincing story attached to them with all corroborative details. He had to be conversant with the behaviour of GAF officers in the Mess, towards superiors, inferiors and one another, acquire the latest slang terms and be thoroughly acquainted with the latest reactions to current events.

Ps/W often became suspicious of microphones and refused to talk within four walls, but did not mind talking in the open air. In such cases it was arranged that exercise in the enclosure be prolonged or given more frequently, the S.P. memorised all information imparted to him and generally wrote it down in the lavatory at the earliest opportunity or arranged a sign to be taken out at once, ostensibly for interrogation. One of such signs was the low humming or whistling of a pre-arranged popular song. Another was the mention of a pre-arranged name, such as General Bagaroff, in connection with the Russian campaign. Needless to say, the latter sign meant that the S.P. for some good reason, wished to be taken away from his companion.

A careful study of Ps/W selected for the centres plus the co-operation of the regular S.Ps, and constant check on conversations between Ps/W enabled recommendations being

Appendix "D"

made to the Naval, Army and Air components of the centres as to which Ps/W would be likely to co-operate willingly. This resulted in a team of Ps/W-stool pigeons being recruited, the results of which proved to be excellent. They were approached on ideological, sentimental or religious grounds and here the Welfare Officer played a most important part. These selected persons were led up to the point of volunteering to obtain information from their fellows. Naval prisoners proved to be the most approachable and the results they produced were of the greatest value. Indeed, some of the information in regard to U-Boat locations and tactics may be described as having been of vital importance. These S.Ps. were given preferential treatment in the form of better quarters, extra cigarettes and beer occasionally. This all sounds simple but great care has to be taken to select properly and to make the approach gradually, employing all the amenities described above.

It is of interest to note that the total number of Ps/W serviced by S.Ps. from 1940 to 1945 was 1506.

Bibliography

Allied Translation and Interpreter Service. 1944. "WO 208/2525: Procedure in interrogating and handling prisoners of war." London: The National Archives, 12.

Anon. 1947. "Building and Launching of HMS Royal Rupert." *The Royal Rupert Times*, 12, 34th ed.

Beesly, Patrick. 2006. *Very Special Intelligence: The Story of the Admiralty's Operational Intelligence Centre 1939-1945.* London: Chatham Publishing.

Bell, Falko. 2015 31:4. "One of our Most Valuable Sources of Intelligence: British Intelligence and the Prisoner of War System in 1944." *Intelligence and National Security,* 556-578. http://www.tandfonline.com/doi/abs/10.1080/02684527.2015.1062319.

Bernstein, Jeremy. 1996. *Hitler's Uranium Club: The Secret Recordings at Farm Hall.* Woodbury, NY: American Institute of Physics.

Busch, Fritz-Otto. 1991. *The Drama of the Scharnhorst.* Translated by Eleanor Brockett and Anton Ehrenzweig. London: Robert Hale Ltd.

CSDIC. c 1945. "WO 208/3256: Mediterranean and Middle East theatres: use of 'X' source (concealed microphones) in interrogation centres run by CSDIC 1940-1945." London: The National Archives.

—. 1944. "WO 208/3468: CSDIC (Canada): fitting POW's with microphones." London: The National Archives.

—. 1944. "WO 208/4132: Interrogation reports on German prisoners of war (CSDIC)." London: The National Archives, 29 Feb.

—. 1947. "WO 208/4140; Interrogation Reports on German Prisoners of War 1111-1264." London: The National Archives, 07.

—. 1943. "WO 208/4145: Interrogation Reports on German Prisoners of War." London: The National Archives, March-June.

—. 1943. "WO 208/4146: Interrogation Reports on German Prisoners of War." London: The National Archives, June-Sept.

—. 1943. "WO 208/4147: Interrogation Reports on German Prisoners of War 2200-2450." London: The National Archives, 11.

—. 1944. "WO 208/4148: Interrogation Reports on German Prisoners of War Nos 2451-2699." London: The National Archives, 31 01.

—. 1944. "WO 208/4149: Interrogation Reports on German Prisoners of War Nos 2700-3500." London: The National Archives, 31 03.

—. 1944. "WO 208/4150: Interrogation Reports on German Prisoners of War Nos 3501-3359." London: The National Archives, 30 04.

—. 1944. "WO 208/4151: Interrogation Reports on German Prisoners of War Nos 3360-3650." London: The National Archives, 31 05.

—. 1944. "WO 208/4152: Interrogation Reports on German Prisoners of War Nos 3651-3790." London: The National Archives, 30 06.

—. 1944. "WO 208/4163: Interrogation Reports on German Prisoners of War Nos 1731-1949." London: The National Archives, 28 02.

—. 1945. "WO 208/4164: Interrogation Reports on German Prisoners of War Nos 1950-2141." London: The National Archives, 31 08.

—. 1944. "WO 208/4196: Interrogation reports on German and Italian prisoners of war (CSDIC)." London: The National Archives, 31 08.

—. 1945. "WO 208/4198: Special extracts from interrogation reports on German and Italian prisoners of war (CSDIC)." London: The National Archives, 31 08.

—. 1945. "WO 208/4200: Special extracts from interrogation reports on German and Italian prisoners of war (CSDIC)." London: The National Archives, 31 03.

Bibliography

—. 1944. "WO 208/5522: Interrogation reports on German prisoners of war: GRS 1-11." London: The National Archive, 27 05.

—. 1944. "WO 208/5551: Consolidated report on German Naval gunnery; SR 1." London: The National Archives, 05 02.

—. 1944. "WO 208/5574: Special Reports on German and Italian prisoners of war: CSDIC Middle East Nos 600-813 (incomplete)." London: The National Archives, 04 06.

—. 1944. "WO208/5508: Interrogation reports on German and Italian prisoners of war: AFHQ 1-107." London: The National Archives, 27 03.

Dailey Jr, Franklyn E, Capt USNR (Retd). 2009. *Joining the War at Sea 1939-1945*. 4th. Alpharetta, GA, 01.

—. 2012. *U-73 speaks from the depths of the Mediterranean*. Accessed 07 12, 2016. http://www.daileyint.com/seawar/aphjtwas.htm.

Dimbleby, Jonathan. 2015. *The Battle of the Atlantic*. London: Random House.

Fisher, Rob. 2002. *The Impact of German Technology on the Royal Canadian Navy in the Battle of the Atlantic*. 14 May. Accessed February 16, 2016. http://uboat.net/articles/44.html.

Fraser, Bruce A. 1947. "Sinking of the German Battle-Cruiser Scharnhorst on 26th December 1943." *ibiblio*. 05 08. Accessed 02 21, 2015. http://www.ibiblio.org/hyperwar/UN/UK/LondonGazette/38038.pdf.

Fry, Helen. 2014. *Spymaster: The Secret Life of Kendrick*. CreateSpace Independent Publishing Platform (10 July 2014).

—. 2017. *The London Cage: The Secret History of Britain's WWII Interrogation Centre*. London: Yale University Press.

—. 2019. *The Walls Have Ears*. 1st. New Haven and London: Yale University Press.

Hall, Leonard, interview by Peter M Hart. 2005. *Imperial War Museum Oral History, Cat No 27271* (04).

Hasselriis, C H W. 1943. "Denmark in Revolt." *University of Toledo Digital Repository*. New York: University of Toledo.

http://utdr.utoledo.edu/cgi/viewcontent.cgi?article=1240&context=ur-87-68.

Helgason, Gudmundur. 2016. *uboat.net.* 07 09. Accessed 09 17, 2016. http://uboat.net/index.html.

Hinsley, Francis Harry, and C A G Simkins. 1990. *British Intelligence in the Second World War.* Vol. 4. London: HMSO.

Hinsley, Francis Harry, Edward Eastway Thomas, C F G Ransom, and R C Knight. 1984. *British Intelligence in the Second World War.* Vol. 3 Part 1. London: HMSO.

1944. "HW 18/250: Teleprinted translations of decrypted Second World War German U-boat (or U-boat command) radio messages." London: The National Archives, 03 Feb.

Jackson, Robert. 1964. *A Taste of Freedom.* London: Arthur Barker.

Jackson, Robert. No 17, 1977. "German POWs in England." Edited by Winston G Ramsey. *After the Battle* (Battle of Britain International Ltd) 48-53.

Jackson, Sophie. 2012. *British Interrogation Techniques in the Second World War.* Stroud, Gloucestershire: The History Press.

Jacobsen, Alf R. 2001, 2003. *Scharnhorst.* Translated by J Basil Cowlishaw. Oslo, Stroud: Sutton Publishing Limited.

Jago, Michael. 2013. *The Man Who Was George Smiley: The Life of John Bingham.* London: Biteback.

Kahn, David. 1985. *Hitler's Spies: German Military Intelligence in World War II.* New York: Collier Books.

Kirby, Geoff. 1972. "A History of the Torpedo Parts 3-4." *Journal of the Royal Naval Scientific Service* 27 (2): 78-105.

Kirkwood, Henry. n.d. *U Boat Archive.* Accessed Jul 22, 2014. http://www.uboatarchive.net/U-593CalpeActionReport.htm.

Kleinman, Steven M, Major, USAFR. 2006. "The History of MIS-Y: US Strategic Interrogation During World War II." *Master's Thesis.* Washington, DC: Joint Military Intelligence College, 21 04.

Lincoln, Ashe. 2017. *Secret Naval Investigator: The Battle Against Hitler's Secret Underwater Weapons.* Barnsley: Frontline Books.

Bibliography

2014. *List of successful U-boat commanders.* 7 June. Accessed July 22, 2014. http://en.wikipedia.org/wiki/List_of_successful_U-boat_commanders.

McCue, Brian. 1990. *U-Boats in the Bay of Biscay: An Essay in Operations Analysis.* Washington DC 20319-6000: National Defense University Press. Accessed 08 15, 2016. http://www.dtic.mil/dtic/tr/fulltext/u2/a229582.pdf.

McGann, Marie-Claire. 2015. *MV Kerlogue.* Accessed 11 16, 2015. http://lugnad.ie/kerlogue/.

McLachlan, Donald. 1968. *Room 39: Naval Intelligence in Action 1939-45.* London: Weidenfeld and Nicholson.

MI9. 1941. "WO 208/3269: Dulag Luft (Oberusel): RAF personnel." London: The National Archives, 06.

militaryhistory. 2008. *The Wartime Experiences of an RNR Officer.* 31 01. Accessed 02 21, 2015. http://www.bbc.co.uk/history/ww2peopleswar/stories/33/a8999833.shtml.

Naval Intelligence Division. 1944. "ADM 1/16833: Information Obtained from Prisoners of War ex Scharnhorst." London: The National Archives, 16 01.

—. 1944. "ADM 186/809: Interrogation of German naval survivors." London: The National Archives, Jan.

—. 1943-1944. "ADM 199/1032: Various convoys: reports:." London: The National Archives.

—. 1944. "ADM 199/2478: Director of Naval Intelligence: movements of small craft and personnel to Mediterranean, questionnaires and Prisoners of War statements: includes CX material." London: The National Archives, 31 12.

—. 1944. "ADM 199/464: Anti-U-boat operations in the Mediterranean reports 1943-1944." London: The National Archives.

—. 1941-1944. "ADM 199/549: German - Japanese blockade running: reports." London: The National Archives.

—. 1943. "ADM 199/913: Sinking of SCHARNHORST." London: The National Archives.

—. 1943. "ADM 199/966: SL, KMS and MKS convoys: reports MKS 1 - 32 MKS 34, SL135, SL 136, SL 137, SL 138, SL 139, SL 140, SL 141, SL 142, SL 143, SL 144." London: The National Archives.

—. 1944. "ADM 223/120: NID UC Reports: Nos 251-500." London: The National Archives.

—. 1943. "ADM 223/141: Summary of statements by German prisoners of war." London: The National Archives, 30 06.

—. 1943. "ADM 223/142: Summary of statements by German prisoners of war July-September 1943." London: The National Archives, 30 09.

—. 1944. "ADM 223/144: Summary of statements by German prisoners of war." London: The National Archives, 01 04.

—. 1945. "ADM 223/209: Photocopies of Papers Cited in History of Iintelligence 1939-1945 Vol 3 Pt 1: Chapter 35 (War at Sea - U boats): references 159 and 161." London: The National Archives.

—. 1944. "ADM 223/286: Operational Intelligence Centres: formation and history." London: The National Archive, 04.

—. 1947. "ADM 223/297: Notes and extracts from volumes of paper collected by Admiral Godfrey." London: The National ARchives.

—. 1943. "ADM 223/353: DNI Notes." London: The National Archives.

—. 1944. "ADM 223/354: DNI Notes." London: The National Archives, 03.

—. 1943. "ADM 223/354: DNI Notes." London: The National Archives.

—. 1944. "ADM 223/355." *DNI Notes Vol 2*. London: The National Archives, 06.

—. 1943. "ADM 223/467: NID Monograph NID (I)." London: The National Archives.

—. 1943. "ADM 223/468: NID Monograph NID (II)." London: The National Archives.

Bibliography

—. 1948. "ADM 223/473: NID memoranda: training and administration 1933-1948." London: The National Archives.

—. 1947. "ADM 223/475: Intelligence Collection Methods." London: The National Archives.

—. 1945. "ADM 223/501: 30 Assault Unit: targets." London: The National Archives.

—. 1950. "ADM 223/619: The Navy and Naval Intelligence 1939-1942: afterthoughts by Admiral J H Godfrey (former DNI)." London: The National Archives.

—. 1945. "ADM 223/792: NID 12 Selections from History - Volume 1 - History, Organisation and Material." London: The National Archives.

—. 1943. "ADM 223/8: Special intelligence summaries." London: The National Archives.

—. 1937-1945. "ADM 223/84: Photocopies of papers cited in history of intelligence." Vol. 1. London: The National Archives.

—. 1944. "ADM 223/877: NID UC Reports: Nos 315-500 (incomplete)." London: The National Archives.

Neitzel, Sönke, and Harald Welzer. 2013. *Soldaten: On Fighting, Killing and Dying.* Translated by Jefferson Chase. London: Simon & Schuster UK Ltd.

Nudd, Derek. 2020. *Castaways in Question.* Portsmouth: Cottage Grove Editions.

Offley, Ed. 2011. *Turning the Tide.* New York: Basic Books.

2014. *Operation Stonewall.* 19 Jun. Accessed Jul 27, 2014. http://en.wikipedia.org/wiki/Operation_Stonewall.

Oswald, John. 2004. *An Interrogator's Life (Part 1).* 27 10. Accessed 09 01, 2016. http://www.bbc.co.uk/history/ww2peopleswar/stories/61/a3189161.shtml.

Patterson, K G Lt, RANVR. 1998. "Documents.7766: Private Papers of Lieutenant K G Patterson RANVR." London: IWM, 03.

PWIS. 1945. "WO 208/3256; Mediterranean and Middle East theatres: use of 'X' source (concealed microphones) in interrogation

—. 1941. "WO 208/3442: Prisoners of war holding strong anti-Nazi views." London: The National Archives.

—. 1942. "WO 208/3443: War Office camps for X and Y prisoners of war." London: The National Archives, 02.

—. 1943. "WO 208/3458; CSDIC's and PWIS's: general policy." London: The National Archives.

—. 1943. "WO 208/3461: CSDIC's: inclusion of Allied personnel." London: The National Archives.

—. 1940. "WO 208/3513: Training of Intelligence Officers in interrogation of POWs." London: The National Archives, 12.

—. 1941. "WO 208/3515: Use of Polish officers for interrogation." London: The National Archives, 31 07.

—. 1943. "WO 208/3524: Inter Service Detailed Interrogation Centres described as transit." London: The National Archives, 01.

—. 1943. "WO 208/3525: Publication in the press of information regarding the interrogation of POWs." London: The National Archives, 06.

—. 1944. "WO 208/3527: Special camp for Anti-Nazi POWs: suggested transfer from No 1 Camp to No 7 Camp." London: The National Archives, 31 07.

—. 1945. "WO 208/3535: Possible use CSDIC reports in propaganda." London: The National Archives, 31 08.

—. 1944. "WO 208/3553: Shipment of POWs to Canada." London: The National Archives, 02.

—. 1945. "WO 208/4203: Propaganda: information obtained from enemy prisoners of war." London: The National Archives, 03.

—. 1946. "WO 208/4642: Dulag Luft, Oberursel, Germany: ill-treatment of allied airmen." London: The National Archives, 09.

Bibliography

—. 1945. "WO 208/4970: The Story of MI19." London: The National Archives.

Rennison, John P. 2013. *70th Anniversary of the Alsterufer sinking.* 27 Dec. Accessed 07 26, 2014. http://fcafa.wordpress.com/2013/12/27/70th-anniversary-of-the-alsterufer-sinking/.

Scotland, Lt Col Alexander P. 1957. *The London Cage.* London: Evans Bros Ltd.

Special Operations Executive Personnel Files HS9/491/1. 1946. "Charles William EVERETT - born [1908]." London: The National Archives, 31 12.

Sullivan, Matthew Barry. 1979. *Thresholds of Peace: German Prisoners and the People of Britain 1944-1948.* London: Hamish Hamilton.

Thomas, Roger J C. 2003. *Prisoner of War Camps (1939-1948).* Swindon: English Heritage.

United States Holocaust Memorial Museum. 2011. *The Joshua family stands outside the Jordanbad sanitorium near Biberach a few months after their liberation.* 05 07. Accessed 06 11, 2016. http://collections.ushmm.org/search/catalog/pa1174416.

USAAF. 2014. "NAZI INTELLIGENCE: German WWII Interrogation Methods (720p)." *YouTube.* 22 10. Accessed 09 17, 2016. https://www.youtube.com/watch?v=uUeWMpWLJlM.

Van Cleve, Lt Col Thomas C. 1945. *The Activities of Two Agencies of the CPM Branch, MIS, G2, WDGS.* Washington: US Army. http://www.militarymuseum.org/Camp%20Tracy%20History.pdf.

Vincent, Jeff. No 70, 1990. "The Combined Services Interrogation Centre." Edited by Winston G Ramsey. *After the Battle* (Battle of Britain International Ltd) 44-52.

Weir, H R. 1943. *Woolsey Action Report.* 17 12. Accessed 07 27, 2014. http://www.uboatarchive.net/U-73WoolseyActionReport.htm.

Welbourn, Donald Burkewood, Lt Cdr. 2008. *An Engineer in Peace and War: A Technical and Social History.* Edited by Margaret Hardy. Vols. 1 - 1916-1952. 3 vols. Lulu.com.

—. 1999. "Documents.8279: Private Papers of Lieutenant Commander D B Welbourn RNVR." London: IWM, 08.

Welbourn, Donald Burkewood, Lt Cdr, interview by Conrad Wood. 1999. *Imperial War Museum Oral History, Cat No 18777* IWM, (17 04). Accessed 11 08, 2016. http://www.iwm.org.uk/collections/item/object/80017864.

Wernard, Alfred Conrad, interview by Conrad Wood. 1998. *Imperial War Museum Oral History: capture and interrogation after sinking of U-187 (Cat No 18573)* IWM, (04 11).

Wikipedia. 2014. *German battleship Scharnhorst.* 16 09. Accessed 10 07, 2014. http://en.wikipedia.org/wiki/German_battleship_Scharnhorst.

Winton, John. 2000. *Death of the Scharnhorst.* London: Cassell.

INDEX

A713 (stool pigeon), 89, 190
Alsen, W, 84, 85, 152, 185
Alsterufer. See MV Alsterufer
Altendorfer, A, 112
Atkinson, Lt L F, 65
Averkamp, T, 81
Backhaus, H, 21
Barron, Evelyn, 62
Bey, Konteradmiral E, 18, 19, 22, 172, 200
Birke, R, 185
Bismarck, 129
Bletchley Park, 10, 18, 43, 130
Blumenberg, W, 37, 81, 149, 150, 190
Bohle, G, 21
Böhme, Oblt K, 34, 37, 86, 87, 88, 102, 133
Brandi, Klt A, 102, 103
Brest, 12, 17, 164, 166, 174, 187, 188
Breuker, H, 71, 189
Broughton Rectory, 88
Brünning, Kptlt H, 102
Casablanca Conference, 74
Charlotte Schliemann, x
Churchill, W E, xvii, 38, 50, 96
Close, K, 186
Cope, Lt Cdr B S R, ix, xii, 38, 60, 61, 62, 64
CSDIC, ix, xi, xiii, xv, 15, 25–43, 43, 45, 46, 47, 48, 49, 50, 54, 56, 57, 58, 62, 63, 64, 65, 66, 67, 68, 79, 80, 81, 88, 95, 96, 98, 102, 105, 106, 107, 108, 113, 115, 122, 139, 143, 146, 156, 159, 164, 183, 185, 189, 193, 195, 197, 218
Algiers, 3, 32, 44, 45, 46, 53, 95, 97, 102
Cairo, 43
Latimer House, ix, x, xii, 26, 27, 38, 60, 62, 68, 96, 97
Opinion Surveys, 68–79
Trent Park, 26, 28, 29, 151
Wilton Park, 26, 96
Dabelstein, H, 37, 69, 81
D-Day, xi, xiii, 31, 40, 48, 64, 66, 149, 167, 183–91, 194, 195
Deckert, Olt z See H, 4, 5, 98, 101, 131, 144, 146, 184
Delmer, S, 71, 91, 92
Diessel, R, 149
Director of Naval Intelligence. *See* Naval Intelligence Division/DNI
Doležal, PO O, xii, 11, 12, 15, 40
Dönitz, Großadmiral K, 19, 23, 52, 73, 77, 154
Drugs, use of, 35
Duckwitz, G F, 171
E-boats
  S-147, 148
  S-88, 168
  S-96, 77, 168
Eck, Kptlt H-W, 148
Essman, T, 69, 100, 163

Everett, Lt C W, 62, 66, 93
Ewald, H, 31, 153, 154, 155
Fleming, Cdr I, 47, 63, 64, 195
Flower, Jean, 62
Forward Interrogation Unit, 47, 64, 67, 68, 195
Fraser, V Adm Sir B, 19, 21, 22, 23, 105
Fry, Dr Helen, xii
Furneaux, 2/Off C M, 67
Georg, Olt z See, 77, 90
Gessler, H, 117, 155, 157
Gneisenau, 17, 127, 128
Godfrey, R Adm J H, 39, 41, 92, 128, 160
Görs, W (N1553), 79
Grüter, G (N1485), 89, 101, 148, 153, 154
GSR, xvi, 42, 54, 140–44
Hager, H, 159, 169, 179
Hahn, H, 118
Hallwig, H, 113
Hansen, J, 137
Heinemann, Lt z See K, 104, 116, 154, 177, 184
Hitler, A, xv, 68, 73, 76, 77, 79, 80, 81, 85, 86, 100, 101, 113, 150, 155, 178, 185
HMS *Belfast*, 19, 20
HMS *Calpe*, 2, 3, 6
HMS *Cameron*, 64
HMS *Duke of York*, xii, 19, 20, 21, 23, 96, 106, 110, 145, 199
HMS *Dunottar Castle*, 64
HMS *Eagle*, 4, 102
HMS *Enterprise*, 13, 40
HMS *Glasgow*, 13, 40
HMS *Glorious*, 17, 18, 23
HMS *Graph* (U-570), 59

HMS *Holcombe*, 2, 42
HMS *Jamaica*, 19, 20
HMS *Lagan*, 136
HMS *Lancaster*, 64
HMS *Leeds*, 64
HMS *Matchless*, 21
HMS *Norfolk*, 19, 20, 23
HMS *Rawalpindi*, 17, 18
HMS *Renown*, 17, 18
HMS *Scorpion*, 21
HMS *Seaham*, 14
HMS *Sheffield*, 19
HMS *Tynedale*, 2, 42, 105
Hoffmann, Lt z See A, 148
Hünert, G, 3, 102, 138, 187
Hungershausen, Kptlt H, 34, 87
Izzard, Lt Cdr R W B, 62, 63, 64, 67, 92
Izzard, Ralph, 62
Kelbling, Klt G, 1, 2, 3, 85, 102, 103, 105, 131, 138, 144
Kendrick, Lt Col T J, xii, 38, 56
Kinkele, Lt z See K, 101, 103
Krüger, W, 113
Kruse, W, 172, 185
Kugler, G, 90
La Pallice, 18
Lange, T, 32
LDC, 30, 31, 32, 51, 96
Lemke, 1te Off E, 118, 119, 154, 174, 176, 177, 179
Liebig, Lt (ing) M, 104
Liedtke, K, 157
Ligensa, F, 113, 117, 153, 157
Löffenholz, H, 109, 111, 151, 152
London District Cage. *See* LDC
Losch, W, 98, 100

Index

Lunzer, Lt J P, 67
Lüth, Kk W, 102
Mackenzie, Esmé, 62
Marriner, Lt J S, 65
Marseilles, 6, 100, 164, 184, 185
McFadyean, Lt Cdr J C, 49, 57, 64
Merkle, J, 110
Mers El Kébir, 5, 6
Meyer, E (N1878), 82, 89, 119
MI19, 25, 28, 38, 48, 91, 94, 217
MI9, 25, 29
MV Alsterufer, ix, xii, 9–12, 12, 13, 15, 40, 70, 95, 97, 99, 118–22, 125, 142, 143, 147, 154, 156, 157, 170, 174, 175, 176, 177, 178, 197
MV *Burgenland*, 12
MV *Kerlogue*, 14, 117
MV *Rio Grande*, 12
MV *Weserland*, 12
Naval Intelligence Division
    DNI, ix, xvi, 38, 39, 41, 47, 102, 105, 112, 117, 123, 124, 128, 136, 196
    NID 1/PW, 34, 41, 43, 95
    NID 17Z, 64
    NID 3/PW, 34, 39, 43
Neel-Wall, Gwendoline, 62
Niemöller, Pastor M, 86, 159
Nissen, 2te Off J (Alsterufer), 11, 99, 118, 156, 157, 170, 178
Nissen, U (U-73), 98, 99, 104, 178
Normandy landings. *See* D-Day
Op-16-Z, 63
    Fort Hunt, 47, 63

Osorno. *See* SS *Osorno*
Petersen, H, 112
Piatek, Kpt P, 9, 12, 70, 118, 121, 178, 179
Pohl, G, 166
Prinz Eugen, 17
Prisoner of War Information Bureau, xvii, 28
Prisoner of War Interrogation Service. *See* PWIS
PWIS, xvii, 30, 46, 47, 57
Raithel, H, 167
RDB, xv, xvii, 144, 146
RDS, xvii, xviii, 144
Red Cross, 28, 50, 52, 109
Reimann, E, 110
Reprisal weapons, 3, 73, 153, 149–56
    Peenemünde, 3
Rosenbaum, Klt H, 4
Rossmeissl, F, 165
Röther, Klt J, 103
Rushbrooke, Cdre E G N, ix, 41, 102, 137, 160
Samuel, Lt Cdr W S, 62
SBT, xv, xvii, 42, 146, 148
Schaffrath, P (N2175), 17, 83, 84, 85, 108, 109, 111, 167, 169, 171
Scharnhorst, v, ix, xii, 22, 17–23, 23, 43, 52, 69, 70, 72, 73, 83, 90, 96, 97, 106, 105–11, 116, 118, 127, 128, 142, 145, 151, 152, 159, 164, 166, 167, 169, 171, 172, 179, 185, 191, 197, 199, 200
Scholar, Lt H I, 65, 66
Schöneboom, Olt z See D, 102

Schramm, Olt z See G, 13, 86, 112, 113, 114, 117, 149, 150, 155, 156, 174, 190, 197
Schütz, H, 52, 56
Seehund (Seal), 144
Shippey, Marine F, xii, 96, 123
Speidel, Klt H H, 73
Spitsbergen, 17, 109
Spitz, R (N1552), 31, 69, 70, 79, 80, 89, 90, 100, 111, 155, 163, 164
SS *Germania*, 89
SS *John S Copley*, 5
SS *Osorno*, 9, 10, 167
SS *Peleus*, 148
St Nazaire, 105, 164, 165, 166, 187, 188, 190, 195
Stäger, J, 98, 101, 153, 174
Stool pigeon, 3, 31, 32, 33, 34, 37, 38, 39, 43, 46, 51, 52, 59, 80, 79–91, 97, 100, 101, 109, 113, 119, 142, 147, 148, 149, 154, 155, 159, 169, 173, 178, 184, 188, 190, 193, 217–21
Strater, G, 96, 109
T-25, ix, 14, 12–14, 43, 70, 86, 95, 97, 111–18, 131, 142, 143, 145, 149, 153, 157, 166, 167, 187, 197
Tehran Conference, 74
Tirpitz, 17, 18, 83, 108, 109, 128, 129, 172
Torpedoes, 136–40
    T4 *Falke*, 136
    T5 *Zaunkönig* (Gnat), 2, 6, 33, 42, 136, 137, 138, 139, 193
Toulon, 1, 4, 6, 100, 103, 166, 174, 183, 184, 185
U-boats, 132–35

Type XXI, 134, 135, 139
Type XXIII, 135
U-135, 1, 82, 89
U-172, x
U-175, 149
U-178, 88
U-187, 30
U-223, 32
U-231, x
U-257, x
U-260, 22
U-264, x, 31, 32, 90, 153, 188
U-305, 10
U-309, 12
U-340, 187
U-352, 64, 92
U-380, 103
U-386, x, 37, 69, 81, 149, 190
U-406, x, 54, 71, 143, 165, 189
U-415, 12
U-425, 88
U-431, 102
U-432, 79, 91
U-444, 31, 79, 89, 91
U-450, 34, 37, 45, 86, 102, 133, 134, 183, 184
U-453, 103
U-505, 14
U-506, 88
U-536, x, 132
U-570 (HMS *Graph*), 40, 59
U-593, ix, 1–4, 4, 15, 42, 50, 52, 95, 97, 98, 102–5, 130, 131, 134, 138, 142, 144, 145, 146, 154, 177, 184, 187, 197
U-618, 14

Index

U-642, 102
U-643, 73
U-73, ix, xii, 3, 4–6, 15, 33, 50, 69, 95, 97, 98–102, 103, 104, 123, 130, 131, 134, 138, 140, 142, 145, 146, 153, 163, 166, 173, 178, 184, 186, 197
U-744, 137, 170
U-845, 147, 157, 171
U-848, x
U-85, 64
U-852, 148
U-91, 34, 81, 87
USS *Card*, 10
USS *Edison*, xii, 5, 6, 101
USS *Trippe*, 5
USS *Wainwright*, 2, 6
USS *Woolsey*, 5, 6, 7
Vogt, H, 118, 166
Voigt, R, 171, 208
Völker, K, 149
von Gartzen, Kk W, 111
von Kalckreuth, Olt z See C, 112, 117, 156, 187

von Schlippenbach, Klt E R F, 103
von Werra, Olt F, 36
Wallek, M, 84, 109, 164, 185
Warscheid, F, 118, 119, 122, 147, 176, 178, 179
Weatherby, Cpt J M, 63
Weatherby, Lt Cdr R M, 62, 92
Weatherby, Richard, 62
Wehling, K, 98, 173
Weighardt, Lt z See A, 103, 104
Weispfennig, W, 148
Welbourn, Donald, 62
Welbourn, Lt D B, 59, 65, 88, 91, 92, 93, 124
Wengefeld, G, 79
Wernard, A, 30, 32, 56
Wiebusch, N, 21
Wiest, J, 20
Zanger, R, 152, 159, 191
Zaubitzer, H, 20, 109
Zimmerman, F, 102
Zwietasch, W, 98, 138

About the Author

Derek Nudd's rare blend of arts and science degrees and a career in the defence engineering industry are a valuable grounding for insights into technical intelligence in WW2. He has published two other books and an article, *The Battle of Jutland, through a Looking-Glass*, in the peer-reviewed journal *Mariner's Mirror*. He has written, edited and spoken in the field of naval and maritime history, appeared on television and acted as historical consultant to TV productions.

Armageddon Fed Up with This is the true story of one articulate artillery conscript's journey from raw gunner to professional sergeant, preserving a humorously caustic take on army life along the way.

The tale is told through his letters home, and woven into the social, political and military mayhem going on around him.

"Everyone should own a copy of this book" –
That's Books and Entertainment

If you enjoyed this, you need to read …

Castaways in Question
DEREK NUDD
A story of British naval interrogators from WW1 to denazification

They thought their war was over when they were hauled from the sea.

Instead, captive German sailors were fed, clothed and brought to London where they experienced British intelligence officers' deft skills at extracting vital information from their heads.

Castaways in Question follows the naval interrogators' growing confidence and expertise from their pioneering first steps in World War 1 to their role in dismantling one of the most vicious regimes the planet has ever seen.

> 'This is a good history of the British naval PoW interrogation process and what it yielded across the World Wars. Readable and interesting to newcomers and those familiar with the topic alike.'

Dr Marcus Faulkner — King's College London

Derek's web site is at www.dnudd.co.uk.

Printed in Great Britain
by Amazon